MAKING
FEMINIST
MEDIA

FILM AND MEDIA STUDIES SERIES

Film studies is the critical exploration of cinematic texts as art and entertainment, as well as the industries that produce them and the audiences that consume them. Although a medium barely one hundred years old, film is already transformed through the emergence of new media forms. Media studies is an interdisciplinary field that considers the nature and effects of mass media upon individuals and society and analyzes media content and representations. Despite changing modes of consumption—especially the proliferation of individuated viewing technologies—film has retained its cultural dominance into the 21st century, and it is this transformative moment that the WLU Press Film and Media Studies series addresses.

Our Film and Media Studies series includes topics such as identity, gender, sexuality, class, race, visuality, space, music, new media, aesthetics, genre, youth culture, popular culture, consumer culture, regional/national cinemas, film policy, film theory, and film history.

Wilfrid Laurier University Press invites submissions. For further information, please contact the Series editors, all of whom are in the Department of English and Film Studies at Wilfrid Laurier University:

Dr. Philippa Gates
Email: pgates@wlu.ca
Dr. Russell Kilbourn
Email: rkilbourn@wlu.ca
Dr. Ute Lischke
Email: ulischke@wlu.ca

Department of English and Film Studies
Wilfrid Laurier University
75 University Avenue West
Waterloo, ON N2L 3C5
Canada
Phone: 519-884-0710
Fax: 519-884-8307

MAKING FEMINIST MEDIA

THIRD-WAVE MAGAZINES ON THE CUSP OF THE DIGITAL AGE

ELIZABETH GROENEVELD

WLU PRESS

WILFRID LAURIER
UNIVERSITY PRESS

This book has been published with the help of a grant from the Canadian Federation for the Humanities and Social Sciences, through the Awards to Scholarly Publications Program, using funds provided by the Social Sciences and Humanities Research Council of Canada. Wilfrid Laurier University Press acknowledges the financial support of the Government of Canada through the Canada Book Fund for its publishing activities. This work was supported by the Research Support Fund.

LAURIER ✹
Inspiring Lives.

ONTARIO ARTS COUNCIL
CONSEIL DES ARTS DE L'ONTARIO
an Ontario government agency
un organisme du gouvernement de l'Ontario

Canada Council
for the Arts

Conseil des Arts
du Canada

LIBRARY AND ARCHIVES CANADA CATALOGUING IN PUBLICATION

Groeneveld, Elizabeth, 1977–, author
  Making feminist media : third-wave magazines on the cusp of the digital age / Elizabeth Groeneveld.

(Film and media studies series)
Includes bibliographical references and index.
Issued in print and electronic formats.
ISBN 978-1-77112-120-0 (paperback).—ISBN 978-1-77112-101-9 (pdf).—
ISBN 978-1-77112-102-6 (epub)

  1. Feminism—Periodicals—History—20th century. 2. Feminism—History—20th century. 3. Zines—History—20th century. 4. Women's periodicals—History—20th century. 5. Women—History—20th century. I. Title. II. Series: Film and media studies series

HQ1101.G76 2016   305.4205   C2015-908640-X
                                                        C2015-908641-8

Text design by Sandra Friesen.

This book is printed on FSC® certified paper and is certified Ecologo. It contains post-consumer fibre, is processed chlorine free, and is manufactured using biogas energy.

Printed in Canada

For Mom & Dad

CONTENTS

CONTENTS

LIST OF ILLUSTRATIONS AND TABLES

ILLUSTRATIONS

TABLES

ACKNOWLEDGEMENTS

First and foremost, I wish to thank the creators and editors of third-wave magazines for their creativity and commitment to feminist cultural production. In particular, I would like to thank the magazine founders and editors who took the time to correspond with me by email or speak with me by telephone about their publications: Amy Schroeder, founder and publisher of *Venus Zine*; Nicole Cohen, co-founder of *Shameless*; Lisa Jervis and Andi Zeisler, co-founders of *Bitch*; and Dyann Logwood, co-founder of *HUES*. Dyann was particularly generous in mailing some original and difficult-to-find copies of *HUES* to me.

I hugely appreciate the editors of Wilfrid Laurier University Press, particularly Lisa Quinn for believing in this project. I also thank Rob Kohlmeier and Wendy Thomas for helping me get this book through production. Two anonymous reviewers gave helpful feedback on the manuscript.

This project began in the School of English and Theatre Studies at the University of Guelph, where I completed my doctorate in Literary Studies. I would like to thank the faculty and my peers for their help, encouragement, and support. In particular, I thank Christine Bold for her incredible support and perceptive comments on the early versions of this work. Christine has been an invaluable mentor to me both as an insightful scholar of print culture and as a delightful human being. I also appreciate the detailed feedback and mentoring provided to me by Susan Brown. It was Susan who suggested I look at *BUST*'s fashionable feminists issue, which eventually turned into the fourth chapter of this book. Maria DiCenzo was an invaluable resource for her knowledge of the field of feminist periodical studies. Susan Nance provided thoughtful comments on the relationship between reading and public space that informed my final chapter on *Bitch* magazine's vibrator ad controversy. Ann Cvetkovich gave generous feedback on the manuscript that helped shape its current form. I wish to thank the members of my writing group—Ben Authers, Sally Booth, Debra Henderson, Raman Johal, and Ingrid Mündel—for their encouragement, camaraderie, and generous feedback on the earliest incarnations of this book. The Mündel/Lacelle and Authers/Bugeja households have been welcoming and gracious hosts during my many trips to Guelph over the years.

Making Feminist Media was enriched through my conversations with faculty, staff, and students at McGill University and my extended Montreal community. I thank Chelsea Barnett, Jenny Burman, Cecelia Chen, Amy Hasinoff, Yasmin Jiwani, Krystle Merchant, Claire Michela, Sorouja Moll, Julie Moreau, Lena Palacios, Julianne Pidduck, Camila Rivas-Garrido, Steven Schnoor, Alanna Thain, Monika Viktorova, and Caili Woodyard. A special thanks goes to Carrie A. Rentschler, particularly, for her incisive feedback on the Introduction and Chapter Six of this book, and for her mentorship and fun sense of humour. I thank Samantha C. Thrift for her perceptive comments on my work and, most importantly, for her friendship.

I could not ask for better colleagues than those I have met at Old Dominion University (ODU). I thank the Women's Studies department, particularly Lindal Buchanan, Anita Fellman, Jennifer N. Fish, Vaughan Frederick, Rebekah Joyce, Lee Ellen Knight, Stacey Parks, Cathleen Rhodes, and Moriah Shumpert for all their support. I thank Zack Gehring for his thoughtful comments on my chapter on feminist crafting. I am so pleased to have wonderful colleagues in Shenita Brazelton, Sarah Florini, Vanessa Panfil, Yvette Pearson, Alison Reed, Avi Santo, Michael Smith, Kerstin Steitz, and Nicole Willock. I particularly appreciate Pamela VanHaitsma for the weekly writing sessions that helped me pull this manuscript together. A big thanks to all of my students, especially those in my Gender and Media, Feminist Print Culture, and Feminisms and Sexualities classes at ODU and at McGill, for having conversations about—and making—feminist media with me.

Making Feminist Media benefited tremendously from my visit to the Sallie Bingham Center at the Duke University archives and special collections. Librarian Kelly Wooten deserves special thanks for granting me access to some unsorted boxes of *Bitch* documents that were incredibly useful for my research. The early stages of research and writing this book were also assisted by a doctoral fellowship from the Social Sciences and Humanities Research Council of Canada and an Ontario Graduate Scholarship. Conference audiences at the Banff Centre, the Canadian Association of American Studies, McGill University, the National Women's Studies Association, the Popular Culture Association, Simon Fraser University, University of Alberta, University of Guelph, University of Newcastle, University of Waterloo, and

University of Windsor have all contributed to my thinking about third-wave magazines and making feminist media.

Many thanks to my extended network of friends and colleagues, including Debbie Adams, the Banks family, Ann Brathwaite, Patrick Bugeja, Heather Coiner, Neal Evans, Peg Evans, Amy Erdman Farrell, Peter Fleming, Tim Griese, Shannon Hoff, Trevor Holmes, Pete Johnson, Carl Jones, Tessa Jordan, Jessalyn Keller, Martin Lacelle, Dan Margolies, Erynn Marshall, Sara Matthews, Michelle Meagher, Hannah Naiman, Miriam Novick, Wendy Peters, Scott Prouty, John Russon, Alison Sauer, Elliot Storm, Cullen Strawn, and Ben Stowe. Many thanks to Jackie Lealess for lending me several early issues of *BUST* and *Bitch*, as well as her precious copies of *Sassy*, and to Rachel Torrie, my gracious host in Vancouver and Ottawa, who lent and photocopied key sections from issues of *Bitch* not in my collection and gave thoughtful and incisive feedback on Chapter Five. I thank Anne Hartman for lending her ear to this project and for encouraging me to put more of myself in my writing.

Thanks to my wonderful family, especially my parents, John and Marsha Groeneveld, for all of their love and support, and to whom this book is dedicated in loving memory. And thanks to Chris Banks for his thoughtful comments on this project, for listening to me when things were easy and when things were hard, and for making me laugh.

My work on "Third-Wave Feminism and the Limitations of the Wave Metaphor," which I discuss in the Introduction to this book, and my discussion of Rebecca Walker's *Ms.* article "Becoming Third Wave" in Chapter Three originated from a chapter called "'Not a Postfeminism Feminist': Feminism's Third Wave," published in *"Not Drowning, But Waving": Women, Feminism, and the Liberal Arts*, ed. Susan Brown, Jeanne Perrault, JoAnn Wallace, and Heather Zwicker (Edmonton: University of Alberta Press [2011], 271–84).

"'Be a Feminist or Just Dress Like One': *BUST*, Fashion and Lifestyle Feminism" is an expanded version of the article "'Be a Feminist or Just Dress Like One': *BUST*, Fashion and Feminism as Lifestyle," in the *Journal of Gender Studies* 18/2 (June 2009): 177–90.

"'Join the Knitting Revolution': Representations of Crafting in Feminist Magazines" knits together two previously published works on the politics of feminist crafting: "'Join the Knitting Revolution': Third-Wave Feminist Magazines and the Politics of Domesticity," published in *Canadian Review of American Studies* 40/2 (2010): 259–78, and "Crafting Publics in Feminist Periodicals," published in *Modern Print Activism in the United States*, ed. Rachel Schreiber (Burlington, VT: Ashgate Press, 2013), 205–20.

MAKING FEMINIST MEDIA: THIRD-WAVE MAGAZINES ON THE CUSP OF THE DIGITAL AGE

Where are the girl-friendly places in the mass media? Where are the things we can see and read and hear that don't insult our intelligence? How can we get more of them? We can make them.

—*Bitch* mission statement

When I found your magazine, I felt like singing!!!
—Letter to *Bitch*, archived at Sallie Bingham Center

Beginning in the early 1990s, a new kind of publication appeared on the shelves of independent book and record stores and in the mailboxes of subscribers across the United States and Canada: the third-wave feminist magazine. These periodicals—*Bitch* (1996–), *BUST* (1993–), *HUES* (1992–99), *ROCKRGRL* (1995–2006), and *Venus Zine* (1994–2010)—brought their own particular forms of feminism to bear on topics like popular culture, identity, fashion, domesticity, and the arts. As popular print publications, over the last two decades third-wave magazines have helped create feminist popular cultures and have attempted to make what Lisa Jervis and Andi Zeisler describe in their inaugural editorial for *Bitch* magazine: girl-friendly spaces within a mass media landscape where few such spaces exist.

Third-wave magazines all began as zine publications. Zines are independently produced micro media that differ from most other forms of print publication since the creator (or creators) of a zine usually controls all aspects of the production process: from the content, to the design and layout, to production (usually by photocopier), to distribution.[1] The do-it-yourself (DIY) principles at the heart of zine culture are also central to third-wave magazine publishing. Jervis and Zeisler's inaugural editorial of *Bitch* is emblematic of this ethos, and this framing of the magazine's politics—as carving out a space for the voices of girls and women—has carried through its publishing career. *Bitch* presents itself here, and elsewhere, as a smart alternative to conventional magazines for women and encourages a role for readers as more than consumers, but as also producers and allies. By using the word "we" in this editorial, *Bitch* emphasizes the collectivity of and excitement for the possibilities for feminist print media. Third-wave magazines like *Bitch* emphasize the importance of valuing girlhood while also reworking what constitutes a girl in the first place.

And, indeed, the excitement captured in *Bitch*'s initial editorial is reflected by readers, as is evidenced in the words of the second epigraph, a line from one of the many letters to the editor now archived in the collection of third-wave feminist print artifacts at the Sallie Bingham Center for Women's History and Culture. The words of this reader evoke not only happiness and joy but also the expression of that emotion through song—a feeling that turns into a creative force. The feelings that are propagated between third-wave magazines and their readers are often generative. The act of reading feminist magazines is thus far more than the consumption of information or entertainment: readers often write about their engagement with third-wave magazines in ways that suggest a profound intimacy with the texts, as sites for gaining inspiration and energy through the act of reading, and as places for interacting with and shaping feminist communities.

I came to write this book as one such reader of third-wave magazines. I was introduced to magazines like *BUST* and *Bitch* sometime in the late 1990s or early 2000s: I was immediately hooked. I would read them cover to cover, talk to my friends and partner about the articles that I'd find, and save them all. My favourite part of the magazines was the Letters to the Editor section. In *Bitch*, this section often spanned three or four pages and I felt through reading that I was participating in the debates therein. The letter writers were so engaging, thoughtful, passionate—and often very funny; I felt that I had jumped into a community of cool feminist folks who were reading and thinking about the same things that I was, who were participating in shaping feminist discourse. As a university student who had discovered a lot of her feminism through academic books and journal articles, the contemporariness and freshness of what I found in the pages of third-wave magazines excited me.

These feelings of engagement, passion, and excitement that I felt in my interactions with third-wave magazines are also evident in other readers' letters to the editor, both published in the magazines and archived in third-wave feminist collections. *Making Feminist Media* attempts to capture some of these feminist affects, the hope, wonder, anger, and joy engendered through reading feminist magazines and engaging with the debates therein. Emotions, as Sara Ahmed (2004) argues, are crucial to feminism because they move us into action (175). Rather than framing feminist magazines as passive objects or the act of reading as a passive activity, *Making Feminist Media* demonstrates how these magazines were in engaged in a project of actively "doing feminism" (Rentschler and Thrift 2015) both through creating and shaping feminist discourse on a whole range of topics from the arts, to politics, to sex, and through helping engender a sense of feminist community through the shared act of reading.

Third-wave magazines are sites of negotiation among interrelated groups of editors, readers, distributors, writers, and advertisers about the meanings of contemporary feminism—what it is, what it includes and excludes, and to whom it belongs—as they circulate within the popular print marketplace. Popular discourses on the third wave, and the ways in which these discourses articulate with the politics of race, sexuality, DIY culture, and other feminisms, are far from monolithic both across different third-wave magazine publications and even within the same periodical. These magazines are multivocal texts that present varying and, at times, contradictory messages pertaining to contemporary feminisms. These magazines can thus be seen as microcosms of central debates happening within third-wave feminisms in all their complexity. Through a set of case studies on the politics of race, fashion, crafting, and sexuality, *Making Feminist Media* analyzes some of these debates and the role of third-wave periodicals in helping to shape feminist discourse in the 1990s and 2000s.

Making Feminist Media also engages with two publications for teen girls, *Shameless* (2004–) and *Rookie* (2010–), that started in the 2000s. Because they have slightly different readerships and were not established in the 1990s, these magazines provide some interesting points of contrast with the more recognizably "third-wave" magazine cohort that this book makes its focus. While distinct from third-wave magazines, both *Shameless* and *Rookie* are also fascinating extensions of the third-wave magazine that publications like *BUST*, *Bitch*, and *HUES* helped to cultivate.

Third-wave magazines emerged at a pivotal time in media culture: the cusp of the digital age. Although feminism now has vibrant blogging, vlogging, and Twitter cultures, in the 1990s and early 2000s online feminisms were less accessible and known to a wide audience. Vicki Tobias's article on feminist blogging from 2005, for example, takes great pains to explain to the uninitiated what a blog is and how to find one. The primary medium most

3

feminists were using to engage with feminism in the 1990s and early 2000s was print. This book makes a case for the central but frequently unacknowledged role that print culture played during this period. The point is not to wax nostalgic about a time without Twitter nor to assert clear-cut boundaries between print and online cultures; indeed, *Bitch* and *BUST*, the only two feminist magazines started in the 1990s that have survived beyond 2014, are now hybrids of magazine, zine, and online content, including blogs, social media pages, and Web stores. Nonetheless, I do argue that the kinds of feminist cultures engendered via print are different from those generated by online media because of print's materiality and, in the case of feminist magazines, through the specific genre features of the magazine itself.[2]

While today *Bitch* and *BUST* are multimedia enterprises, all third-wave magazines started as small-circulation, independently produced zines and then quickly made the transition to more widely circulating magazines with circulations in the tens of thousands. Although they often critique pop culture and what Lauren Berlant (2008) calls "women's culture," because third-wave periodicals are not quite underground and not quite mainstream they are also of these cultures, informing and overlapping with them, in ways that challenge easy distinctions between these categories (*Female Complaint* vii–x). Since third-wave magazines rely on the commercial marketplace to stay in business, they provide a fascinating site for asking critical questions about what kinds of feminisms find greater hospitality within capitalism. All the transitions that third-wave magazines have made over the past two decades give us insight into the strategies employed by independent feminist publishers to stay afloat in an inhospitable market climate. As this work shows, the material aspects of production and distribution influence feminist magazines' content and policy and shape what feminisms are—and aren't—articulated within these periodicals. While it might be easy to characterize any feminist engagement with the marketplace simply as "selling out," *Making Feminist Media* attempts to complicate this narrative, by framing the engagement of feminist magazines with the market as a space of compromise and negotiation, which is revealing of what the capitalist marketplace can and can not sustain.

In its broadest terms, *Making Feminist Media* imagines new and more complex ways to think about feminist histories, the politics of third-wave feminism in the 1990s and early 2000s, and the kinds of communities, or feminist publics, fostered through print culture. It does this by bringing together interviews with the editors and publishers of these third-wave magazines; archival research conducted at the third-wave magazine collection at the

Sallie Bingham Center; and discursive analysis of the advertising, articles, editorials, and letters to the editors of these periodicals. It historicizes these publications within the long history of feminist periodical publishing from 1850 onward and situates them within their more immediate context of 1990s punk, DIY, Riot Grrrl, and queer activism. While third-wave feminism is often described through its distinctiveness and divergence from the previous feminist "waves," *Making Feminist Media* shows the continuities between third-wave publications and their predecessors, in ways that challenge conventional understandings of the wave metaphor within feminist thought.

PRINT CULTURE AND ARCHIVES OF FEELINGS

Print culture plays a vital, but often unacknowledged, role in North American feminist movements. For instance, print culture scholars Mary Chapman and Victoria Lamont (2012) observe that, while "most histories of American woman suffrage ... begin with oratory" (253), in fact the movement was also characterized by a "widespread and innovative print culture" (254) that allowed women to influence government policy, attract new supporters, document the movement, and build an imagined community of believers. Similarly, Kathryn Flannery (2005) argues that "retrospective accounts of midcentury feminism tend to discount literacy's role in the movement" (2). Feminist magazines keep readers up to date with the debates and events within the various strands of the movement, but they also help to engender momentum or growth. They can create and shape the terms of debate around various feminist issues. Inherent to third-wave magazines' creation of feminist public cultures is their role as active and vibrant sites of debate and struggle over the various meanings of "feminism" within contemporary popular culture. The generic conventions of magazines—the editorial voice, the use of the collective "we," and the Letters to the Editor section—foster a sense of community and a sense of having a stake in the political debates that are played out on a magazine's pages that are arguably unparalleled within other forms of print culture. Feminist periodicals offer, as Barbara Green (2009) puts it, a counterpublic sphere, "a space for alternative discourses and identity formations" (197). This sense of having a stake or the potential for voice in a periodical, whether through letter writing, subscription, or submission of an article, can also result in a strongly affective dimension to magazine reading

This affective dimension of feminist magazine reading allows third-wave magazines to act as "archives of feelings" (Cvetkovich 2003). In her study of queer cultural production, Ann Cvetkovich argues that texts can act "as repositories of feelings and emotion, which are encoded not only in the content of the texts themselves but in the practices that surround their production and reception" (7). Third-wave magazines are indeed physical archives that document feminist debates, discussions, and interests, but they are also archives of feelings. That is, feminist feelings of joy, hope, frustration, or anger can attach themselves to the magazines as material objects. We see evidence of these feminist affects both through readers' letters and through the widespread practice of collecting and keeping third-wave magazines.

Particularly during the early and mid-1990s, when the Internet was still in a nascent form, getting a feminist magazine in the mail could feel like receiving a postcard from a good friend, and—particularly for readers living in smaller towns—it felt like a whole other world opened up of people who were thinking and feeling similarly. The earliest letters to *Bitch*, archived at the Sallie Bingham Center, demonstrate these kinds of affects. As one letter writer put it, "Your magazine is a breath of fresh air for people like me who are stuck in small towns where the majority of the population is sexist, racist, homophobic and 'conservative.' Sometimes I feel like I am going to drown in all the hate that I am surrounded by, but reading something like *Bitch* reminds me that I can educate others." This letter highlights that third-wave magazines are so much more than repositories of feminist debates: these periodicals create and document feminist communities, serving as identificatory points of connection among strangers. As David Henkin (1998) argues, reading is a process by which individuals come to discern "connections to one another and assume membership in a collective body or a shared cultural formation" (10). While conventionally constructed as a private activity, reading is actually intimately tied to the processes of subject formation and identification or disidentification (Muñoz 1999) with a broader feminist public culture.

The second way that we see third-wave magazines acting as "archives of feeling" is through the readerly practice of keeping magazines after they have been read. The fact that the majority of feminist periodical readers never discard their magazines suggests that these texts have an emotional resonance. In 2006, BUST reported that 95% of their readers either saved entire issues, or parts thereof, or passed them along to others (BUST Media Kit). In 2007, *Venus Zine* reported that 67% of its readers never discarded their copies and 13% gave them to friends (Venus: Advertising Information). According to Carolyn Kitch (2005),

> the very popularity of these kinds of journalistic media products ... suggests that they have personal and collective value, as material culture as well as

information and imagery, to those who buy them. Even, or perhaps especially, as a commodity, a magazine can have profound social meaning to readers who identify with its contents, who treasure and save it as an object, and who believe and remember the story it tells. (8–9)

The act of buying, collecting, and archiving feminist magazines suggests that they have significance for their readers as material artifacts: it is also a political act, given the ways in which minoritarian and social movement histories are often erased or diminished within dominant accounts of the past. Karina Hof's (2006) ethnographic study of scrapbooking finds that scrappers have a similar attraction to the materiality of scrapbooks: "I prefer scrapbooking to a webpage," one participant observed, "because a web site is not something you can have on your coffee table for friends and family to look through. I like to have something you can actually pick up" (374). Unlike the Internet, the materiality of magazines allows for a tangible archive of feminist writing, dialogue, and activity and promotes particular kinds of affective relations. The act of keeping third-wave magazines demonstrates the affective bonds that readers have with them and their key role in shaping feminist public cultures.

FEMINIST PUBLICS AND POPULAR CULTURE
Making Feminist Media engages with and extends the concepts of *public culture, publics,* and *counterpublics* that have developed from Jürgen Habermas's (1987) classic work *The Structural Transformation of the Public Sphere: An Inquiry into a Category of Bourgeois Society.* Habermas defined the public sphere as a realm separate from the state in which citizens could debate and discuss common affairs. He focused his study on the rise of a bourgeois public sphere in the eighteenth century, arguing that the development of this sphere, and the notion of public opinion, was facilitated by the rise of print culture, such as newsletters and newspapers, and the establishment of literary salons and coffee houses, which allowed people to gather and have critical discussions pertaining to art, literature, and the state. Habermas saw the development of nationally circulating print cultures as facilitating the capacity for critical discussions that had the potential to challenge the state and to hold it more accountable to the needs of the bourgeois public. Habermas's argument is important for studying third-wave print culture because it suggests that print has a political function in the way that it can promote critical discourse, community building, and political action.

Habermas's work has been widely criticized by feminist and antiracist scholars because it largely ignores both the print cultures of women, working-class folks, and racialized people in the mid-nineteenth century. Nancy Fraser (1997), for example, has argued that "the view that women and blacks were excluded from 'the public sphere' turns out to be ideological: it rests on a class- and gender-biased notion of publicity, one that accepts at face value the bourgeois public's claim to be *the* public" (75). Further, the valuing of "rational" discussion within Habermas's analysis ignores the way that the very notion of rationality is predicated on very specific kinds of identity performances (maleness and whiteness) and emerges out of a very specific European Enlightenment tradition. Moreover, as Linda B. Chambers, Linda Steiner, and Carole Fleming (2004) note, Habermas's work on the public sphere "dates the decline of public life to precisely that period when women succeeded in articulating their political concerns" (158). Finally, Habermas argues that the bourgeois public sphere declined as capitalism developed into mass culture. The critical reasoning and debate that Habermas valued within public spheres was, as Luke Goode (2005) describes it, "displaced by a culture *consuming* public" (18). Here, Habermas's argument rests on the view that consumption is a passive activity rather than a more active process; it does not account for the ways in which individuals or interpretive communities might engage with a product in unexpected or subversive ways.

Despite the limitations of Habermas's original formulation of the public sphere, the concept remains a useful one for thinking through the relationships between reading, thinking, and acting, and how individuals come to understand and articulate their relationships to identity- or issue-based groups. For these reasons, Habermas's work has found its way into the overlapping scholarship of feminist, queer, and Black theorists who have pushed Habermas's work in new directions. These critiques of the public sphere are useful for the study of third-wave magazines because they remind us that feminist public cultures are also not utopian spaces where all ideas and all people are necessarily welcome. Because the discourses fostered within public cultures must circulate, and because third-wave magazines circulate within the capitalist marketplace, publications that are "friendlier" to capitalism will find greater sustainability. Put bluntly, the straighter, the whiter, the more consumption-based the publication, the more longevity it seems to find.

To greater and lesser extents, and in different ways, third-wave magazines are imbricated in the capitalist marketplace and as such they do not exist outside the larger, dominant sphere of popular culture. To signal this imbrication, I use the phrase "feminist publics" to describe the kinds of life-worlds that feminist periodicals cultivate. Public sphere theorists (Fraser 1997; Warner 2002) argue that there are multiple, competing publics, rather than a single, unmarked public sphere, and that publics that are defined in relation to their tension with a larger, dominant public function as "counterpublics" (Warner, 56). Given the ways in which feminisms have often been understood as having such a relationship with popular culture and the publics it engenders, the term "counterpublic" might seem a particularly apt term to use in characterizing the communities that third-wave magazines help cultivate. However, "counterpublics" implies a separation or disconnect with popular culture, and feminist magazines do not exist fully outside of this realm. Rather, third-wave magazines overlap with and are part of popular culture, even as they are critical of some its facets.

My understanding of *popular culture* is grounded in the work of Cultural Studies scholars (Hall 1997; Hollows 2000; McRobbie 1996) who value popular texts like magazines for what they tell us about the power relations of everyday life. This approach analyzes the dominant discourses and counter-discourses that run through popular culture texts. Discourse, as philosopher Michel Foucault (1978) has famously argued, has material effects in the world: it acts on and produces subjects. But people are not simply passive subjects to discourse. A Cultural Studies approach also considers consumers of media texts as active interpreters who have some agency in taking up, accepting, negotiating, or rejecting the subject positions offered to them.

Public spheres, as Fraser asserts, "are not arenas only for the formation of discursive opinion; in addition, they are arenas for the formation and enactment of social identities" (83). When I write about feminist public culture, therefore, I am referring specifically to the social formations and affects that are enabled through the circulation of print materials within the commercial marketplace. This marketplace enables the existence of these publics through the circulation of the magazine text but also puts constraints upon the kinds of visual and written texts that circulate within it. Because most magazines rely on some form of advertising revenue, publications that represent feminisms, queer sexualities, or complex racial subjectivities generally have a harder time attracting companies that wish to advertise in their pages. The conditions of the marketplace both enable and constrain the discursive formations within third-wave magazines. *Making Feminist Media* focuses on how these discourses have helped define third-wave feminism in the 1990s and 2000s.

THIRD-WAVE FEMINISM AND THE LIMITATIONS OF THE WAVE METAPHOR

In my interviews with magazine founders, I asked how they saw their publications in relation to third-wave feminism and found that most had an ambivalent relationship with the concept. Although *Shameless* founder Nicole Cohen suggests that her publication "shares with other third-wave publications a certain aesthetic, rooted in DIY (do-it-yourself), punk and indie rock culture," she admits, "I have trouble with the term third wave." Similarly, *Bitch* founder Lisa Jervis (2007) argues that while *Bitch* fits the third-wave description chronologically, the term is often used to signify "a chronological category, an ideological description, or an aesthetic.... Folks using the term rarely clarify what they mean," adding, "In my opinion, this leads to a lot of intellectual muddles." While *Venus Zine* founder Amy Schroeder (2006) readily identified her magazine as "third wave," she added, "I spend more time thinking about the entrepreneurial experience than I do waxing philosophical about *Venus*' impact on or involvement with the feminist movement." Finally, while founder Dyann Logwood considers *HUES* to have been third wave because of the period of time during which it was published, and because of the media- and technology-oriented interests of its creators, she stresses that "we respect all of the work that has come before us," "we believe, as most pro-women do, that sisterhood is powerful," and "a lot of our ideas [were] grounded in the second wave."

Like these third-wave magazine founders, I also recognize the term's limitations as a framework for understanding feminist histories. As Lisa Jervis points out, the wave metaphor "wraps up differences in age, ideology, tactics, and style, and pretends that distinguishing among these factors is unimportant" (2006, 14). The wave metaphor thus simplifies the range of debates within feminism and tends to represent each period within feminist history monolithically and often in tension with each other. This tendency is particularly apparent within some third-wave writings about second-wave feminism.[3] The authors of one third-wave website assert, for example, "We are putting a new face on feminism, taking it beyond the women's movement that our mothers participated in, bringing it back to the lives of *real women* who juggle jobs, kids, money, and personal freedom in a frenzied world" ("The 3rd Wave" 2006). In this passage, second-wave feminists are the out-of-touch mothers who have exhausted their potential. This discourse assumes that second-wave feminism is a coherent whole and implies that second-wave feminists ignored the complexities of work, reproduction, and political agency. Clearly, this is not the case. Many second-wave feminists have advocated, and *continue* to advocate, for precisely the "real women" described in this statement. Similar rhetoric contrasting 1990s feminism with the 1970s pops up in *BUST*. For example, in their 1997 Goddess-themed issue, Celina Hex [Debbie Stoller] stated that the word "Goddess" had "become a wishy-washy unicorns-and-rainbows concept to me, done to death and almost ruined by all those goddess-worshipping freaked-out frizzy-haired femmes of the '70s" (2).[4] The wave metaphor often functions to obscure many similarities between second- and third-wave feminisms. As Jervis argues, "Much has been said and written about the disagreements, conflicts, differences, and antagonisms between feminists of the Second and Third Waves, while hardly anything is ever said about our similarities and continuities" (14). These discursive tendencies are not only inaccurate but unproductive for building political alliances and lines of communication that cross generational divides.

Another limitation of the wave metaphor is that it implies that very little happened during the "lulls." For example, according to Astrid Henry (2004),

> Feminists who came of age in the late 1970s to mid-1980s ... must necessarily go missing from feminism's narrative of its generational structure. They are subsumed under the category "second wave." ... As they can be understood as neither "mothers" nor "daughters" within feminism's imagined family structure, such feminists are frequently absent from recent discourse of feminism's (seemingly two) generations. (4)

By examining this temporal gap between the second and third waves, it is clear that this conceptualization of feminist movements elides significant developments within feminist theorizing during the 1980s, by U.S. Third World feminists bell hooks (1981), Cherríe Moraga and Gloria Anzaldúa (1981), and Audre Lorde (1984). Within the wave structure, however, this body of theorizing either falls through the cracks or is framed in a "helper" role that assists in ushering in third-wave feminism (Hemmings 2011, 43). Similarly, a heated set of debates in the 1980s known as the "lesbian sex wars" from which the position of sex-positive feminism emerged do not easily fit into the wave structure. A variety of legal and constitutional amendments were also proposed and, sometimes, achieved during this period: marital rape became a legally recognized crime in Canada and in many U.S. states;[5] Catharine MacKinnon and Andrea Dworkin helped introduce an ordinance to ban pornography in Minneapolis, a significant legal challenge, regardless of whether or not one agrees with it; and, while the Equal Rights Amendment was defeated in 1982, it was reintroduced in every subsequent session of the U.S. Congress. The 1980s may be predominantly characterized by social and economic conservatism, but this does not mean that it was a time during which feminists stopped fighting.[6]

The wave metaphor fails to acknowledge the important feminist work that is done in coalition with other social movements, feminism outside of a Western context, woman of colour, and indigenous feminisms. Coalition work that includes feminist mobilization concerning the AIDS crisis, gay rights, anti-poverty, anti-racism, and the environment is often left out of feminist histories conceptualized in terms of waves. Further, as Suzanne Staggenborg and Verta Taylor (2005) assert, the use of wave language "obscures the range of activities that might be counted as feminist, including the work of poor and working-class women and women of color worldwide" (38). While the wave metaphor may fit the dominant histories of feminisms in Canada, the United States, and the United Kingdom, it tends not to resonate with non-Western feminisms. Even within Canada, the United States, and the United Kingdom, the wave metaphor primarily describes the gains of the feminist movement that have most benefited white women (Springer 2002, 1059). Winning the right to vote, for example, is usually considered the defining feature of first-wave feminism of the early twentieth century, but not all women were enfranchised at the same time—in Canada, Aboriginal women were not enfranchised until the 1960s, while in the United States the Voting Rights Act of 1965 attempted to address the racist barriers that prevented many African American women and men from voting in elections.

Despite the limitations of the wave metaphor as a whole, the cohort of publications that *Making Feminist Media* takes as its subject has been widely identified as emblematic of third-wave feminism (Baumgardner and Richards 2000; Conrad 2001; Heywood and Drake 1997; Munford 2004; Snyder 2008). In naming BUST, *Bitch*, HUES, *Venus Zine*, and ROCKRGRL as *third-wave* magazines, I am primarily identifying the temporal context out of which these publications emerged. Like Amber Kinser (2004), who argues that the "third wave is less about differences in *politics* than it is about the differences in *climate*," I am not interested in defining and reifying the "third wave" as a recognizable set of practices, subjectivities, or interests (132). Third-wave feminism is a discursive construct, insofar as it unites a range of disparate practices and strategies under a common umbrella term. I use the term "third wave" because of its rhetorical force as a way of identifying the dual contexts of second-wave legacies and intensified backlash/post-feminist discourse out of which these 1990s periodical publications emerge.

In identifying *Shameless* and *Rookie* as *post-wave* publications, I signal the emergence of these magazines from a slightly later temporal context. Moreoever, identifying a post-wave context highlights the increasing dissatisfaction with the wave metaphor within feminist thought (Berger 2006; Garrison 2005; Groeneveld 2011; Lauglin et al. 2010).

RESEARCHING FEMINIST MAGAZINES

Research on third-wave magazines often feels like a treasure hunt: it's frustrating and onerous, with lots of dead ends, but sometimes results in a great find. Periodical research often involves amassing one's own personal collection, hunting around various libraries, trolling online auction sites, relying on the gifts and loans of friends from their prized collections, visiting the women's centres at university campuses, and seeking out zine libraries in coffee shops and artists' spaces. Online databases can be useful for the content of the periodicals (some text-only content from *HUES*, for example, was at one time available online through the GenderWatch database), but frequently the materials that are integral to a periodical's meaning—advertisements, covers, images, and the relationality between these various aspects of the text—are lost. Even the dog-eared corners of a friend's copy of *Sassy* tell their own stories. These are the unofficial archives of periodical culture.

Because magazines are ephemeral texts and "unacademic," they rarely find their way into the collections of university libraries. Conducting this research in a Canadian context posed an additional challenge, as most of the public libraries will favour Canadian magazine subscriptions for their shelves. Luckily, some feminist periodical and zine publications have also found homes in official archives, thanks to the efforts of a small handful of librarians, at places like Duke University's Sallie Bingham Center and the Barnard Zine Library (Eichhorn 2013, 23). The Duke archives gave me access to back issues that were not part of my personal collection, as well as financial documents, correspondence among members of the editorial staff, and published and unpublished letters to the editor. Cobbling together these official and unofficial archives of third-wave culture allowed me to work with complete runs of *BUST* from 1993 to 2010; *Bitch* from 1996 to 2010; and *ROCK-RGRL* from 1995 to 2006. I worked with partial runs of *Venus Zine* from 1994 to 2010; *Shameless* from 2004 to 2010; and *HUES* from 1993 to 1996. I was able to work with the entire archive of *Rookie*, as an online publication. The archival materials on *BUST* and *Bitch* that I accessed at the Bingham Center allow for a more trenchant analysis of the particular moment at which these magazines emerged, and how the magazines, and readers' relationships to them, began to shift over the course of the 1990s and into the 2000s. Early print letters to the editor from the mid-1990s, for example, carry a different valence from print letters sent to the editor in the mid-2000s due to the ease of access to email. What is included in and excluded from the archives is a text in itself, capable of being read in a way that shows what stories are valued and how shifts in media technologies—the entrance of these texts into the digital age—have altered how readers interact with these texts.

Reader responses to third-wave magazines, whether through letters to the editor or through online exchanges, are an important part of analyzing these texts. There are a range of reader relationships with feminist periodicals, and such work highlights more than the text itself but allows for a consideration of how texts have social lives, and how stories these texts tell play a role in our everyday lives, shaping our understanding of ourselves and the world and the stories that we tell about ourselves. This approach owes its debt to earlier feminist media critics who have used sociological and ethnographic methods to examine how and to what extent readers take up, reject, and/or negotiate the various subjectivities made available to them within a given text. The landmark studies of Ien Ang (1985), Janice Radway (1984), and Janice Winship (1980) on the pleasures of soap operas, romance fiction, and women's magazines, respectively, for consumers, has led to the adoption of more ethnographic and sociological approaches to the study of popular texts.

These methodologies have also been employed by other magazine scholars, such as Dawn Currie (1999), whose work on girls magazines, *Girl Talk: Adolescent Magazines and Their Readers*, consists of a feminist materialist analysis of interviews with forty-eight girls between the ages of thirteen and seventeen who read adolescent magazines, such as *Sassy, Elle,* and *Seventeen*. Additionally, Angela McRobbie (1996) and Elizabeth Frazer (1996) have each advocated ethnographic approaches in their separate studies of the British teen magazine *Jackie*, a method that allows for an examination of the ways in which readers are only ever partially subject to ideologies. I seek to achieve a similar end through the consideration of readers' letters to the editor, not only to demonstrate the ways that readers negotiate their own meanings in relation to the magazine text, but also to highlight the ways in which readers' letters play a crucial role in constructing—writing—the discourses of the magazine itself. This approach shares commonality with Amy Erdman Farrell's study of *Ms.* magazine. Her book, *Yours in Sisterhood* (1998), blends semiotics, discourse analysis, and materialism and focuses on the historical trajectory of *Ms.* magazine from the 1970s through to the 1990s, with an additional chapter devoted to letters to the editor. This approach allows Farrell to highlight how the content and style of *Ms.* have shifted over the course of its existence, how the conditions of its publication have shaped the magazine, and how dialogue developed between editors and readers.

Making Feminist Media also highlights the material aspects of magazine production, paying careful attention to the financial constraints under which feminist magazine producers are frequently working, and the ways in which these constraints influence magazine content and policy. Classic feminist scholarship, such as the work of Ros Ballaster, Margaret Beetham, Elizabeth Frazer, and Sandra Hebron (1991), Rosalind Coward (1987), Marjorie Ferguson (1983), Betty Friedan (1963), and Ellen McCracken (1993), has analyzed magazines in terms of the ideological messages conveyed to readers. Other scholars, such as Amy Erdman Farrell (1998), Nancy Walker (1998), and Janice Winship (1980), have built on these studies through either discursive analyses or ethnographic/sociological approaches that engage more directly with readers' responses to periodical texts; very few studies have engaged with the important role that economic formations play in the lives of feminist periodical publications, although Anna Gough-Yates's (2003) study of women's magazines is an important exception. My own approach blends discourse analysis and reader response and pays attention to the frequently invisible economic formations that shape the content and form of periodicals.

THIRD-WAVE MAGAZINE SCHOLARSHIP
Although feminist work on women's magazines is growing as a scholarly field, thus far little critical work has been focused on third-wave magazines.[7] One exception is the work of scholar Courtney Bailey. In *"Bitch*ing and Talking/Gazing Back: Feminism as Critical Reading" (2003), Bailey argues that reading feminist magazines is an act of *critical reading* through her semiotic analysis of a *Bitch* magazine cover from the year 2000. According to Bailey, the magazine's use of irony, parody, and pastiche on its front covers produces a kind of Brechtian alienation effect (*Verfremdungseffekt*) in which the reader is encouraged to think critically about the visual and textual signs through the distancing effect produced by parody. This kind of visual and rhetorical technique relies on a body of shared knowledge among readers who need to be able to recognize and decode the parodic elements of the text. In this sense, as Bailey argues, "*Bitch* both relies upon and invokes a particular discursive community, which means that the ability to engage in its vision of feminism depends on certain privileges, such as those accruing from education, socioeconomic class, and geographical location" (15). Nonetheless,

and as Bailey points out, *Bitch* also presents a version of feminism that is constructed as a site of contestation and debate, and, through its focus on reading popular culture critically, the magazine tacitly acknowledges the active role of readers in shaping and creating meaning.

A similar approach to Bailey's is taken in Alison Piepmeier's *Girl Zines: Making Media, Doing Feminism* (2009), which includes discussions of *Bitch* and *BUST*. Piepmeier argues that *Bitch* cultivates a "pedagogy of active criticism" in its pages that allows the reader to participate in feminist criticism alongside and in response to the articles (172). In her discussion of *BUST*, Piepmeier focuses on the ways in which the publication seeks to "celebrate femininity and the pleasures of femininity" (106). Piepmeier's work includes *Bitch* and *BUST* as part of a larger study of girl zine cultures in which she argues that zines help cultivate "embodied communities" (18). While *BUST* and *Bitch* have both transitioned from zine to magazine, Piepmeier's work suggests that it is because of their roots in zine culture—and the embodied community zine culture engenders—that the two publications have been able to sustain themselves through financial challenges.

The work of Suzy D'Enbeau (2009) examines *BUST* magazine's feminine and feminist transformations of popular culture in issues of the magazine published during 2005 and 2006. Drawing on the philosophical work of Mary Daly, D'Enbeau argues that *BUST* "uses humour as a means of resistance" and "employs the power of language to combat patriarchal social control" (17). In response to critiques that *BUST* is not "feminist enough," D'Enbeau argues that the magazine "'BUSTs' through negative connotations of feminism to present a contestable, flexible, and more accessible version of feminism" (17). While I agree with D'Enbeau's assessment, I argue in subsequent chapters that *BUST*'s "accessible version" of feminism is more accessible to privileged subjects, primarily young white women, and that this accessibility is often predicated on the denigration of other, "less fashionable" subject positions.

While *BUST* and *Bitch* are not the focus of her work, Rebecca Munford's scholarly writing (2004) on Riot Grrrl, girlie, and post-feminisms includes consideration of these magazines. Munford argues that these two periodicals exemplify "girlie feminism," a term that she borrows from Jennifer Baumgardner and Amy Richards's *Manifesta: Young Women, Feminism, and the Future* (2000). In it, Baumgardner and Richards define "Girlies" as "girls in their twenties or thirties who are reacting to an antifeminine, antijoy emphasis they perceive as the legacy of second-wave seriousness. Girlies have reclaimed girl culture, which is made up of such formerly disparaged girl things as knitting, the color pink, nail polish, and fun" (80). Based on *BUST*'s anthologized collection of readings, *The BUST Guide to the New Girl Order* (Karp and Stoller 1999), and *Bitch*'s website, Munford's argument is that, "by focusing its critique on cultural manifestations of dominant social forms rather than the institutions which maintain them, Girlie risks reinforcing a binary between culture and politics that privileges individual over collective empowerment" (149). While this certainly is a risk, Munford's argument does not take into account the dynamic ways in which readers may take up and engage with these periodical texts.

Appearing in the same anthology as Munford's article is Melanie Waters's (2004) analysis of contemporary feminist perspectives on pornography, which includes a discussion of *The New Girl Order*. The work of *BUST* may be "inclusive and non-judgmental," Waters argues, but the "refusal to acknowledge the continued contentiousness of pornography speaks to the third wave's desperation to expel the spectre of anti-pornography feminism from the contemporary landscape" (259). Indeed, *BUST* may be subversive, but ultimately the edginess of *BUST* frequently comes at the expense of its feminist forerunners.

This scholarly work is an important contribution to the growing field of feminist periodical scholarship, but—as yet—no study has undertaken a comprehensive and sustained analysis of these periodicals as a group. No study to date has attended to the ways in which these texts, *as magazines*, have shifted and developed over time, issue by issue; the important differences among these publications; and the ways in which for- and not-for-profit status shapes the kinds of magazines that are produced. *Making Feminist Media* attempts to provide such an analysis: through contextualizing these publications within the broader history of feminist periodical production; by situating these magazines within the 1990s and early 2000s feminist climate known as *the third wave*; by analyzing the ways in which the material context of the marketplace affects these periodicals; through assessing the political benefits and limitations of these magazines; and through case studies of exemplary moments within the lives of specific periodicals.

CHAPTER OVERVIEW

Making Feminist Media is divided into two parts. Part One: Historicizing Third-Wave Magazines contextualizes this group of publications within both the long history of feminist periodical publishing in the United States and Canada and the more recent feminist media landscape of the 1990s. Since third-wave feminisms are often constructed as completely distinct or divergent from the previous "waves," historicizing these publications helps demonstrate some of the fascinating continuities across different decades. Chapter One supplies an overview of the publishing trajectories of BUST, *Bitch*, HUES, ROCKRGRL, *Rookie*, *Shameless*, and *Venus Zine*, providing a fuller introduction to these magazines for readers unfamiliar with the publications. The chapter situates the emergence of these periodicals within the girl cultures propagated by *Sassy* magazine and Riot Grrrl music and zines in the early 1990s. Chapter Two contextualizes third-wave magazines within the long history of feminist periodical publishing and highlights the continuities between and differences among these late-twentieth-century publications and their forerunners, with regard to content, ethos, and engagement with the marketplace. The commercial marketplace plays a critical role in mediating the relationship between readers and magazines and determining the financial success of a periodical. The chapter analyzes the relationship between feminist periodicals and the marketplace, since engaging the commercial marketplace has been fraught with challenges for feminist magazines. These publications usually lack capital, advertisers, and a large base of readers; moreover, some feminist publications that have found a measure of success are often widely perceived as having "sold out." This chapter challenges these reductive analyses by recasting the relationship between feminist periodicals and the market as a relation characterized by negotiation, compromise, and adaptation.

Part Two: The Politics of Third-Wave Magazines is built on a set of four case studies that illuminate some of the key issues discussed and debated within these publications, including the politics of race, fashion, domesticity, and sexuality. These chapters analyze the coverage (or lack of coverage) of these topics within these magazines to illuminate how third-wave magazines were contributing to feminist discourse in the 1990s and early 2000s. This analysis demonstrates how the constraints of the marketplace helped shape the kinds of discourses that were possible. Chapter Three, for example, examines the increased popularity of niche marketing in the magazine industry during the 1990s and links the rise of identity-based marketing with the intensification of identity-based politics and the consequences of this intensification for HUES, a publication predicated more on an intersectional politics of alliance than of identity. The chapter probes the systemic racism of the magazine and advertising industries, drawing on co-founder Dyann Logwood's own accounts of commercial companies who declined to advertise within HUES. Finally, I use Logwood's narrative to reflect on the relative commercial success—and whiteness—of BUST and *Venus Zine*, which fit more readily with the format of niche marketing.

Chapter Four on fashion and lifestyle feminism engages with *BUST* magazine's 2006 call to "be a feminist or just dress like one." Taking *BUST*'s fashion issue as a case study, this chapter contextualizes *BUST*'s particular take on fashion within both a broader history of feminist perspectives on the politics of dress and the negative backlash against feminism that gained particular strength during the 1980s. It argues that *BUST*'s fashion issue is an ambivalent text that offers, on one hand, homage to feminism's "past" and, on the other hand, a rather simplistic view of that history. Given the complex and historically fraught relationship between dress and feminism within the United States, an examination of the dynamics of fashion and feminism, and the *BUST* spread particularly, crystallizes my broader interest in the politics of representation, recuperation, and money within popular feminisms in the early 2000s.

A key feature of these publications is their promotion of reclaiming and repoliticizing activities traditionally associated with the domestic sphere, particularly knitting. Chapter Five, "'Join the Knitting Revolution': Representations of Crafting in Feminist Magazines" critically examines and historically contextualizes the discourses on the "new" knitting within the letters to the editor, editorials, articles, and advertisements of third-wave feminist periodicals and argues that contemporary feminist craft cultures sit at a politically ambivalent nexus of privilege, complicity, and resistance. By historicizing the promotion of knitting, this chapter sheds light on the changing ways in which the domestic sphere has figured within the broader history of U.S. feminism and suggests that, despite their appeals to the "new," these periodicals are in conversation with what is to some extent an imagined feminist past.

The final chapter, "Dildo Debacle: Advertising Feminist Sexualities in *Bitch* Magazine" analyzes the controversy surrounding the placement of a full-page advertisement for a purple dildo on the back cover of *Bitch* magazine. It contextualizes the controversy within the history of the feminist "sex wars" and one of its main outcomes, sex-positive feminism. Sex-positive feminism is articulated within third-wave periodicals, particularly *BUST*, in a way that tends toward presenting primarily heteronormative subject positions for readers. As a much more ambivalent–queer–image of feminist sexuality, the *Bitch* ad, and its location on the magazine's back cover, generated a debate among readership that I read as primarily a preoccupation with what feminism should look like in public. That is, at stake in the vibrator controversy is the question of how feminism represents itself to a broader "unmarked" public that is constructed as unsympathetic to feminist concerns and supportive of heteronormative social relations.

CONCLUSION

Making Feminist Media analyzes the discursive patterns within third-wave periodicals—their key debates, tensions, and trends—in order to assess the benefits and limitations of their brand of feminism, to examine the subject positions made available to readers, and to consider the ways in which readers take up, negotiate, or reject these positions. It examines the ways that these discursive frameworks are enabled, shaped, and constrained by the capitalist marketplace in which they circulate. These material concerns of markets and money have indelibly shaped feminist periodicals, not only in the late twentieth and early twenty-first centuries but also in the past. By examining these contemporary periodicals within the context of their historical precursors, the book highlights significant continuities, as well as breaks, between third-wave magazines and their feminist antecedents. Many of the debates and interests that are constructed as "new" within third-wave periodicals in fact have fascinating and revealing historical precedents. Taken together, what these historical and contemporary texts demonstrate is the crucial role that periodical culture has played, and continues to play, in shaping contemporary feminism.

PART ONE

HISTORICIZING THIRD-WAVE MAGAZINES

CHAPTER ONE

"SOMEONE ELSE ACTUALLY CARES AS MUCH AS ME": SASSY MAGAZINE, GRRRL ZINE CULTURE, AND FEMINIST MAGAZINES

In 1996, *Bitch* launched its inaugural issue, featuring a special section called "*Sassy* Sucks." Its second issue featured a follow-up article entitled "*Sassy* Update: The New Staff of the New-and-Not-Improved *Sassy* Get Defensive in the Face of their Critics" (Jervis 1996b). *Bitch*'s vitriol for *Sassy* magazine certainly struck a chord with readers. In a letter to the editor archived in *Bitch*'s records at the Sallie Bingham Center, one reader writes in: "I was so excited to read [*Bitch*] and discover that someone else actually cares as much as me about *Sassy*'s sad demise.... [M]y friends thought I was crazy to care so much about a silly teen magazine." Years later, when former *Sassy* editor Jane Pratt launched a new magazine, *Jane*, *Bitch* ran an article called "10 Things to Hate About *Jane*: New Rag from former *Sassy* editor Raised Our Hopes and Then Dashed Them on the Jagged Rocks of the Newsstand" (Zeisler, Jervis, and Hao 1999). What was it about *Sassy* magazine that elicited such strong responses from its readers, including the founders of *Bitch*?

For many women now in their thirties and forties, *Sassy* (1988–96) was a touchstone, a magazine that did not talk down to its readers, a cutting-edge girls magazine that was the first publication of its kind to run condom ads, a magazine that was subject to a mass boycott by right-wing religious groups in the United States, a magazine that introduced many readers to zine culture for the first time, and—finally—a magazine that left many readers feeling utterly betrayed in its final year of publication. This chapter introduces the girl culture climate of the 1990s that inspired third-wave magazine publications, a culture in which *Sassy* magazine played an integral role. The chapter situates third- and post-wave magazines within the context of the 1990s, focusing on *Sassy* and grrrl zine culture. It then provides an overview of the publishing trajectories of third-wave magazines, as well as post-wave *Rookie* and *Shameless*, outlining the philosophies, content, and financial struggles of each publication.

Responding to the lack of writing on girls' subcultures in the late 1970s, Angela McRobbie and Jenny Garber (1976) described the private spaces of girls' bedrooms as key sites for the cultivation of unique girl cultures, which involved experimenting with makeup and hair, gossiping with friends, and reading and discussing teen magazines. Simon Frith and Angela McRobbie (1978/79) argued that "[t]eenage girls' lives are usually confined to the locality of their homes; they have less money than boys, less free time, less independence of parental control" and thus the subcultural lives of girls are shaped by the space of the bedroom (50). Both *Sassy* and grrrl zines are part of what characterized a new kind of girls' bedroom culture in the 1990s. Both *Sassy* and grrrl zines constructed their ideal readers as smart and creative. Grrrl zine makers, particularly, often encouraged their grrrl readers to become zine makers for themselves, while *Sassy* encouraged their readers to explore music, art, and film outside of the mainstream (Leonard 1998, 110; Stockburger 2011, 18). This chapter argues that the girls' bedroom cultures propagated by *Sassy* and grrrl zines were the ideal petri dish for the growth of third-wave magazines and that the anger and betrayal that many readers felt when *Sassy* radically changed its publishing profile were intensely generative for many third-wave magazine producers.

THE STORY OF *SASSY* MAGAZINE

Sassy was the most immediate precursor to third-wave feminist magazines. The publication was founded by Sandra Yates, who worked for the Australian-based Fairfax Publishing at a time when the company was interested in entering the American marketplace. Yates wanted to create a U.S. equivalent to Australia's *Dolly* (1970–), a frank teen magazine and the highest-selling girls periodical per capita worldwide. *Sassy* had been up and running for only one month in 1988 when its publisher, Fairfax, dumped its U.S. properties. This move prompted Yates and co-publisher Anne Summers to form Matilda, which purchased both *Sassy* and *Ms.* magazine. In 1989 the magazines were purchased first by Lang Communications and then Petersen Publications in 1994. Under Petersen, the entire magazine was overhauled, rendering it virtually unrecognizable to its readers as "*Sassy*."[1]

Sassy was a breath of fresh air in the sphere of girls magazine publications in a number of significant ways, including Sandra Yates's early decision to hire as editor the relatively unknown Jane Pratt, whose innovative approach made the publication a cult classic. Pratt encouraged her staff writers to develop their own individual personae through their writing, a technique that was unheard of within the magazine industry. Unlike other magazines that would receive letters to the editor, all the *Sassy* staff, including Pratt, would receive individualized letters from readers who identified with them particularly. In their homage to *Sassy*, Kara Jesella and Marisa Meltzer write, "Readers got to know the staff so well that by the end of the first year, writers signed their stories with their first names only" (20). This older sister rather than parental tone cultivated a stronger bond between *Sassy* writers and readers. As Jesella and Meltzer argue, "Though *Sassy* was never able to match the advertising or circulation of other teen magazine giants of its day, the magazine more than made up for this lack in terms of reader devotion" (vii).

While *Sassy* was not an overtly feminist publication, it also set itself apart from other teen magazines because it ran content that was inflected by feminism and was generally considered more socially progressive than the other teen magazines that were its contemporaries. Under its ownership by Matilda, the publication was considered a "little sister" to *Ms.* magazine. Jesella and Meltzer argue, "*Sassy* was like a Trojan horse, reaching girls who weren't necessarily looking for a feminist message" (29). For example, as a consumer magazine, *Sassy* published articles on fashion and beauty but also tried to promote positive body image within them. However, the range of body types the periodical showed in its pages was quite narrow: pictures of plus-sized models were never featured in the context of fashion or beauty. In this sense, *Sassy* did not radically reconfigure the genre of girls magazines but rather attempted to bring a slightly feminist slant to the existing columns common to the genre.

Another way that *Sassy* was special was its frank discussion of sexuality, a practice virtually unheard of within the teen magazine genre in the late 1980s and early 1990s. The magazine was sympathetic to homosexuality and was the first teen magazine in the United States to accept condom ads. This difference from other girls magazines was more than a matter of contrasting editorial approaches; Jesella and Meltzer argue that, "[a]s teen-pregnancy rates soared, AIDS became a very real threat, and debates over what kids should be taught about sex in school raged, the magazine heralded a new way of thinking about girls and sexuality" (vii). However, this more open approach to discussing girls' sexuality led to a boycott of the publication and the companies that advertised within its pages. One article in particular, entitled "Losing Your Virginity: Read This before You Decide," drew the ire of a U.S. right-wing fundamentalist Christian group called Women Aglow. The initial boycott soon drew further support from the influential socially conservative groups Focus on the Family, American Family Association, and Moral Majority. As a result, almost every advertiser pulled out of *Sassy*, a move that was clearly more about business than moral outrage, given that the same companies continued to advertise in *Dolly*, which in many ways was still a much bolder publication than *Sassy*. In their discussion of the *Sassy* boycott, Jesella and Meltzer assert that "[Sandra Yates] had never really understood the dire threat the right wing posed. No one from Australia did" (37). The magazine was forced to pull articles dealing with sex in the following issue and Yates was asked to step down as publisher (40). From that point forward, the publication continued to moderate its sexual content in order to maintain its existing advertising contracts and in order to prevent another damaging boycott.

When *Sassy* was purchased by Petersen, the entire staff was replaced with new writers, and the amount of fashion and beauty content was increased, a move that deeply angered many of *Sassy*'s readers, many of whom wrote letters of complaint to the magazine. According to Mary Celeste Kearney (1998), "Readers' criticisms of the new *Sassy* ranged from 'lameass,' 'boring,' and 'repetitive' to '*Sassy* should be renamed YMII or *Seventeen, The Sequel*,' 'Some of your articles make me want to yak,' and 'Did YM have you buy out *Sassy* or are you merely doing the work of Satan?'" (296). In response, the new staff took the unprecedented approach of writing an editorial to the unhappy readers, telling them, "[T]hat you are capable of such whiny evil is disheartening and pretentious. Quit your bitchin', lighten up, and cut us some slack" (quoted in Jesella and Meltzer, 107). For a magazine that had cultivated such an innovative and progressive approach to the girl magazine genre and had fostered such strong bonds between readers and writers, this kind of treatment understandably saddened and angered many readers. Under Petersen, the magazine changed into a more conventional teen publication and folded after just a few months.

THE LEGACY OF *SASSY*

The impact that *Sassy* had on third-wave magazine creators would be difficult to overestimate. In many cases there are direct links between *Sassy* and third-wave magazine founders: both Lisa Jervis and Andi Zeisler, founders of *Bitch* magazine, did internships at the magazine, and Tali Edut, co-founder of *HUES*, worked on one of the "reader-produced" issues. On *Bitch*'s website, Jervis and Zeisler cited *Sassy*, along with *Ms.*, as two of the magazines that inspired them to start their own publication. In a 2001 interview, *Venus Zine* founder Amy Schroeder stated, "*Sassy* magazine was my first biggest inspiration" (Schroeder 2001). *Sassy* also gets special mention in BUST magazine's inaugural editorial: in the context of complaining about women's magazines, Celina Hex [Debbie Stoller] and Betty Boob [Marcelle Karp] (1993) write,

> Only *Sassy* magazine, devoted to the newly found freedom and sexuality of the teenage girl, seems to understand that being a girl can be really fun. That being independent is a cool thing, that girls make great friends, that boys are only part of the story, that the way you look doesn't matter all that much and that beauty comes in many shapes and colours, that you buy clothes because it's fun to buy things you like, fun to listen to music that floats your boat, excellent super fun to say yes to cute boys, yes to wild car rides, and yes to life. Those of us older girls who get off on reading *Sassy* do it as a sort of guilty pleasure: sure, it makes us feel good, but it also makes us feel like losers because the only magazine we can relate to is meant for teenagers! (n.p.)

As Hex and Boob's editorial demonstrates, despite toning down its sexually progressive voice, *Sassy* was able to push the boundaries of teen girl culture in other ways. Unlike other teen consumer magazines of its day, *Sassy* devoted attention to aspects of both celebrity and underground culture, making the magazine popular with both teen girls and an older demographic of people involved in indie culture. Thurston Moore and Kim Gordon of the band Sonic Youth, for example, were both self-declared fans of *Sassy* and later wrote articles for the magazine. And one of *Sassy*'s covers, featuring Kurt Cobain and Courtney Love, accompanied by the tagline "Ain't Love Grand?" is now an iconic image of the 1990s.

It's clear that *Sassy* influenced third-wave magazines, but it did so in different ways depending on the type of interaction individual magazine creators had with the publication, as well as the year that they started their own magazines. Hex and Boob's editorial celebrates *Sassy* at its best: *Sassy* revisioned girlhood as fun; the magazine valued independence and encouraged whimsy, pleasure, and saying yes to things.[2] This revisioning of girlhood was—and in many ways, still is—quite radical in that it imagines girls as active agents, a stark contrast to a cultural milieu in which girls are often depicted as passive consumers and as sexual objects, which, as Deborah Tolman (2002) argues, "precludes having desire of their own" (82).[3] In many ways, *Sassy* was an important forerunner of the sex-positive feminism that would shape the politics of sexuality in magazines like *BUST* and *Bitch*.

Tali Edut's experience working on *Sassy*'s second reader-produced issues was formative for her later co-creation of *HUES*.[4] In 1989, *Sassy* began publishing one issue per year created entirely by readers. As Caryn Murphy argues, this practice empowered *Sassy* readers "to understand the process of magazine production, and to see themselves as the focus of that process" (517). For Edut, the process of creating the reader-produced issue was more than a little educative. For this issue, the participants had wanted to feature two women on the cover, one African American and one Filipino American, but were explicitly asked by the executives of the publishing company to include at least one white woman in order to help sell the publication at newsstands. *Sassy*'s regular staff also had a similar fight to put a photograph of an African-American woman, Sala Patterson, voted "Sassiest Girl in America" by readers, on the cover by herself in 1992. In the industry, the cover of the magazine is its most important selling feature because it attracts newsstand buyers to the product. The magazine cover is crucial, as David Crowley (2003) argues, in that it labels both the periodical and the consumer (7). Through the process of identification, the image on the magazine cover is designed to reflect back to the consumer a more perfect and attainable, but always just-out-of-reach, version of themselves. Sadly, *Sassy*'s publishers only saw white middle-class femininity as an aspirational and relatable identity. As a multicultural pro-woman publication, *HUES* almost always featured more than one woman on its cover and, although white women sometimes made the cover, they were never featured alone.

Since *Bitch* was launched in 1996, two years after *Sassy* was sold to Petersen, the tenor of the magazine's relationship to *Sassy*, and later *Jane*, was quite different from the admiration expressed by Hex and Boob in their 1993 inaugural editorial for *BUST*. As the opening of this chapter demonstrates, much of *Bitch*'s early fodder for critique was *Sassy* and *Jane*, and many of *Bitch*'s early letters to the editor held in the Sally Bingham Center archives were from disaffected *Sassy* readers. The primary affect characterizing the early *Bitch* articles on *Sassy* is rage. The subject headings in Jervis's first article on *Sassy* progress are shaped by an affect arc: from indignation ("Who are you and what have you done with my favourite magazine?") to "I'm getting upset" to "If you don't stop I'm going to scream," culminating in "AAAAAAARRRRGGGGHHHH!!!!!," and concluding with "Don't forget to breathe." The changes that *Sassy* underwent are figured as a form of violence; Jervis (1996a) characterizes the magazine as "mutilated beyond recognition." Jervis's writing takes the reader through her copy of the "new" *Sassy*, using her gradually mounting rage as a site for building feminist media critique. Jervis notes and dismantles the discourses that girls' sexualities are dangerous and that feminism is no longer relevant, which appear in the pages of her Petersen-published issue. Anger, as Sara Ahmed (2004) argues, "moves ... into an interpretation of that which one is against, whereby associations or connections are made between the object of anger and broader patterns or structures.... Anger is creative; it works to create a language with which to respond to that which one is against, whereby 'the what' is renamed, and brought into a feminist world" (176). Anger thus becomes a site of theory generation. In *Bitch*, anger about *Sassy* is also shaped by the love that Jervis, and other readers, have for the magazine. Jervis's "what have you done with my favourite magazine?" gives a sense of the kind of ownership and protectiveness that readers felt toward *Sassy*.

The generativeness of this feminist anger about *Sassy* was also in its capacity to bring together the readers and editors of *Bitch* in a new feminist public. As the letter to the editor that frames this chapter demonstrates, the idea that "somebody else actually cares as much as me" becomes a way for one *Bitch* reader to build a feminist community of disaffected *Sassy* readers now also reading *Bitch*. This letter further demonstrates *Sassy*'s popularity with an older cohort of readers, as evidenced by the fact that the reader's friends can't understand why she would care about a "silly" teen magazine. This statement speaks both to the specialness of *Sassy* and to the ways in which the products of girls' culture, generally, are rarely valued and seen as important. In its focus on feminist response to popular culture, *Bitch* promised to deliver a critique that was shaped by care and love, as well as anger.

Sassy magazine inspired and shaped the production of third-wave magazines that started in the 1990s. Because they began publication in the 2000s, this context is less germane to *Shameless* and *Rookie*. Notably, however, founder and editor-in-chief of the online feminist magazine *Rookie* (2010–), Tavi Gevinson (2010), gives her very first inkling to her blog readers that she will start *Rookie* that same year in a post about reading old issues of *Sassy*: "Maybe [reading about *Sassy*] is even enough to inspire someone to make Generation Y a *Sassy*. Maybe it already has." Like Gevinson's creation of a line between *Sassy* and *Rookie*, *Shameless* has also been positioned as part of a lineage started by *Sassy* and continued by other progressive girls magazines. In a blog post announcing the death of *Jane* magazine in 2007, *Shameless* reposted this comment from Canadian music video station *MuchMusic* on their website: "First *Sassy*, then ELLEgirl, and now *Jane*—all have folded. Where have all the great girl mags gone? And what exactly are they making room for? At least we still have *Shameless*" (quoted in Fowles 2007). It's also notable that the word "sassy" has found its way into *Shameless*'s description of its readers as "smart, strong, sassy young women and trans youth" ("About *Shameless*" 2014). For third-wave magazines, the idea of being sassy, that is, to be bold, smart, and perhaps a little cheeky, is an aspirational quality, and while *Sassy* magazine can't take all the credit for that, the magazine certainly left an indelible mark on feminist periodical publishing in the 1990s and beyond.

RIOT GRRRL AND GRRRL ZINE CULTURE

Beginning on the west coast of the United States and Canada in the early 1990s and then spreading nationally and internationally, Riot Grrrl was a feminist punk scene that arose out of young women's frustration with and anger about sexism and other social injustices.[5] While each Riot Grrrl chapter was different, many started consciousness-raising (CR) groups, organized self-defence workshops, formed music groups, and created zines. A do-it-yourself (DIY) ethos permeated each of these activities. The DIY ethos of punk enabled girls to create their own cultural productions, challenging the construction of girls as only passive consumers. Riot Grrrl encouraged other girls to start bands, even if they didn't yet know how to play instruments, and most Riot Grrrl zines encouraged their readers to start making zines, too. Riot Grrrl was about the process of doing feminism on the ground. For young women who were angry about social injustices, Riot Grrrl also gave a space to participate in cultural critique where one did not previously exist.

Zines were a significant part of Riot Grrrl. As I discussed in the introduction to *Making Feminist Media*, zines can take a variety of forms, but they are usually small, independently produced publications that are handmade and photocopied. Riot Grrrl zines often contained manifesto-like statements that described the meaning of Riot Grrrl from the perspective of the zine makers. As Stephen Duncombe (1997) points out in his analysis of one such manifesto, "RIOT GRRRL (to me)," "[T]he authors and contributors go out of their way to stress that what follows is only their point of view" (68). In keeping with a DIY approach, Riot Grrrl encouraged other girls and women to create their own meanings of Riot Grrrl and to define the scene and their participation within it for themselves. Zine culture is part of what enabled the spread of Riot Grrrl chapters across the United States and Canada, as other girls and women discovered zines like *Bikini Kill*, *Riot Grrrl*, and *Action Girl*—whether through having them sent in the mail by friends, finding them randomly, or ordering them after reading about one in *Sassy* or in a zine catalogue like *Factsheet Five* or *Broken Pencil*.

Although Riot Grrrls did not self-identify as such, the goals, strategies, and underlying philosophies of this network of feminists have been retrospectively cast as the vanguard of third-wave feminism. "Riot Grrrl is seen by many third wave feminists," according to Jennifer Heywood and Leslie Drake, "as one of feminism's most active sites, one that spawned a new, specifically third wave feminist culture" (204). Similarly, Jennifer Baumgardner and Amy Richards assert that Riot Grrrls "pioneered a feminist voice that was both political and distinctly new" (78). In distinction to these writers, Andi Zeisler

(2008) argues that "Riot Grrrl was a direct descendant of the radical feminism of the late 1960s and early 1970s" (106). Indeed, there is a direct line between the CR groups and self-defence workshops of Riot Grrrl and the tactics used by many radical feminist groups in the 1960s and 1970s. The declarative manifestos in Riot Grrrl zines share a lineage with earlier radical feminist publications, such as the *Redstockings Manifesto* (1969) or the Radicalesbians' *The Woman-Identified Woman* (1971). Riot Grrrls may have also drawn inspiration from Valerie Solanas's (1967/1971) *SCUM* [Society for Cutting Up Men] *Manifesto*, in that Riot Grrrl groups did not shy away from advocating violence as a means of retribution for crimes such as rape and sexual assault. While Riot Grrrl was indeed new, in that it emerged out of, and in response to, a different temporal and social context, many strategies and tactics of Riot Grrrl share continuities with earlier radical feminisms.

Riot Grrrl also shared some of radical feminism's limitations, insofar as the scene was often unable to adequately address issues pertaining to race and class, as well as racism and classism within the subculture itself. Mimi Nguyen's (1997) compilation zine "Evolution of a Race Riot" was inspired by Nguyen's own experiences of racism within punk scenes and includes over forty submissions by punk people of colour (POC) writing about racism and identity. The zine is now available online through the POC Zine Project, an activist project, which has as its mission statement to make more zines by POC "easy to find, distribute, and share" (People of Color Zine Project, 2014). Despite the participation of women and queers of colour in Riot Grrrl, the scene's normative subject was coded as young, white, and female.

"WE WERE BASICALLY EVIL": WHEN *SASSY* MET GRRRL ZINES

As it grew and spread, Riot Grrrl gained national media attention and was the subject of several patronizing articles in the mainstream press. A 1992 *Newsweek* article calling the more "extreme" Riot Grrrls "sanctimoniously committed" to the subculture is emblematic of this coverage ("Revolution, Girl Style" 2014). In response, Riot Grrrls self-imposed a media blackout by refusing to speak with reporters, due to fears of co-optation by, and misrepresentation within, the mainstream.

Sassy was also writing about grrrl zine cultures like Riot Grrrl. *Sassy* writer Christina Kelly launched "Zine Corner" in 1991, which featured a "zine of the month" in every issue. The zine feature in *Sassy* had mixed results: on the one hand, it encouraged and inspired many girls to start their own zines. On the other hand, many of the zines that were featured in "zine corner" soon ceased publication due to the overwhelming amount of orders the creators received following their publication's promotion in *Sassy*. Due to the photo-copying and postage costs associated with making zines, most zine-makers barely broke even on their publications: larger scale publishing was not sustainable. Despite its drawbacks, *Sassy*'s coverage of underground culture constructed alternative cultures as a potential space of belonging for girls who felt like outsiders in their own communities. One prominent Riot Grrrl zine maker, Nomy Lamm, remarked of living in Olympia, Washington, "It never seemed cool to me until I read about it in *Sassy*" (quoted in Jesella and Meltzer, 79). Lamm's comment demonstrates *Sassy*'s integral role in con-structing particular geographical and cultural locales as having subcultural cachet, and its influence on inhabitants' own perceptions of where they lived and how they inhabited that space.

Sassy played a key role in spreading the message about Riot Grrrl, but some felt that through publicizing the subculture, *Sassy*, as a mass-market publication, was also contributing to its demise. Kelly summed up the criti-cism thusly: "We weren't punk enough; we were co-opting the scene; we were basically evil" (quoted in Jesella and Meltzer, 78). The coverage of under-ground culture in *Sassy* became a point of tension, since the magazine was perceived by some as exploiting a small but vibrant community of politically minded artists and musicians. And many members of subcultural groups like Riot Grrrl valued their outsider status: publicity was seen as a quick way to kill the scene.

In the 1990s, there were heightened tensions around the idea of selling out; Kelly's comments that some saw *Sassy* as "basically evil" for covering grrrl zine culture highlight this broader cultural climate. It was one of the first periods during which alternative music broke into the mainstream—and not always willingly—as typified most strongly by the grunge band Nirvana. These categories of mainstream and alternative, which now seem much more permeable and overlapping, seemed much more bounded in the 1990s (even if this wasn't necessarily so) and questions of selling out or co-optation were especially salient to people involved in alternative cultures such as Riot Grrrl.

THE LEGACY OF 1990s GRRRL ZINES

The influence of 1990s grrrl zine cultures on third-wave magazines is clear: BUST, *Bitch*, HUES, ROCKRGRL, and *Venus Zine* all started as zine publica-tions. Amy Schroeder described the making of the first-ever *Venus Zine* as a nineteen-year-old freshman at Michigan State University to me in a 2006 interview:

The first issue took me one night to produce. It was a straight-up fanzine—a personal zine, or "perzine." It wasn't particularly good—it was just me spouting off about my experience as a freshman in college who was interested in feminism. I produced one issue per year throughout college. Each issue was better than the last. The more I learned about editing and writing from working at my college newspaper, the better *Venus Zine* became. I recruited my friends to write for the magazine, which helped it progress from perzine to zine with interviews and essays.

Schroeder's account of the development of *Venus Zine* is similar to the story of *HUES*, which began as a zine publication of a few hundred copies, also on a university campus—this time, the University of Michigan. But, while Schroeder's *Venus Zine* developed into a nationally circulating magazine quite organically, *HUES* co-founders Dyann Logwood, Tali Edut, and Ophira Edut began to pursue the national distribution of *HUES* as a deliberate goal almost immediately following the unexpectedly warm response to the first issue.

As third-wave periodicals have developed from zines to magazines, so too has the cultural landscape they inhabit. While the prominent Riot Grrrl bands of the 1990s are no longer active, the new musical projects of musicians belonging to Riot Grrrl bands in the 1990s are frequently the subject of stories in *BUST*, *ROCKRGRL*, and *Venus Zine*. For example, in 1991, Corin Tucker was a member of prominent Riot Grrrl band Heavens to Betsy but by 1994 had formed Sleater Kinney with Carrie Brownstein. Sleater Kinney has graced the covers of both *ROCKRGRL* and *Venus Zine*. Similarly, Kathleen Hanna, of the former Riot Grrrl band Bikini Kill, went on to form Le Tigre, which has made the covers of both *BUST* and *Venus Zine*. The albums of these groups and other post-Riot Grrrl bands are reviewed in these publications, as well as in *Shameless*, *Rookie*, and *Bitch*.

While *BUST*, *Bitch*, *HUES*, *ROCKRGRL*, and *Venus Zine* became more widely known as magazine publications, they have retained aspects of grrrl zine culture. *BUST* magazine, for example, retains the cut-and-paste aesthetics and playful, ironic tone that characterized grrrl zines. In the early 2000s, its website would regularly feature pictures of 1940s-style pin-up girls on its home page, while the early issues of the print magazine often featured images of 1950s-style housewives and clip art from old magazines. The contemporary feminist craft cultures propagated by *BUST* also emerge out of the DIY ethos of grrrl zines. Similarly, the sarcastic, witty discourse within *Bitch* may also be read as a continuation of the common rhetorical strategies of critique used in grrrl zine publications. Even as they have left the temporal context of the 1990s, grrrl zine culture continues to make its mark on these publications.

FEMINIST MAGAZINES ON THE CUSP OF THE DIGITAL AGE

Third-wave magazines—*Bitch* (1996–), *BUST* (1993–), *HUES* (1992–99), *ROCKRGRL* (1995–2006), and *Venus Zine* (1994–2010)—and post-wave magazines—*Rookie* (2010–) and *Shameless* (2004–)—have emerged as a distinct genre, but they also share characteristics with other women's magazines, zines, and leftist periodicals. For example, each print magazine uses a layout typical of commercial women's magazines: they contain letters from and to the editor, departments, short articles, features, book and music reviews, and advertising. *BUST* and *Venus Zine* also contain fashion spreads (clothes for sale), while *HUES* and *Shameless* contain style pages (discussions about clothes). As an online publication, *Rookie* has a hybridized style department that is framed as discussion about clothes and makeup but which also provides hyperlinks to the websites of clothing and makeup companies featured in its photos. The boundaries between what one might think of as a "feminist magazine" and a "women's magazine" are thus more permeable than one might at first imagine.

Unlike conventional magazines for women, however, third- and post-wave periodicals are known for covering independent music and culture, offering sharp-witted critiques of popular culture and politics, serving as forums for debating the dynamics of contemporary feminism, reclaiming activities like crafting and burlesque as empowering pastimes, and embracing sex, sex toys, and feminist pornography as powerful and pleasurable. With the exception of *BUST* and *HUES*, these periodicals do not feature works of fiction. (*BUST*'s fiction offering is a "one-handed read," an erotic short story, at the end of every issue, while *HUES* included poetry submitted by readers.) As independently published periodicals, the print magazines lack the backing of large publishers and distributors that deliver more mainstream magazines into grocery stores, pharmacies, and corner stores. Rather, third-wave magazines established in the 1990s had to be sought out in independent bookstores, major bookstore chains, or record stores alongside other independently produced, politically minded publications like *Mother Jones* (1976–), the *UTNE Reader* (1984–), or the now-defunct *Punk Planet* (1994–2007). Thus, despite their similarities to women's magazines, third-wave print periodicals' feminist content shapes how these publications are identified, marketed, and placed on the shelves.

The growth of online culture has changed the ways in which readers now access these magazines. Many book and record stores have now folded across the United States and Canada, and periodicals have had to adapt to this change. All of the feminist periodicals now in circulation have robust websites through which readers can order individual copies of, or subscriptions to, the magazines. Indeed, when people ask me about my research and I tell them about *Making Feminist Media,* I've found that some know of *Bitch* magazine as a website but are not always aware that there is also a print version. *BUST* and *Bitch* now provide subscriptions to an online version of the magazine at a discounted rate and *Rookie* publishes entirely online. It would now be more accurate to conceptualize of *BUST, Bitch, Shameless,* and *Venus Zine* as multimedia enterprises of which the print magazine is just one part.

This section introduces the periodicals on either side of the cusp of the digital age—*Bitch, BUST, HUES, ROCKRGRL, Rookie, Shameless,* and *Venus Zine*—and describes their genesis, content, and material conditions of production. It provides a sense of how these periodicals emerged, what they initially looked like, what kinds of topics are covered, how their editorial tones resemble and diverge from each other, and where they are heading. While third-wave periodicals all made the transition from zine to magazine, a move that increases their ability to reach a larger, broader readership, this move into commercial culture has also raised different kinds of questions about financial sustainability in comparison to the relatively low costs of small-scale zine production. Thus, this section also pays attention to the kinds of financial pressures that bear upon commercial feminist periodicals and introduces some of the strategies that the magazines have used to adapt to these challenges.

BITCH (1996–)

Bitch: Feminist Response to Popular Culture is a not-for-profit magazine that critiques representations of gender within and highlights the contributions of women who are making their own interventions into the realm of mainstream media culture. A typical issue contains feature articles, shorter columns, letters to the editor, an editors' letter, a list of people or things that are liked by the editors (the "bitch list"), and reviews of books and music. The magazine also features a regular section called "Love It/Shove It" (renamed "Department of Everything" in the Winter 2016 issue) in which contributors respond either positively or negatively to current mainstream mass media productions. Because of this organizational format, *Bitch* is more of a journal-style publication than its counterparts, *BUST* and *Venus Zine*, which are produced more in the style of glossy women's magazines.

Issues of *Bitch* are always organized around a central theme. Past themes have included food (Winter 2014); fame and fortune (Summer 2012); noir (Winter 2008); super (Spring 2007); and style and substance (Summer 2006). As this list demonstrates, some of *Bitch*'s themes are clearly subject-based, while others are more conceptual. *Bitch* tends to offer feature-length articles that interpret the given theme in a variety of ways. For example, *Bitch*'s Winter 2014 issue contains seven food-themed features on the topics of "Craving the Other: One Woman's Beef with Cultural Appropriation"; "Why Labour Is the Real Food Movement"; "Nine Artists Inspired by Food"; the Sistah Vegan project; an interview with *Meaty*'s Samantha Irby; and an analysis of the gender dynamics of food TV. The thematic approach thus allows *Bitch* to open up to readers a range of possible critical feminist perspectives on a given theme without prescribing any one particular form of feminism.

The first issue of *Bitch* was a black-and-white zine publication created by Lisa Jervis, Andi Zeisler, and Benjamin Shaykin. The premier issue contained seven articles, including the above-mentioned special section "*Sassy* Sucks," a discussion of the founders' love/hate relationship with the media, an analysis of the representation of women on *MTV*, as well as music and book reviews. The issue concluded with a short homage to John Travolta. The inaugural editorial, a manifesto statement written by Jervis entitled "This Magazine Is about Speaking Up," (1996d) argues that bitching is important

> [b]ecause—*regardless of those who still think it's an insult—it's an action.* Because a confrontational stance is powerful. Because *Bitch* connotes anger, and I agree with bell hooks when she says, "Confronting my rage, witnessing the way it moved me to grow and change, I understood intimately that it had the potential not only to destroy but to construct. Then and now I understand rage to be a necessary aspect of resistance struggle." (1)

The publication thus takes the word "bitch" and redeploys it as an active force that helps make sexism visible so that it can then be combatted. The action of "bitching," as it's used within the magazine, invites readers to engage critically with the world around them, as well as with the material within the magazine itself, offering what Alison Piepmeier calls "a pedagogy of active criticism" (157). Reading both magazine and popular culture with a critical eye is constructed within *Bitch* as a feminist act.

The inaugural editorial's citation of prominent African American feminist theorist bell hooks suggests an anti-racist feminist politics that acknowledges the intersection of gender, race, class, and sexuality and that values anger and rage as important sites from which to build feminist movements. While *Bitch*'s early issues did not always live up to this intersectional framework—in its third issue, Jervis (1996c) wrote an editorial apologizing for the omission of *Essence* and *Today's Black Woman* from an article comparing women's magazines—*Bitch* has demonstrated a commitment to including topics that, and writers who, represent a range of identities, as well as accountability for when it's missed the mark. The feminist rage that hooks writes about is generative and valuable; Jervis uses hooks's formulation of rage to value anger as a feeling that matters.

Jervis emphasizes the importance of anger to link her personal rage to a larger context that devalues feminism. Her repetition of the word "because" is an intervention into and defiance of a post-feminist discourse that sees feminism as no longer relevant and as unimportant. Post-feminism, as feminist Cultural Studies theorist Angela McRobbie (2009) argues, is the peculiar phenomenon by which feminism is actively undermined through often celebratory claims that equality has already been achieved. Jervis was writing out of this wider cultural context, which had just seen the sale of the beloved *Sassy* and the emergence of mass culture's makeover of Riot Grrrl: the Spice Girls. Jervis insists that feminism matters, that feeling angry matters, and that creating space for alternative and dissenting voices matters. *Bitch*'s goal was to create such a space for editors, writers, and readers alike.

Bitch's title performs the action of reclaiming the word "bitch" as a positive term in both noun and verb. This refashioning of "bitch" is part of a larger third-wave context. As Melissa Klein (1997) argues, "Our [third wavers'] politics reflects a postmodern focus on contradiction and duality, on the reclamation of terms. S-M, pornography, the words *cunt* and *queer* and *pussy* and *girl*—are all things to be re-examined or reclaimed" (208), and Stephanie Gilmore (2005) asserts that an "important cultural task third wave feminists have undertaken is reclaiming the derisive terms that accompany women's sexuality" (107).[6] Within the context of the magazine, the word "bitch" thus becomes a signifier of sharp-wittedness and critical thought, applicable both to the woman who reads the publication and to how she engages with the mainstream cultural productions critiqued within the popular text's pages: she bitches about them.

Despite the magazine's attempt to recuperate the word "bitch" within its publication, the magazine's title has at times been a hindrance to the publication's development. Due to its title, *Bitch* had some difficulties in securing a phone listing under its actual name and, in Issue 19, the editors admit "there've been plenty of occasions when our name has held us back from some juicy media coverage" (Jervis and Zeisler 2003, 5). Nonetheless, in their 2006 introduction to *Bitchfest*, their tenth anniversary compendium of selected articles from the magazine, Zeisler and Jervis (2006) reaffirm their commitment to the name:

> If being an outspoken woman means being a bitch, we'll take that as a compliment, thanks. And if we do so, it loses its power to hurt us. Furthermore, if we can get people thinking about what they're saying when they use the word, all the better. Last, but certainly not least, "bitch" is efficiently multipurpose—it not only describes who we are when we speak up, it describes the very act of making ourselves heard. (xxi)

While not being massively successful in reinventing the meaning of "bitch" for a broad audience, *Bitch* magazine has opened up and developed a conversation about sexist discourse and the ways in which it is used to silence women. The struggles *Bitch* has faced regarding its name, however, are just one aspect of the challenges this feminist magazine has encountered in trying to expand and sustain itself.

Bitch has had its share of financial difficulties. In a 2001 editorial, the editors announced that the issue (tellingly titled "Near Death Experience") had almost been their last, citing day jobs, printer bills, and burnout (Jervis and Zeisler 2001, 5). Nonetheless, after much discussion and debate, the editors decided to quit their day jobs and commit to *Bitch* as a full-time project. While *Bitch* published as a successful quarterly publication for the next eight years, in an interview I conducted with Andi Zeisler (2007), she stated, "It's just getting more and more difficult to publish a print magazine, financially. Everything gets more expensive every year—paper, postage, shipping, fuel.... Not to sound too pessimistic, but we always feel relieved when we look at our cash flow and see that we can make it to another issue." That same year, *Bitch* moved from San Francisco to Portland in an attempt to help defray costs ("Our History" 2014). In early 2008, publisher Debbie Rasmussen and editor Andi Zeisler created a video called "Save Bitch" (posted on YouTube and *Bitch*'s website) that helped launch a fundraiser for the magazine. Citing financial difficulties, the decline of the print industry, and misogyny within that same industry, Rasmussen and Zeisler appealed for donations, in order to help the magazine raise $40,000, the amount that is required to put out one issue of the magazine. Although the campaign was successful—it raised $74,000—the financial sustainability of *Bitch* remains precarious.

The material constraints on print publishing have meant that *Bitch* has had to constantly adapt in order to stay financially viable. *Bitch* changed its name to *Bitch Media* in 2009, appointed its first executive director, and became a "nonprofit multimedia organization" of which the magazine is now just one part ("Our History" 2014). In 2013 and 2014, the organization launched a "May Match" campaign, during which all donations were matched by an anonymous private donor (up to $25,000 in 2013 and $30,000 in 2014). Their 2014 campaign was kicked off by an open letter, written by Kathleen Hanna, about the value of *Bitch* magazine to her. It is *Bitch*'s willingness to adapt—changing locations, becoming a multimedia organization, emphasizing fundraising—that has kept *Bitch* in print. Through all of these changes, however, *Bitch* has never strayed from its mandate to deliver a clever and witty feminist critique of popular culture.

BUST (1993–)

BUST began as a black-and-white photocopied zine by Debbie Stoller and Marcelle Karp. The editorial of the premier issue is a manifesto written in a confessional style that locates the impetus for the magazine in a kind of generational angst among "girl-women" in their late twenties and early thirties. Writing under their *noms de plume* of Celina Hex and Betty Boob, Stoller and Karp assert that these girl-women are caught somewhere between wanting their own "radical bohemian thrift-store" version of the trappings of a conventional life (marriage and children) and wanting to remain "girls" (Hex and Boob 1993, n.p.). The co-founders define *BUST* as a more grown-up version of *Sassy*: their magazine is for "Generation XX," a clever reworking of "Generation X" that signals their focus on women (through the reference to the XX chromosome)—those women slackers who are "more than two boys away from being virgins" (Hex and Boob 1993, n.p.). The tone of the inaugural editorial runs through the early issues of *BUST*; that is, in a style typical of a perzine (or personal zine), writers share first-person narratives dealing with body image, sex, men, growing up, motherhood, and pop culture.

BUST quickly became a full-fledged magazine; a typical issue now includes features, short articles, reviews, a fashion spread, and classified ads. *BUST*'s regular departments are "Broadcast," a "news and views" section, which includes short articles on politics, quotations from celebrities, a "boy du jour" (a picture and profile of an up-and-coming male actor/ musician), a pop-culture-related quiz, and "the museum of femorabilia," which is an article on a kitschy vintage product targeted towards women or girls; "Real Life," a section devoted to craft and cooking projects and products; "Looks," which contains a fashion spread and fashion-related product reviews; and "Sex Files," which contains a sex advice column, a "one-handed" read, and a short sex-related article. As *BUST* has developed, celebrity interviews have become a more prominent part of the publication: one difference between such interviews in *BUST* and its non-feminist counterparts is that *BUST* interviewers always ask the question "Are you a feminist?"

Despite being the longest-running feminist magazine from the 1990s' zine explosion, *BUST* has experienced financial difficulties. A 2001 article in *The Phoenix* indicates that Stoller and publisher Laurie Henzel had run out of money in August of 2000 and were looking for a buyer (Willdorf 2001). The two women sold *BUST* to Razorfish Studios, a company that wished to relaunch the quarterly as a ten-times-a-year publication. An article about Stoller and Henzel's relaunch appeared in the *New York Times* on September 10, 2001 (Kuczynski). However, following the September 11, 2001, attacks on the World Trade Center and the subsequent economic downturn, Razorfish dumped *BUST* and the entire staff was laid off. Stoller and Henzel reorganized, repurchased the magazine from Razorfish, and relaunched the magazine as an independently published periodical in the spring of 2002. *BUST* has remained independently published ever since, which has given the publication a great deal of autonomy, but this move did not spell the end of economic difficulties for the publication.

In early 2009, the periodical launched its first ever appeal for subscriptions, due to the global economic recession. Many of *BUST*'s advertisers, Stoller asserted, "from bigger brands to smaller crafty companies, have had to cut their marketing budgets" and "independent companies like *BUST* are feeling the pinch in a big way" (2009, 6). In contrast to *Bitch* magazine, which had made an appeal for donations a few months prior and was subsequently criticized on the popular blog *jezebel.com* for "reinforcing the negative stereotype that women are shit when it comes to business" (Egan 2008), Stoller stated that *BUST* was "not asking for a handout" but was eliminating the middleman through getting readers to subscribe directly rather than purchase through the newsstand (2009, 6). This rationale is an interesting contrast with *Bitch*'s contemporary appeal for donations. While the not-for-profit *Bitch* now relies on both subscription revenue and donations, as a for-profit publication *BUST* relies instead on the rhetoric of economic resourcefulness, actively eschewing an interpretation of its request as charity. *BUST* was able to stay afloat financially and its subscription rates have held steady at around

90,000 since (Chafin 2014). Like *Bitch*, part of *BUST*'s continued viability as a publication has been due to its ability to adapt to the changing climate of the publishing industry.

HUES (1992–99)

HUES began as a zine co-created by Dyann Logwood and sisters Tali and Ophira Edut as a Women's Studies undergraduate assignment that asked students to create a project that would "forever change the lives of women" (Logwood 1995). In an interview I conducted with Logwood (2007), she recounted that following the release of the inaugural issue, "we started to receive a lot of positive feedback, and then we got letters from people as far away as Africa. We had letters from women in different countries because the students had gone home and just kind of picked up a copy out of the dorm and took it with them. People kept telling us that we should do it 'for real.'" From that point forward, Logwood and the Edut sisters began publishing subsequent issues of *HUES* with the goal of becoming a nationally circulating pro-woman magazine.

The first nationally circulating issue appeared on newsstands in 1995; the main feature was an article on Republican Women of Colour (entitled "Red, White, and Clueless?"), written by a left-leaning woman of colour seeking to understand "the more colorful side of the right" (Longroño Guerrero 1995, 18). Other features included a round table of Indian women discussing dating and marriage, the "Woman's Guide to Car-Shopping," and a photo-essay on Jackson Heights, New York, an Indian-American neighbourhood. In addition to feature articles, the national issue also had a "body and soul" department, which contained short articles on the morning-after pill, reviews of "ethnic makeup," and a section devoted to profiles of individual women's lives (Logwood 1995, 9). It also contained profiles of lesbian cartoonist Diane DiMassa, Oshun priestess Luisah Teish, and women in the hip-hop groups Arrested Development, the Digable Planets, and The Coup. As *HUES*'s first national issue demonstrates, the magazine was committed to being a multicultural publication that represented a range of identities and experiences.

To raise money to publish *HUES*, the co-founders and other volunteers held hip-hop dance parties as fundraisers and were initially able to access campus funding through the University of Michigan. Unfortunately, after going national, the magazine was no longer recognized as a student group on campus; as a result, the publication was sustained for some time with the help of family support, including the Edut sisters' grandfather, a Holocaust survivor who, as Logwood put it in our interview, "really appreciated our chutzpah." However, after a while, the founders felt guilty about accepting money from family members and decided to take out a loan to finance the magazine; the loan had only recently been paid back at the time of the interview, eight years after the periodical had folded. As a multicultural pro-woman publication, HUES was never able to garner the large advertising contracts (with one exception, a Levi's jeans ad) or larger publishers that magazines without a political agenda or commitment to diversity can.

As the co-founders drew to the end of their university careers, Logwood and the Edut sisters decided to sell the magazine to New Moon, which produced the teen magazine *New Moon: For Girls and Their Dreams*. While the decision to sell HUES was a difficult one, a decision Logwood likened to giving a baby up for adoption, she recalled in our interview that the families of the co-founders had started to say, "We love you. We support you. But you all need to get real jobs." Indeed, the work of producing HUES had truly been a labour of love with little financial reward. As Logwood recounts, they had approached a few larger publishers and realized that they "would change the focus of the publication and [this] would turn it into something that we couldn't stand behind." While New Moon promised to preserve the integrity of the publication, it was able to carry HUES for only a few more issues. Producing two magazines had been more work than the publishers had anticipated, and HUES was placed on permanent hiatus. Despite having been retired from circulation, HUES's ability to publish nationally for four years in a climate that was inhospitable to representations of multiracial women and to feminist and womanist discourse is nothing short of remarkable.

ROCKRGRL (1996–2005)

In 1996, musician Carla DeSantis founded ROCKRGRL as a music trade publication for women. Citing sexism against women in the music business by fans and fellow musicians, women's visual representation in music videos as sexual playthings, and their relative absence from leading music magazines, DeSantis designed the magazine to introduce readers "to the women of the past, present, and future who have contributed to and succeeded in the music business" and to give female musicians practical information specific to the industry, such as advice about record labels, legal issues, and equipment (DeSantis 1995, 2). The premier issue featured profiles of and interviews with musicians Gretchen Seager and Queen Latifah and bands That Dog, Tilt, The Go Go's, and The Au Pairs, as well as columns on legal language and approaching record labels. In addition to the print magazine, ROCKRGRL also started a Women In Music Conference, which celebrated and promoted women in the music industry and was held in Seattle in 2000 and 2005. *ROCK-RGRL* was the go-to music trade publication for women, providing a valuable resource for musicians who did not always have access to the same networks as their male counterparts. Despite its important purpose, like other third-wave magazines *ROCKRGRL* frequently had financial difficulties.

The first evidence of financial trouble appeared in 1996, when DeSantis appealed to readers to purchase subscriptions (in the unambiguously titled editorial "Send Us Your Money!") due to the lack of advertising revenue brought in by the magazine. DeSantis wrote of her own dislike of advertising in magazines, but she added, "I am obviously late in learning that ads are the bread and butter of any publication" (3). Indeed, in the editorial for the ultimate issue of the magazine, DeSantis (2005) thanked Fender for being the first big company to take the magazine seriously and advertise regularly within it. In the final issue of *ROCKRGRL*, DeSantis cited a poor economy, rising printing and postage costs, and the growth of the Internet as factors in the demise of the periodical. "Without proper funding—and even with," observed DeSantis, "independent print magazines are in a constant struggle to survive" (2005, 4). Due to these factors, *ROCKRGRL* was just one of many independent print magazines to fold during the 2000s. One of these compatriots was *Venus Zine*.

VENUS ZINE (1995–2010)

Venus Zine began as a zine publication, which was gradually developed into a nationally circulating magazine by its founder, Amy Schroeder (Schroeder 2006). *Venus Zine* was focused on and targeted to women who are musicians, visual artists, and craft practitioners, with a focus on independent culture. A 2006 media kit for the magazine indicated that the average reader was a white woman with or in the process of attaining a college education, with a median income of $29,700, living in a large city (Schroeder 2014). As Schroeder described it in our 2007 interview, "We're a lifestyle publication for hip, creative, smart women. As far as I'm aware, *Venus Zine* is the only internationally distributed publication that focuses on women in the arts." While *Venus Zine* circulated mainly in the United States, it was also distributed in Canada, Europe, and Japan. Despite its international circulation, the magazine frequently featured artists from its home base of Chicago, as well as artists from across the United States.

A typical issue of *Venus Zine* includes "arteest," a section that profiles individual visual artists; "penus," a department containing articles about male visual or musical artists; music, fashion, and film departments; book reviews; and feature articles. For example, the features in the Fall 2008 issue were an article called "The Bicycle Warriors," which profiled individuals who are obsessed with biking as well as all-girl bike groups; a how-to article on professional blogging; and an article profiling young American women voters called "Coming of Age in the Bush Era." As *Venus Zine* developed, its articles increasingly focused on entrepreneurship, particularly how women who were independently blogging (as in the 2008 issue), crafting, or making art could potentially turn these activities into small business ventures. One of *Venus Zine*'s other developments was its name change.

Initially called simply *Venus*, in 2006 the publication appended the word *Zine* to its name, perhaps as a way of marking the DIY roots of the publication as it became more glossy and less recognizably informed by a zine aesthetic. *Venus Zine* most closely resembles *BUST* in look and feel. Unlike *BUST*, however, *Venus Zine* generally did not openly identify itself as feminist and did not claim the activities promoted within it (such as DIY crafting) as political ones. While Schroeder herself considered the magazine to be feminist, she commented in our interview that "some of the readers *Venus Zine* targets don't necessarily identify themselves as feminist, even though I consider them to be." This identification of *Venus Zine* as feminist shifted when the publication was sold to Sarah Beardsley in 2010.

Venus Zine went through a number of shifts in editorial and publishing staff, beginning in 2006, when Schroeder sold the publication to publishers Anne Brindle and Marci Sepulveda, but none so dramatically changed the tenor of *Venus Zine* as the magazine's sale to Beardsley. Although Beardsley's (unrealized) goal, to dramatically increase circulation from 60,000 to 200,000, was admirable, it seemed to come at the expense of the magazine's feminist base. Beardsley characterized the publication's new take on feminism this way: "We don't use that particular F word around here. It just doesn't seem relevant" (quoted in Miner 2010). Whether the magazine's change in perspective, its inability to produce more subscriptions, or the print publishing climate generally, *Venus Zine* did not make it to 2011.

SHAMELESS (2004–)

All of the above periodicals commenced publication in the early to mid-1990s as zine publications and gradually grew into nationally circulating magazines that have maintained some form of zine aesthetic, which is mainly expressed through a dedication to independent or fringe artists, musicians, and designers. *Shameless*, in contrast, began in 2004 as a magazine, co-founded by Nicole Cohen and Melinda Mattos. Despite its differences from third-wave magazines, in an interview for *Making Feminist Media* Cohen described *Shameless* as sharing

> with other third-wave publications a certain aesthetic, rooted in DIY (do-it-yourself), punk and indie rock culture; the magazine has a certain irreverence to it, although we do tackle serious issues; and, although it is a magazine proper, [*Shameless*] has the heart of a zine. The politics of the magazine are broad, as the politics of our contributors are broad, but there is a large focus on arts and culture, representations of women in popular culture (this theme has particularly emerged on our weblog), frank discussions of sexuality and queer issues, as well as a commitment to a broad range of issues and representations.

Shameless also differs from most of its counterparts in being both a Canadian and a not-for-profit publication. The magazine also has a smaller circulation of about 3,000 copies, and is aimed at a slightly younger, teenage audience. Despite these differences, *Making Feminist Media* includes *Shameless* because of its important thematic similarities to these other U.S.-based publications. Because *Shameless* began in the 2000s, I identify both *Shameless* and *Rookie* as post-wave publications that draw on third-wave and other feminisms but do not share the context of the 1990s in the same way that third-wave magazines do.

Like most other magazines, *Shameless* is composed of feature articles, shorter reads, and reviews. Each issue of *Shameless* includes profiles of inspiring women, news briefs, an advice column, style profiles, and guides to DIY crafts. In the first years of publication, *Shameless* also featured a rant on the last page of each issue that analyzed the politics of language (the premier issue took the slang term for a tank top, "wife-beater," to task). While retiring the "Last Word" column in 2010, *Shameless* continues to publish articles that foreground the significance of language. Its 2014 issue, for example, discusses what the term "two-spirited" means. Like *Bitch*, the editors of *Shameless* recognize the power of reclaiming and critiquing language, and most importantly what we invoke when we use the words that we do.

The premier issue in 2004 (see Figure 1) emphasized the magazine's aesthetic links with DIY and indie culture; the front cover features hand-drawn pictures of three girls, with signifiers closely associated with punk/indie culture: multiple piercings and ripped fishnet stockings and boots. The cover was designed to look as though it was composed of four separate pieces of paper that had been cut up and reassembled, giving the paper a cut-and-paste collage aesthetic, a hallmark of zine production. Inside, the magazine's

FIG. 1 Inaugural-issue cover, *Shameless* (2004)

first issue contained feature-length articles on globalization, comedians Mae Martin and Sabrina Jalees, and girls' involvement in community radio. The tone of *Shameless* is that of a smart and cool older sister, creating a version of girlhood that is active, fun, and political. The magazine's inaugural tagline, "for girls who get it," encapsulates this philosophy.

The tagline, "for girls who get it," constructs readers as girls who are savvy, intelligent, witty, youthful, and—above all—"in the know." That is, the tagline gestures toward a reader who has a kind of insider knowledge (the "it" of the phrase is left deliberately vague). As a publication that attempts to offer an alternative to fashion-and-makeup-centred girls magazines, *Shameless* constructs "getting it" as being aware that the norms perpetuated by mainstream girls magazines are patriarchal and capitalist. "Getting it" also implies insider knowledge of independent cultural productions (music, crafting, art, and so on), which are constructed as cooler and better than corporate-sponsored productions. This distinction between corporate/mainstream and independent/alternative is an important one for Cohen. In articulating the differences between *Shameless* and some of its U.S. counter-parts, Cohen argues that

> *Shameless* is more rough-around-the-edges than BUST, which has higher production values. I think *Shameless* covers more activism than BUST and *Bitch*, which is a large part of our mandate and a way in which to try support the small active feminist activist community in Canada. BUST is much more consumer-oriented than *Shameless*, in a way that moves the magazine closer to mainstream women's magazines than we position ourselves. (2007)

The girlhood that *Shameless* thus envisions for and with its readers is a politically engaged one that positions itself in opposition to the perceived values of mainstream women's magazines. At the beginning of 2011, *Shameless* changed its tagline to "talking back since 2004," in order to reflect the magazine's trans-inclusive mandate. As editor Sheila Sampath (2016) puts it, *Shameless* positions itself as "a feminist magazine rooted in principles of social justice and anti-oppression."

ROOKIE (2010–)

Rookie is an online post-wave magazine founded by Tavi Gevinson in 2010. Gevinson is known for the style blog *The Style Rookie,* which she began in 2008 at the age of twelve. Unlike most other publications for teen girls, *Rookie* was actually founded by a teenager and is staffed by a combination of teens and young women. *Rookie* functions like a magazine in that it organizes its writing around monthly themes and has regular departments, including music, sex, fun, fiction, and style pages, as well as an advice column. Unlike a magazine, however, *Rookie* updates its content on a daily basis and relies entirely on advertising revenue to support the site.

    Rookie is partnered with Say Media, a digital advertising company that offers promotional blog posts, branded videos, inclusion in gift guides, video pre-roll (the advertisements that play before viewing a video), among other services to its clients. Advertising in *Rookie* is thus often embedded within the website content itself, particularly its style department, rather than through dedicated ad space, of which there is very little. A recent style article on experimenting with bright makeup contains no fewer than eight product placements complete with hyperlinks to the advertised products. While online publication certainly avoids many of the challenges that print magazines face in revenue generation, the Internet is also not a free space that exists outside of the demands of marketing.

CONCLUSION

This chapter has argued that both *Sassy* and grrrl zine cultures helped redefine girlhood in significant ways in the late 1980s and early 1990s and have had an indelible influence on feminist magazine publishing. Because they reimagined girlhood so differently than most other media representations, readers of *Sassy* and grrrl zines developed strong bonds with these publications. It's not surprising, therefore, that readers also felt very protective of both *Sassy* and zines. As I have discussed, these attachments manifested in a variety of different ways—from feelings of betrayal, when *Sassy* radically changed its content, to anger over *Sassy*'s coverage of grrrl zines. These affects, however, were also remarkably generative for third-wave magazines in that they provided a ground from which to build critical feminist media discourse.

This chapter has also provided overviews of feminist magazines on either side of the digital age's cusp. What emerges from the publishing trajectories of each magazine is a sense that feminist periodicals are in an almost constant state of flux because they must adapt to changes in the wider media marketplace. This condition of magazine publication is far from new, of course. As the next chapter demonstrates, the challenges that feminist magazines have faced in the realm of commercial culture date back to the very beginnings of commercial culture itself.

CHAPTER TWO

"SERIOUS AND MATERIAL BUSINESS": THIRD-WAVE MAGAZINES AND THE MARKETPLACE IN HISTORICAL PERSPECTIVE

In 2013, Nancy Fraser penned a widely circulated article in *The Guardian* on "how feminism became capitalism's handmaiden." For many feminists (hooks 1994; Mohanty 2003), feminist movements are also *necessarily anti-capitalist*. What does it mean, then, that feminist magazines rely on a capitalist marketplace for their circulation? Does this make them non- or anti-feminist? This chapter engages with how third- and post-wave magazines have negotiated the capitalist marketplace, taking as its starting point this assertion by historian Nan Enstad (1999): to argue "that consumer culture is serious and material business is not to claim it as an arena of freedom, nor to claim that it made [or makes] women radical" (6). The goal of this chapter, then, is not to adjudicate whether capitalism is "good" or "bad" for feminism. What the chapter does do is treat the realm of commercial culture, of which feminist magazines are a part, as an important but uneven terrain characterized by negotiation and compromise.

This chapter places the negotiations and compromises undertaken by third- and post-wave magazines within the long history of feminist periodical publishing. While third-wave feminisms, particularly, have often been framed as radically divergent from their forerunners, this chapter demonstrates the continuities between feminist magazines across different eras.[1] One of these continuities is the simple fact of how difficult it is to sustain a feminist magazine. In their remarkable survey of feminist periodicals, Kathleen Endres and Therese Lueck (1996a) argue, "Whether they were started in the nineteenth century as an abolitionist newspaper or in the twentieth century as a voice of feminism, these periodicals shared a common financial future: bleak" (xii). To place in perspective the publishing trajectories of the now defunct *HUES* (1992–99), *ROCKRGRL* (1995–2006), and *Venus Zine* (1994–2010) discussed in Chapter One, Endres and Lueck found that over one-third of the seventy-six feminist publications included in their study had a life span of less than ten years (xii). While publications can become defunct for a whole variety of reasons, what this chapter also demonstrates is that publications that are politically radical and/or committed to decentring whiteness tend to have shorter life spans.

The final goal of this chapter is to complicate the narrative of "selling out" or of co-optation that frames much of the criticism levelled at feminist magazines. Chapter One detailed the way that *Sassy* magazine received criticism, when it began covering grrrl zine culture because it was seen as co-opting the scene for its own gain. Similar charges arise when feminist magazines accept particular kinds of advertisements or adopt more hierarchical roles for staff.

The discourse of co-optation is, however, an overly simplistic account of what happens when feminism goes to market. As Amy Erdman Farrell (1998) argues, "[T]he notion of 'co-optation' suggests that feminism itself, as a social and political movement, exists as a pure space, uncontaminated by struggles among its participants for power and resources until it comes into contact with commercialism. Certainly we know that this is not true" (9) The idea of co-optation suggests a unidirectional flow of action, whereby the marketplace magically empties oppositional cultural productions of their political force. This discourse neither considers the role people play in interpreting, adapting, and appropriating aspects of commercial culture for their own, sometimes subversive, ends nor does it account for the ways that progressive cultural productions can and do influence the broader public sphere. The discourse also assumes that the politics of a given cultural text were radical in the first place. What this chapter shows is that this is not the case: magazines that are more moderate to begin with are more likely to find some measure of success than their radical counterparts. Thus, the narrative of co-optation does not bear out, when examining the history of feminist magazine publication; yet this narrative has shaped and continues to shape major studies of feminist periodicals.

Studies of feminist and other women's magazines tend to replicate a problematic and inaccurate dichotomy between feminism and commercial culture. For example, Nancy Humphreys's (1989) sourcebook for American women's magazines places *Ms.* in the section on twentieth-century women's magazines, rather than the section "Feminist Periodicals," given that *Ms.* is a commercial, glossy publication (viii–ix). Similarly, Endres and Lueck's (1996) two-volume guide to women's periodicals in the United States (one volume on social and political issues and the other on commercial publications) places *Ms.* and *Sassy*, vital precursors to third- and post-wave publications, in the volume devoted to commercial publications. The organization of these volumes suggests a division between "commercialism" and "politics." *Ms.*

and *Sassy* clearly challenge the mutual exclusivity of these categories. Yet the dichotomy remains in place, in ways that foreclose more nuanced conversations about how feminist magazines engage the realm of commercial culture and misrepresent what happens when feminism goes to market.[2] Feminist engagement with the marketplace might be best characterized as a process of negotiation over incredibly uneven terrain, wherein the choices available to feminist publications are shaped by their politics. This pattern is illuminated when we look more closely at the politics of magazine names, for- vs. not-for-profit status, advertising, and other funding sources in the long history of feminist periodical publishing.

THE POLITICS OF MAGAZINE NAMES

Chapter One of *Making Feminist Media* discussed the ways in which *Bitch* magazine has attempted to reclaim the word "bitch" but that the magazine has also paid a price, at times, for the project of remaking and revaluing this word. The struggles *Bitch* has faced because of its name are not new to feminist magazines, however, as is evidenced by the politics of naming within two suffrage-era publications: the moderate publication *The Woman's Journal* (1870–1931) founded by Lucy Stone in Boston, Massachusetts, and the more radical and short-lived *Revolution* (1868–1870), owned and managed by Susan B. Anthony and edited by Elizabeth Cady Stanton in New York City.

From the period of 1917 to 1928, *The Woman's Journal* was known as *The Woman Citizen*, a name change prompted by the consolidation of *The Woman's Journal* with two other suffrage periodicals, *The Woman Voter* and *National Suffrage News* (Spencer 1996, 476). All three publications were purchased by Carrie Chapman Catt, then leader of the National American Woman Suffrage Association (NAWSA) and the New York Women's Suffrage Association. The purchase was made possible by a significant sum of money bequeathed to Catt by Mrs. Frank Leslie to aid the suffrage cause, and new publication was funded with money from the Leslie Suffrage Commission. The name of *Woman Citizen* is clearly more directly linked to the cause of suffrage (Endres 1996d, 433). It announces the periodical's belief that women are, and should be treated as, citizens with all the attendant rights that come with citizenship. However, after suffrage was won in 1920, the publication struggled to stay afloat financially, losing a minimum of $25,000 annually (Finnegan 1999, 166). According to Margaret Finnegan, the publication justified these financial losses as a sign of its refusal to capitulate to less high-minded ideals (140). Nonetheless, *The Woman Citizen* did capitulate in one respect: it changed its name.

In 1928, *The Woman Citizen* changed its name back to *The Woman's Journal* in the hope of further boosting subscriptions and advertising revenue. The magazine's advertising department asserted that the *Citizen's* name "conjure[d] up the militant woman" (a woman who wanted to be treated as a fully enfranchised citizen) and was thus a "handicap, both in attracting new readers and in appealing to advertisers for their business" (quoted in Endres 1996d, 433). *The Woman's Journal* was selected as the new name, since it "[did] not imply a limited political field for the magazine" (quoted in Endres 1996d, 433). In order to build a sustainable publication that drew in new readers and appealed to advertisers, the strategy clearly was to avoid the political stridency implied by the word *citizen*. In this instance, the political views of the periodical were at cross-purposes with its need for advertising revenue and desire to draw in new readers. For this reason, *The Woman's Journal* adapted to stay alive, which it did until 1931 when it folded due to the Great Depression. *The Woman's Journal's* adaptation to its post-suffrage context did not mean greatly changing the mandate of the publication, however. *The Woman's Journal* was always a more moderate publication than its radical counterpart *The Revolution*, which treated a potential change to its name very differently.

Unlike *The Woman's Journal*, *The Revolution* held a more radical position. In addition to championing a national suffrage campaign (some moderate suffragists favoured a piecemeal, state-by-state approach), according to Patricia Smith Butcher (1989), *The Revolution* also "advocated legalized prostitution and easy divorce" (10). Denied funding by suffrage organizations like the NAWSA, which wished to distance itself from the more radical participants in the suffrage movement, *The Revolution* increased its operating deficit monthly. Moreover, *The Revolution* initially refused to carry advertisements for "quack remedies" or any other products in which co-founders Stanton and Anthony did not have confidence. Thus, when the prominent Beecher family offered financial support for the periodical, it seemed like the perfect solution to the publication's fiscal woes. However, this financial support was contingent on a name change to make the publication more palatable and less threatening for an audience outside of the suffrage movement. Stanton refused. In her analysis of *The Revolution*, Marion Marzolf argues that "conservative members of the women's movement" were horrified by the more radical views within the periodical, as well as its "connection of various other social reforms to the woman's cause" (1977, 227). During the suffrage period, there was clearly a trade-off between having a radical, narrowly targeted, but short-lived publication and having a more moderate publication with greater longevity and potentially broader appeal; the apparent incompatibility of the marketplace with radical publications is a factor that continues to resonate within the contemporary realm of popular print culture.

This section has demonstrated the consequences, both positive and negative, for feminist magazines that have chosen to change their titles or decided not to. The politics of magazine names are important: they brand the magazine to readers and to the broader public, especially those encountering the publication for the first time. A magazine changing its name is, then, quite literally a change in identity. For more radical publications, a name change can feel like—and actually involve—going against everything for which a publication stands. For more moderate publications, changing one's name can mean access to the pockets of advertisers and private donors. The questions of how to engage the marketplace and foster financial sustainability run through the long history of feminist publishing, questions that magazines have sought to address through a variety of funding avenues, including for- and not-for-profit routes.

THE POLITICS OF FOR- AND NOT-FOR-PROFIT STATUS

Third- and post-wave magazines have approached the issue of how to adequately raise the funds for publication in different ways. The major distinction among these funding routes is the for- or not-for-profit designation. Both *Bitch* and *Shameless* are not-for-profit publications: one of the main advantages of not-for-profit status is that it allows for tax exemptions, but it also means that these publications cannot engage in direct political activities, such as endorsing political candidates. In contrast, *BUST* and *RookieMag* are for-profit publications; *Rookie*'s costs are substantially lower, however, insofar as the online publication does not have to pay for printing and distribution. The now-defunct *HUES*, *ROCKRGRL*, and *VenusZine* were also for-profits. As I discussed in the last chapter, while *HUES* was for-profit, it also relied on private funding from the Edut sisters' grandfather to survive. As the defunct status of *HUES*, *ROCKRGRL*, and *Venus Zine* suggests, there is a difference between "for-profit" and "profitable."

The distinction between "for-profit" and "profitable" also characterizes feminist magazines established in the 1960s and 1970s, which were often run by volunteer staff who never saw their magazines generate revenue. The vast majority of second-wave periodicals were independently published and mainly supported through a combination of subscription revenue and personal funds. The broad-based *Chrysalis: A Magazine of Women's Culture*

(1977–80), for example, had an entirely unpaid staff (Johnson 1996, 62) and radical feminist magazine *off our backs* (*oob*) (1970–2008) had one paid staff member by 1996 (Endres 1996c, 267). Given their reliance on volunteers, as well as their frequent revenue problems, most second-wave publications were fairly short-lived and published on a small scale: according to Sammye Johnson (1996), *Chrysalis*'s break-even point was calculated at 33,000 but circulation never reached more than 13,000 (61). In contrast, Marion Marzolf (1977) finds that *Ms.* magazine, which had much greater material and industry resources, had a subscription base of 350,000 and an estimated readership of 1.4 million by September of 1973 (243).[3] Despite its much larger subscription base, however, *Ms.* also had difficulties sustaining itself as a commercial feminist magazine, leading to its application for and gain of tax-exempt status in the late 1970s.

Ms. magazine's tax-exempt status meant a savings of hundreds of thousands of dollars in postage costs, resulting in greater financial stability for the publication. *Ms.*'s new status also had an unexpected benefit: Valerie Salembier, head of the ad sales department, recounts in Mary Thom's (1997) memoir of *Ms.* magazine that she was able to sell more advertisements because being a government-approved publication helped make skittish companies feel more at ease (171–72). In this sense, not-for-profit status worked as a kind of legitimation narrative for the magazine, making the publication appear unthreatening to potential investors. And perhaps, in some ways, it was: not-for-profit status meant, for example, that the magazine could no longer participate directly in electoral politics. As a politically moderate publication, *Ms.* was able to successfully negotiate the vetting process for organizations applying for nonprofit status, a negotiation not possible for or rejected in principle by the magazine's more radical contemporaries.

Although applying for nonprofit status as educational publications was an option for many feminist periodicals, most did not take advantage of this funding avenue, despite the eligibility for grants and discounted postage costs associated with government support. For instance, *oob* considered an application for not-for-profit status but was wary of potential conditions attached to grant money (Endres 1996a, xv). Feminist publications that did become nonprofits did not necessarily have an easier time: for example, the radical feminist publication *Big Mama Rag* (1972–84) applied for nonprofit status in 1974 and was rejected by the Internal Revenue Service District Director in Austin, Texas, due to, among other factors, the publication's "articles, lectures, editorials, etc. promoting lesbianism" and politically "doctrinaire stance"; this rejection was later overturned, but not until 1980, in *Big Mama*

Rag, Inc v. United States of America. The differences between the relative ease and long struggle of *Ms.* and *Big Mama Rag*, respectively, to gain nonprofit status illuminates my broader claim that politically radical publications and publications that seek to expand or challenge who counts as worthy of representation within the public sphere generally do not have access to the same kind of revenue streams as their more moderate counterparts.

The political and cultural context in which third- and post-wave magazines find themselves is different from the terrain that second-wave feminist magazines navigated in the 1970s. Fights in court to access government funding and debates around the politics of accepting such money in the first place are absent from the lives of third- and post-wave publications—or, at the very least, not visible to readers of the magazines. Third- and post-wave magazines like BUST and *Venus Zine* are or were for-profit publications, not because they reject the state in principle. As commercial lifestyle magazines, BUST and *Venus Zine* are not, or would not have been, intelligible as educational publications. The long history of funding for not-for-profit feminist magazines demonstrates that politically radical publications had a much harder time accessing such funding or rejected this option in principle because of its links to an oppressive nation-state. Not-for-profit—or 501(c)3— status became a potential option for U.S.-based feminist publications, following the Revenue Act of 1954, and thus was not an option for earlier suffrage publications (Arnsberger et al. 2008, 106). In addition to subscription and advertising revenue, suffrage publications often relied on support from women's rights organizations to supplement the costs of production. However, the politics of organizational funding, like government funding, often came with its own set of "strings attached" that made it difficult, if not impossible, for radical publications to access this revenue source.

THE POLITICS OF ORGANIZATIONAL FUNDING

One of the major paradigm shifts in feminist publishing is that no third- or post-wave publications primarily receive funding from women's organizations. This shift may be due to the different context out of which third-wave publications emerged, particularly the deliberately leaderless and decentralized feminist zine scenes of the 1990s, such as Riot Grrrl. As I have argued in the previous chapter, Riot Grrrl zine culture was a significant generative force for third- and post-wave magazines. The radical goals of Riot Grrrl—to redefine girlhood and to fight oppression in all its forms—did not lend themselves to liberal feminist organizations, which have historically fought for access to existing systems rather than changing the systems themselves. The only third-wave publication that received any kind of institutional support was *HUES*, which was supported by the University of Michigan as a student group, until it became a nationally circulating magazine. The success of *HUES* on a national level and its growth as a magazine meant that it no longer qualified for university funding as a student club. In a sense, the qualities of the magazine no longer matched up with the institutional mandate. In examining the history of funding for women's rights periodicals, it is clear that publications with some form of formal funding have struggled to negotiate between editorial vision and the goals of their funding organs. While organizational affiliation brought more economic stability for earlier women's rights publications, the trade-offs that accompanied affiliation were often more than what radical publications wished to sacrifice. The goal-oriented approach of some women's organizations also meant that publications became less sustainable after those goals had been achieved. This irony is particularly evident in the case of suffrage publications.

Throughout the nineteenth and early-twentieth centuries, organizational support played a vital role in helping more moderate women's rights periodicals maintain a more stable economic base. For example, *The Woman's Journal* was supported by the American Woman Suffrage Association (AWSA) and adopted as the official voice of the National American Woman Suffrage Association (NAWSA) in 1910 (Spencer 1996, 476). As Finnegan notes, this partnership resulted in a rise in both subscriptions and donations (which rose to make up 28% of their revenue in 1910, up from 20% the previous year). In contrast, more radical publications, such as *The Revolution*, had difficulty finding institutional support and, as a result, constantly faced financial hardship. *The Revolution* increased its operating deficit monthly, its circulation never rose to more than 3,000, and it relied primarily on the private funds of co-founder Stanton and Anthony to survive. The absence of institutional support for *The Revolution* was a critical factor in its demise.[4] The refusal of Stanton and Anthony to compromise any of their beliefs in response to pressures from the moderate faction of the women's movement meant that they maintained their principled position but it also spelled the end of their periodical after just two years of publication (in contrast to *The Woman's Journal*'s sixty-one-year publication trajectory). Another publication, the popular *Woman's Tribune*, seemed to be denied organizational support because it covered a variety of topics and therefore lacked the kind of singular focus on suffrage desired by the NAWSA.[5] The institutional support that *The Woman's Journal* received from the NAWSA clearly helped sustain the publication, and the periodical's moderate stance made it an attractive vehicle for the promotion of the organization's work. The dearth of financial support for more radical or innovative publications is a pattern that runs through the long history of feminist publishing, and suggests that evaluating the success a publication by longevity alone is an inadequate measure of its accomplishments.

Dyann Logwood's account of the demise of *HUES* magazine is resonant with the overall pattern of innovative feminist publications' lifespans. *HUES* did not present itself as a politically radical magazine, but the editors did want to represent a range of identities in complex ways that challenged what bell hooks calls the interlocking systems of "white supremacist capitalist patriarchy" (1992, 22). In an interview for *Making Feminist Media*, Logwood stated that many publishers wanted to "change the focus of the publication and ... turn it into something that we couldn't stand behind. So, rather than to sell out, even though, trust me, so many people said, 'well, if you sell out just a little bit, it will help the magazine survive,'" the magazine editors chose to hand *HUES* over to New Moon, a progressive company that published a magazine for young teens. Almost immediately, *HUES* was put on permanent hiatus as a result of the sale. Years later, Logwood clearly did not regret the decision: "Selling out just a little bit is still selling out," she stated. What these histories reveal is that when it comes to adapting one's message in order to access funding channels, the stakes are much higher for more radical publications than for moderate ones, for publications that seek larger gains than simply integrating into an existing and flawed system, and for publications like *HUES* that sought to challenge white supremacy. "Selling out" as a discourse suggests a kind of gradual emptying of a publication's radical goals or ethos, but what the history of feminist publishing suggests is that most radical feminist periodicals went out of business rather than giving up on their principles. However, the discourse of selling out does seem more apt in describing the processes of compromise that some moderate feminist publications underwent.

Despite the limitations of conceptualizing feminism's relationship with the market as one of "selling out," there is clear evidence that moderate periodicals have had to engage in processes of negotiation between its different constituencies. After having been adopted by the NAWSA, for example, *The Woman's Journal* was forced by the organization to make some changes to its size and look. The NAWSA increased the size of the paper and asked for a more commercial look, changes to which the *Journal* acquiesced, despite the opposition of then owner and editor Alice Stone Blackwell, whose interests lay mainly in publishing a political magazine.[6] These kinds of tensions between organizational funding and the political goals of magazine editors have changed, insofar as the funding sources for third- and post-wave feminist magazines are no longer liberal feminist organizations. This difference signals the shifts in the temporal and political contexts out of which third- and post-wave magazines emerged. In her discussion of the "new racism" as part of a matrix of oppression, Patricia Hill Collins (2004) argues that while formal discrimination has been outlawed, a variety of institutional, symbolic, and individual social practices produce "virtually identical racial hierarchies" (32) that come to appear "natural, normal, and inevitable" (34).[7] The goal of liberal feminism, to seek access to existing institutions rather than radically changing or dismantling them, is thus an inadequate way to address the late capitalist, white supremacist, patriarchal context that characterizes the late twentieth and early twenty-first centuries. It is not surprising, then, that feminist publications emerging out of this particular moment have sought to address some of the more symbolic ways in which gender, race, and sexual hierarchies perpetuate themselves. (*Bitch*'s analysis of pop culture representation is a perfect example of this different focus.)

Despite the relative absence of organizational funding for contemporary feminist magazines, there is a resonance between women's rights periodicals and the feminist magazines that emerged in the late twentieth century, particularly with regard to the kinds of choices that feminist magazines have available to them when they are looking at various funding sources. It is clear that moderate publications have an easier time negotiating the demands of institutions—whether those are governmental, educational, or organizational—than radical or innovative publications, which have much more to lose when it comes to making concessions to their funders. One of the key areas where these kinds of compromises become readily apparent is in relation to advertising.

THE POLITICS OF ADVERTISING

All third- and post-wave magazines carry advertising of some kind. In an interview I conducted, co-founder of *HUES* magazine Dyann Logwood recounted how just one major advertisement for Levi's jeans gave the publication enough revenue to publish its first issue that circulated nation-wide. Similarly, as I discussed in Chapter One, *ROCKRGRL* founder Carla DeSantis went so far as to thank Fender for being the first big company to take the magazine seriously and advertise regularly within it in her final editorial for the magazine, when it was folding due to its inability to generate enough ad and subscription revenue. *BUST* contains the highest percentage of advertising out of all third- and post-wave magazines; this feature of the magazine may be attributed to *BUST*'s capability in attracting advertising for a spectrum of different products and through pinpointing—and arguably *creating*—a specific target market.

From its inception, *BUST* identified a specific target market: Generation XX. As discussed in Chapter One, Generation XX was the term coined by editors and co-founders Debbie Stoller and Marcelle Karp (writing pseudonymously as Celina Hex and Betty Boob) to describe women in their twenties and thirties during the early 1990s—a witty modification of the term "Generation X." As the inaugural editorial describes the Generation XX woman, a picture of her emerges: like her male counterpart, she is a slacker with difficulties committing to jobs, responsibility, and adulthood, with the additional gendered fears of having children and being single for life (Hex and Boob 1993, x). She is in debt and without savings, yet still has access to the "yuppie bullshit" dream of getting married to a man with a successful career and having children. The reader of *BUST* is thus coded as a straight, likely college-educated and likely white woman, whose debt is temporary. She is a bohemian, living an artistic life on the fringes of society, by choice, and thus with a certain measure of privilege. Unlike *HUES*, which had immense difficulties in attracting advertisers due to its stated intention to reach all women of all races and ethnicities, *BUST*'s isolation of a particular demographic that is, or may become, upwardly mobile seems to have served the publication well in garnering advertising revenue.

A comparison of the number of advertisements and percentage of advertising pages across *BUST*, *Bitch*, and *ROCKRGRL* clearly illustrates the greater success *BUST* has had in the area of advertising relative to its counterparts.[8] Table 1 compares the number and percentage of advertisements in all three magazines after ten years of publication. This comparison helps make sense of where the publications sat in relation to advertising after having had a decade to grow from zines to magazines and establish themselves as internationally circulating periodicals. As is evident, *BUST* was head and shoulders above the other two publications when it came to number of advertisements and percentage of advertising pages. This difference may be partially attributed to *BUST*'s apparent success with smaller and more affordable "classified" advertisements (eight pages in total in its Winter 2003 issue) that each occupy one-ninth of a page. Neither *ROCKRGRL* nor *Bitch* included advertising sections of this kind.

TABLE 1 Comparison of Advertising after Ten Years of Publication

	BITCH Summer 2006	*ROCKRGRL* Fall 2005	*BUST* Winter 2003
Number of advertisements	29	29	125
Number of ad pages	9.75	14.75	39
Percentage of total pages	10%	22%	31%

TABLE 2 Comparison of Advertising in 2003

	BITCH Winter 2003	*ROCKRGRL* Winter 2003	*BUST* Winter 2003
Number of advertisements	31	41	125
Number of ad pages	9.5	12	39
Percentage of total pages	9.5%	15%	31%

Table 2 takes the same Winter 2003 issue of *BUST* and compares it with the Winter 2003 issues of *Bitch* and *ROCKRGRL*, in order to account for the differences in year of publication in the first table. What the second table demonstrates is that 2003 was not simply an anomalous year when all feminist magazines drew in massive amounts of advertising revenue. The number of advertisements and percentage of advertising in *ROCKRGRL* and *Bitch* stay relatively consistent, while *BUST* remains well above the latter in both categories. What accounts for these differences?

The differences between *BUST*, *Bitch*, and *ROCKRGRL* may be attributed to a number of factors, including the style of publication and target demographic. As a not-for-profit, *Bitch* can rely a little less on advertising revenue than its for-profit counterparts. The difference between *ROCKRGRL*'s and *BUST*'s advertising levels is more complex: while *ROCKRGRL* was targeted to a particular demographic—women musicians—this category denotes a pastime or career, rather than an identity or *type of person*. Conversely, *BUST* markets to a more readily identifiable "type," as discussed above, who may have a range of possible interests, thereby expanding the number of possible advertisers who might be attracted to publishing within the pages of the magazine. While all but four of the advertisements in *ROCKRGRL* are music-related, *BUST*'s advertisements are slightly more varied. Each section of *BUST*'s reviews of music, film, and books is accompanied by advertising of related products, and the magazine's regular sex advice column is paired with advertising for vibrators and women-friendly sex shops. The bulk of the advertisements, particularly in *BUST*'s classifieds section, are for independent companies selling all manner of jewellery, clothing, soap, and vintage fabrics, a phenomenon I discuss further in Chapter Five. A small handful of advertisements for larger companies (e.g., the Showtime television network and PF Flyer shoes) also graces *BUST*'s pages. Despite the monetary importance that large-scale advertising contracts can have for feminist magazines, taking such contracts can also draw criticism. For this reason, most third- and post-wave magazines have policies about what kinds of advertising they will and will not accept.

Because of their feminist politics, third- and post-wave magazines not only have difficulty attracting advertisers but also have to think about how they would address a company with questionable politics wanting to advertise within their pages. As a not-for-profit organization, *Bitch* magazine has addressed this conundrum in its advertising policy by choosing to carry advertisements only from companies that meet its selection criteria of social responsibility, commitment to anti-sexism and anti-racism, and adherence to fair labour practices (Bitch Media 2012). *Bitch* uses a discourse of sponsorship and strategic partnership in its media literature, emphasizing a shared mission of social justice that is consistent in all aspects of the magazine, including its advertising. Similarly, *Shameless* "reserves the right to publish any ad that is in contradiction with [its] mandate" (Shameless 2014). Logwood of *HUES* magazine also recounted to me that their publication refused to take ads for products such as diet pills on principle. Taking advertisements from larger companies or businesses with politics that seem to contradict a magazine's mandate can have consequences for feminist magazines in the form of angry letters to the editor and cancelled subscriptions from readers. For this reason, feminist magazines like *Bitch* have been known to refuse particular advertisements.

Bitch magazine has had its share of advertising debacles—Chapter Six of *Making Feminist Media* focuses on one controversial and now infamous advertisement for a vibrator that appeared on the back cover of the publication. In 2000, the magazine chose to reject an advertisement featuring "faux-lesbian porno iconography" (Jervis 2000, 91). In place of the ad, the magazine ran a stark blank page with a centred text box explaining the ad, and the magazine's rationale behind rejecting it, and inviting commentary from readers. The magazine ran three pages of readers' letters in its subsequent issue, representing just a small selection of the "tremendous volume of mail" received, as well as a pie chart with a statistical breakdown of how readers had responded (Jervis and Zeisler 2000, 6).[9] The vast majority of readers supported *Bitch*'s decision. In making visible to readers the inner workings of the magazine—its decision not to run an ad and the editors' rationale—and inviting reader commentary, *Bitch* was able to open up a conversation about advertising with its readers, giving them a sense of having a stake in what kind of advertising content would appear within the magazine's pages. It was also able to avoid a backlash against the advertisement, had it chosen to run the ad, and to build loyalty and community among readers by creating a forum space within its pages.

Clearly, advertising is "serious and material business" for feminist magazines. Large-scale advertising contracts from big-name companies are far more rare in the world of feminist magazines because large businesses do not often want to associate themselves with feminist publications and because feminist magazines do not always want to associate themselves with big business. For these reasons, the bulk of advertising that one finds in the pages of feminist magazines are for smaller independent businesses that are often feminist or woman-centred. These relationships between feminism and advertising are not new and run through the long history of feminist periodical publishing, a history that reveals varied approaches to the question of ads.

Due to the emergence of radical feminism from new left movements in the 1960s and 1970s, some feminist magazines publishing in these decades did not accept advertising of any kind on principle. *No More Fun and Games* (1968–73), published by the radical separatist group Cell 16 in Boston, exemplified this approach (Endres 1996b, 247). Similarly, the radical feminist magazine *Up from Under* (1970) editorialized in its inaugural issue that "women deserve a magazine ... that is not designed to push useless products" (3). However, most periodicals of this era, such as *Chrysalis* and *oob*, did accept some advertisements, which typically were for other feminist organizations and companies. According to Linda Chambers, Linda Steiner, and Carole Fleming (2004), "few [second-wave periodicals] were able to get as many advertising accounts as they wanted and needed, especially since many of those that carried advertising limited the kind of advertising they were willing to carry" (163). Indeed, the only second-wave magazine that had any real degree of success at garnering ad contracts from large companies was *Ms.* magazine (1971–).

Of all second-wave magazines, *Ms.* was an exception to the rule in almost every way: the publication was, and continues to be, by far the largest and most widely circulating feminist magazine with the highest circulation number; Marion Marzolf (1977) notes that *Ms.* had a subscription base of 350,000 and an estimated readership of 1.4 million by September of 1973 (243). Nonetheless, many companies were unwilling to attach their names to a feminist publication, even a fairly moderate periodical like *Ms.* This reluctance, coupled with both *Ms.*'s own mandate to reform the ad industry through refusing sexist advertisements and the negative, highly critical reader responses to some of the ads that ran in the magazine, meant that advertising in *Ms.* was fraught terrain. One of the few industries willing to run ads in *Ms.* was tobacco, a necessity that Gloria Steinem later described as "a kind of prison," as concerns about the health impact of cigarettes mounted in the 1980s (quoted in Thom 1997, 136). Tobacco money made up such a large proportion of ad revenue that the publication could not afford to lose it, even when readers voiced their concern. For *Ms.*, accepting advertisements was a thorny issue: ads helped fund the magazine, giving it the ability to circulate widely, but these same ads also alienated readers. Advertisements for tobacco made the publication appear hypocritical, advocating for women's health on the one hand, but putting it at risk on the other (Minkler, Wallack, and Madden 1987). The advertising conundrums faced by *Ms.* are resonant with some of the debates about ads in *Bitch*. Prior to the 1960s, however, some women's rights publications openly *embraced* advertising.

The suffrage-era *Woman's Journal* was arguably the women's rights periodical with the most success in harnessing the marketplace. For example, the publication avoided discussing controversial issues, such as divorce, adultery, infanticide, and free love, so as not to scare away potential advertisers (Rodier 2004, 108). *The Woman's Journal* also engaged in "puffery": the practice of giving complimentary copy to advertisers. Finally, in 1904, then editor Charlotte Perkins Gilman wrote that the publication "needed to jump on the bandwagon and produce its own 'bait'" (i.e., subscription lists for advertisers) in order to increase circulation (quoted in Finnegan 1999, 146). Gilman's rhetoric commodifies *The Woman's Journal* readers and demonstrates the *Journal*'s interest in using increasingly popular commercial strategies to ensure the magazine's success. The magazine's commercial strategies exemplify Margaret Finnegan's argument that "particularly during the 1910s, suffragists incorporated modern methods of advertising, publicity, mass merchandising, and mass entertainment into their fight for voting rights" (2). Indeed, this cohort of suffrage magazines was publishing during a time of rapid change in the landscape of commercial culture, a climate that some women's rights publications sought to use to their advantage.

Beginning in the 1890s, a huge shift in the economies of magazines left an indelible mark upon the genre. Printing technologies made mass printing possible, and the possibility of capturing the attention of a mass audience drew advertisers. In turn, magazine publishers noted that they could cut the costs of subscription rates through running cheap advertisements, thereby increasing the number of subscriptions and their profit. As Ellen Gruber Garvey (1996) argues, this move was a watershed moment in periodical history because it both marked a major shift in magazine economics and drew in a new audience of people who had not previously subscribed to the older elite magazines (9). In the 1890s, on average, magazine ad and circulation revenue were equal, but by the late 1920s ad revenue was three times more than subscription money (Schmidt 2002, 994). Given the dramatic effects of these technological advancements upon periodical publications, Richard Ohmann (1996) asserts that "a national mass culture was first instanced in the United States by magazines," meaning that for the first time *readers* became commodities to be sold to advertisers (vii). *The Woman's Journal*, particularly, made use of these new strategies, but other suffrage-era publications at the turn of the twentieth century also recognized the importance of advertising for revenue generation. Nonetheless, this kind of revenue was frequently scarce, since suffrage was a contentious issue. Both *The Woman's Chronicle* (1888–93), founded by Catherine Campbell Cunningham in Little Rock, Arkansas, and Clara Bewick Colby's Beatrice, Nebraska-based *Woman's Tribune*, for instance, mainly were supported by the private incomes of their editors (Endres 1996e, 478). Publications that steered away from the more controversial aspects of women's rights were more successful in garnering advertising dollars. While the women's rights periodicals of this period took advantage of the birth of modern commercial culture, they nevertheless put limitations on the kinds of advertising they would accept.

Suffrage publications rejected particular kinds of advertising on principle. For example, *The Woman's Journal* would not accept ads from alcohol or tobacco companies. *The Revolution* refused to carry advertisements for "quack remedies" or any other products in which co-founders Stanton and Anthony did not have confidence, although the publication was eventually forced to take such advertisements due to financial hardship. Pre-Civil War suffrage publications, such as the Cincinnati-based *Genius of Liberty* (1851–53) refused advertising on principle, while the Providence-based *Una* (1853–55) took ads in its later years for items like *The New York Tribune*, vapour baths, carpeting, and books. In her analysis of *The Una*, Agnes Gottlieb (1996b) speculates that this move may have been due to the periodical's flagging subscription revenue (391). What these different publications reveal is a great deal of variation in willingness to accept advertising. Although some suffrage publications embraced aspects of the emerging commercial culture, most had difficulty attracting advertisers due to the controversial nature of their content and thus relied on primarily subscription revenues or the private funds of their founders to survive.

As the above has demonstrated, the publishing climate for magazine publications from the 1890s onward has necessitated some engagement with advertising. From open embrace to partial acceptance to outright rejection, feminist magazines have taken varying perspectives on the place of advertisements within their pages. While most early women's rights publications were willing to engage this aspect of the marketplace, advertising played a minor role in the lives of periodicals circulating prior to the 1880s and was clearly not politicized in the ways that would later inform debates about ads in second- and third-wave magazines. Editorial decisions about what ads to accept often polarized readers of feminist magazines in the mid- to late twentieth century, potentially resulting in lost subscription and newsstand revenue for publications. The politics of advertising in these feminist magazines may thus be characterized as a kind of fine balancing act between principles motivating the ads, the readers, and the editors. For this reason and, moreover, the general dearth of companies willing to advertise in feminist magazines in the first place, these publications must rely much more heavily on subscription revenue and other funding sources to continue producing issues, in comparison with their non- or not-overtly feminist counterparts. In addition to financial support through reader subscription, feminist magazines have plumbed different kinds of funding avenues, including organizational, private, and public funds, each of which is accompanied by its own benefits and limitations.

CONCLUSION: FEMINISM AND THE MARKETPLACE

This chapter has discussed some of the challenges that third- and post-wave magazines confront in their engagement with the realm of commercial culture, placing these struggles in historical context. Each decision that the editors and publishers of feminist magazines make—from their publications' names to their funding sources to their advertising policies—influences publications' capability of negotiating the marketplace and the shape of that negotiation, and has implications for how readers respond to and interact with the magazine. Each of these decisions takes place within a broader market context that shapes what kinds of choices are available to magazine editors and publishers in the first place. This process might best be characterized as a kind of negotiation of the uneven terrain of the capitalist marketplace, rather than a process of selling out or co-optation.

As this chapter has demonstrated, the discourse of selling out or of co-optation is not useful or accurate in considering how feminist magazines engage the marketplace either now or in the past. First, it is inaccurate to characterize feminist engagement with the marketplace as "selling out" because it implies that the market gradually drains out any spark of radical politics. While clearly the stakes of negotiation and compromise are much higher for radical, innovative, anti-racist publications, what this chapter has shown is that radical publications tend to fold rather than compromise on their beliefs and that commercial feminist publications tend not to have radical politics in the first place. The discourse of "selling out" simply does not bear out in the publication histories of feminist magazines.

Second, the narrative of selling out implies that commercial feminist magazines are utterly apolitical. This is not the case. Certainly, commercial feminist magazines, such as *Ms.*, BUST, or *Venus Zine*, are *differently political*, and their politics are rarely radical, yet these publications are making important interventions into the realm of popular culture. As Amy Erdman Farrell (1998) argues in her assessment of the impact of *Ms.*, although *Ms.* did not radically change the commercial magazine industry, it did adapt elements of magazine culture for its own ends: for example, it redefined self-help and daily life (31). That is, while *Ms.* spoke the language of other women's self-help magazines, through using an intimate voice promising personal transformation or an individualized narrative of one woman making a difference in the world, *Ms.* politicized these narratives and used them to encourage its readers to become politically engaged. Furthermore, when more commercial feminist magazines are dismissed out of hand as apolitical or as "feminism lite" (Baumgardner and Richards 2000, 139), some important conversations are elided among feminists about what it means for feminism to be "popular." Nonetheless, this problematic binary between "commercial culture" and "politics" persists in the literature on feminist magazines.

Both feminism and commercial culture have changed dramatically over the course of the late nineteenth and twentieth centuries. Engaging the commercial marketplace has always been fraught with challenges for feminist magazines, since these publications usually lack capital, advertisers, and a broad base of readers. Nonetheless, historically, some feminist publications found ways to successfully harness the marketplace for their own ends. These strategies resonate differently across historical contexts, due to changes within both feminism and the marketplace itself. In the 1960s and 1970s, engaging the capitalist marketplace was politicized far differently for second-wave periodicals than for the forays made by the early women's rights periodicals. With the exception of *Ms.*, second-wave periodicals either chose to eschew the trappings of commercial culture as a matter of principle or they lacked adequate funding to subsist as a commercial publication in any kind of sustained manner. Nonetheless, as Maria DiCenzo (2000) has written of the British suffrage periodical *Votes for Women*, "the capitalization of the press and the reliance on advertising was not always at odds with political activism" (116). Indeed, this chapter demonstrates that feminist magazines have historically interacted with the marketplace in various ways, often adapting and appropriating aspects of commercial culture for their own ends. Nonetheless, most feminist periodicals have historically also struggled to maintain financial stability. For this reason, "success" for feminist publications should not be defined solely in terms of commercial sustainability.

The history of feminist print culture demonstrates that periodicals have been vibrant sites of debate and have played an integral role in broadening and expanding the movement, as well as making visible and challenging representations of women within popular culture and carving out a space for feminism within that sphere. Third- and post-wave magazines have been and continue to be part of this project.

PART TWO

THE POLITICS OF
THIRD-WAVE MAGAZINES

HUES MAGAZINE, THE POLITICS OF ALLIANCE, AND CRITICAL MULTICULTURALISM

HUES is by, for and about the advancement of women. You could call us womanist or pro-woman if you like. And for the record, being pro-woman does not make us anti-male. We are, however, anti-sexism and against any form of discrimination.

— Dyann, Ophira & Tali

The need for unity is often misnamed as a need for homogeneity....

— Audre Lorde

In 1992, three University of Michigan students—Dyann Logwood and twin sisters Ophira and Tali Edut—submitted a group project for an Introduction to Women's Studies class in response to a class assignment asking students to create something that would forever change the lives of women. This project was the first issue of *HUES* magazine. *HUES* grew to circulate internationally in Canada and the United States during its seven-year run as a magazine dedicated to the advancement of women. Indeed, as the opening epigraph suggests, *HUES* was committed to representing all women through an intersectional lens (Crenshaw 1989), centring the experiences of women of colour as sites of knowledge production. In this sense, *HUES* was a popular print culture manifestation of Black feminist thought (Collins 2000; Lorde 1984; Walker 1984).

In this chapter, I argue that *HUES* used an intersectional approach in its editorials and articles. The magazine fostered a politics of unity of the kind so famously advocated by Audre Lorde, a unity that acknowledged, valued, and celebrated differences among women. In contrast to many women's magazines, including some third-wave feminist publications, *HUES* decentred whiteness as the normative racial identity that codes notions of citizenship, feminism, and idealized femininity. Instead, through both visual and textual strategies, *HUES* produced a multicultural women's magazine that took up the complexity and contingency of identity and that was committed to viewing sexism as part of a larger "matrix of oppression and privilege" (Ferber, Herera, Samuels 2007; Collins 2002, 3). Because of its commitment to representing a range of women and its womanist/pro-woman approach, *HUES* often struggled to find advertisers and a larger publisher who could help financially sustain the magazine.

A NOTE ON METHODOLOGY AND ARCHIVING THIRD-WAVE FEMINISMS

As I discussed in the Introduction, researching periodicals can be a rewarding but challenging task due both to the availability of materials in archives and to the fact that magazines not available in university or local libraries are rarely circulated through interlibrary loan, if at all. Research on third-wave magazines tends to involve trips to archives, often at personal financial cost, a material reality that makes accessing complete runs of publications difficult for many researchers. In the case of *HUES*, these problems are compounded by the fact that well-known third-wave feminist archives at the Barnard Zine Library and the Sallie Bingham Center for Women's History and Culture do not have a complete run of the magazine in their holdings. For a period of time, editorials from *HUES* were available through the GenderWatch database, but they appeared in "text only" format and now seem to be no longer available. The difficulties inherent in researching periodicals, and similar ephemeral cultural productions, and the particular issues with accessing *HUES* speak to larger questions concerning the archiving of both magazines and third-wave feminism.

The absence of *HUES* from archives of third-wave feminism speaks to a set of broader concerns about how third-wave feminism is documented and remembered. Michel Foucault (1969) argues that archives do not simply reflect the past; rather, in the archive we have a "density of discursive practices" that are implicated in power relations (128). Questions of what we remember, who we remember, which stories are centred and which are marginalized, are political ones and have particular urgency for feminist social movements. As Susan Stanford Friedman (1995) asserts, "[Q]uestions feminists have asked of masculinist history about the erasure and distortion of women's lives must be put to feminist histories," as well (20). Given that *HUES* had a remarkable seven-year publication run, was written about in a well-known anthology of third-wave feminism (Heywood and Drake 1997), was promoted as an education resource at annual conferences of the National Women's Studies Association, and at one point had an advisory board that included prominent feminists Rebecca Walker and Gloria Steinem (Edut and Edut 2014), it is surprising that *HUES* is not a part of these archives.[1] Some feminist historians (Gilmore 2008; Roth 2003) have critiqued the erasure of women of colour and working-class women from second-wave feminist histories, focusing instead on the distinct trajectories of, and coalition work across, Black, Latina, and white feminisms. It is crucial that archives of third-wave feminisms pay particular attention to the production of materials by women of colour and women who are not middle or upper class.

The digitization of print culture ephemera has opened up access to these materials to a much wider audience, including periodical researchers. However, the digitization of magazines sometimes excludes materials that are integral to how one might interpret these texts. In the case of the text-only digitization, important materials such as covers, advertisements, and illustrations are not available. As Sean Latham and Robert Scholes (2006) argue, regarding the exclusion of advertising from magazine digitization projects, "[A]dvertising is a vital, even crucial, part of [periodical studies]. The archival decision to excise the commercial matter from these documents arises from a fundamental misunderstanding of periodicals as unique cultural and material objects" (521). While text-only format is beneficial insofar as it provides access to the editorials and articles of a magazine publication, the interpretive framework is limited by this approach since it does not allow for an exploration of the relationships between text and image, or how, for example, different components of a magazine issue might resonate with each other. For example, in Chapter Six, I examine the politics of a controversial advertisement for a vibrator on the back cover of *Bitch* magazine, which ran in the same issue as an editorial discussing the fact that some readers complained about the publication's articles on lesbians. In light of the ways in which some negative responses to the vibrator ad drew on homophobic understandings of sexuality, there is a notable irony in the pairing of this advertisement and editorial. A text-only format of *Bitch*, or an online edition that did not include the original advertising, would not allow for a discussion of these important relationships. While the digitization of print culture ephemera thus represents a significant advance for periodical research, access to physical copies of magazines continues to be crucial.

Due to the scarcity of physical copies of *HUES* and their absence from major third-wave feminist archives, in this chapter my analysis is limited to three original copies of the magazine: Issue 2, Issue 5 (its first nationally circulating issue in spring/summer 1995), and Issue 6 (Winter 1996). Dyann Logwood generously mailed these issues to me. I also draw extensively on a detailed, two-part telephone interview with Logwood, in my analysis of the advertising and publishing context out of which *HUES* emerged. Despite the small number of issues I was able to work with, my interviews with Logwood and secondary research on *HUES* suggest that these issues are representative of the overall content and aesthetic of the publication.

INTERSECTIONALITY

The term "intersectionality" was first coined by legal scholar Kimberlé Williams Crenshaw (1989; 1995) to identify the ways in which "systems of race, gender, and class domination converge" ("Mapping," 358). Arguing that the law is predicated on additive theories of identity as if gender, race, class, and sexuality stack on top of each other like bricks (Razack 1998, 158), Crenshaw concludes that the law frequently fails Black women because of its privileging of only one axis of identity at a time. Instead, Crenshaw advocates an intersectional approach as an interpretive framework for understanding how Black women's lives are structured by both race and gender simultaneously, as well as sexuality, class, and age. She also champions an intersectional framework for anti-racist and feminist political organizing. By coining the term "intersectionality," Crenshaw gave a name to the kinds of thinking and organizing that Black feminists have been doing for generations (May 2012, 155).

Although *intersectionality* has become a buzzword within the academic discipline of Women's and Gender Studies (Nash 2008, 3), the analysis of racism, sexism, classism, and heterosexism as interlocking processes that converge and diverge in complex ways is not new. Vivan May (2012) notes, for example, that late-nineteenth-century Black feminist activist Anna Julia Cooper developed intersectional methods of analysis in her work (156). The collaboratively written Combahee River Collective Statement (1980), which states, "We see as our particular task the development of integrated analysis and practice based upon the fact that the major systems of oppression are *interlocking*" (1, my emphasis), also exemplifies an intersectional analysis that infuses the work of Black feminism. While intersectional analysis has a long intellectual history within Black feminist thought, the term "intersectionality" as a name for this set of analytic practices and politics emerged and gained purchase in a particular context and set of conditions: the United States in early 1990s, the same cultural moment out of which *HUES* came forth.

The cultural climate of the United States in the early 1990s was shaped in large part by the Anita Hill/Clarence Thomas scandal. Thomas, an African American judge, was nominated to the Supreme Court by then president George Bush. The nomination was instantly controversial because of Thomas's conservative views on issues such as affirmative action but became the subject of a huge amount of media scrutiny when law professor Anita Hill accused Thomas of sexual harassment when she had worked for the judge. Thomas denied these allegations, famously calling the resulting nomination hearings "a high-tech lynching for uppity blacks.... [I]t is a message that unless you kowtow to an old order, this is what will happen to you. You will be lynched, destroyed, caricatured by a committee of the U.S. Senate rather than hung from a tree" (Hearing 1991). In using the highly charged discourse of lynching, Thomas shifted the terms of the debate, portraying himself as the victim of a racist attack, sidelining Hill's claims of harassment. The Hill/Thomas scandal is revealing of the early 1990s climate of racial and gender politics in the United States: Hill commented retrospectively on the affair, "I had a gender and he had a race" (quoted in Lithwick 2014). That is, despite Hill's identity as an African American woman and Thomas's identity as an African American man, the confirmation hearing became a larger contest of gender vs. race, as if the two were mutually exclusive. The impact of this hearing and the media coverage surrounding it was far-reaching, remobilizing feminists to find ways of challenging intersecting systems of oppression.

In 1992, less than one year after Thomas was successfully confirmed to the Supreme Court, *HUES* magazine was created and Rebecca Walker (1992) wrote, "I am not a postfeminism feminist. I am the Third Wave" in a *Ms.* magazine article that introduced the term "third-wave feminism" into the lexicon (41). Walker's article was a critical response to the Anita Hill/Clarence Thomas affair, and served as a rallying cry for younger women of Walker's generation to renew their efforts in the fight for social justice and equality. In *HUES*, the Hill/Thomas scandal was invoked as an important context for an article on violence against women in the magazine's first national issue (1995). In it, the Anita Hill story is used to explain why many women do not come forward: as the article asserts, her perpetrator was "not only let off the hood, but exalted to a sickening hero status" ("Violence" 1995, 23). The Hill/Thomas affair was part of a more general climate of intensified race relations in the early 1990s in the United States.[2] The media coverage surrounding this event highlights the ways in which gender and race were seen as somehow incommensurate. *HUES* challenged these views.

DOING INTERSECTIONAL FEMINISM

The intersectional politics of *HUES* is identified immediately by the magazine's title, which emphasizes multiplicity, difference, and a spectrum of colours. According to Jennifer Nash (2008), Crenshaw's formulation of intersectionality emerged as a response to identity-based politics, which did not account for the complexities of intra-group difference and saw identity positions instead as relatively fixed and stable (2).[3] *HUES*'s name foregrounds race as a crucial part of identity; however, the name does not fix this aspect of identity to any one particular group. A name like *HUES* recognizes that everyone has a skin colour that shapes their lived experience. The name *HUES* shares similarities with "woman of colour," in the sense that the term "woman of colour" is a political identity of affinity (Haraway 1991, 155–61; Moraga 1981, xv; Muñoz 1999, 7). Like "woman of colour," *HUES*'s name recognizes race as a political ground for organizing, emphasizing through its one word—but plural—name the importance of unity in diversity and of respect for difference.

The recognition of race as an important and complex dimension of gendered lived experience that shapes how one views the world is built into *HUES*'s name. In an interview I conducted, Dyann Logwood talked about how the magazine's title was designed to reflect the creators' own diverse backgrounds:

> We thought about our friends and the fact that Ophi and Tali are Israeli Jews and their mom's family, I believe, is from Germany. My family is also an ethnic mix of African-American, Native American, Caucasian, I have a relative who comes from India, so we didn't want the magazine to be pigeon-holed as a magazine for blacks and Jews, you know? ... When you looked at our staff and when you looked at the people in our families and the people who we spent most of our time with, it was people from all different backgrounds.

HUES was thus a publication designed to reflect the creators' lived experiences as women with mixed heritages and with identities that did not fit neatly into conventional identity categories.

An early *HUES* article by Ophira Edut (1993) emphasizes the complexity and contingency of identity across different contexts. Edut wrote, "My skin is white, but my looks and attitude often feel very foreign amongst non-Jewish whites. At the same time, I'm not a woman of color as the term is defined.... It is far easier for a white, American Jew to assimilate into a white mainstream than it is for a person of color. Many of us have. But every club has its dues" (3). Here, Edut discusses white privilege through personal narrative. *HUES* writers often practised an intersectional standpoint epistemology that uses lived experience as a site for theorizing and acknowledges that subjects are multiply located (Collins 2002; Haraway 1988). According to Abigail Brooks

(2007), feminist standpoint epistemology asks "that we take women seriously as knowers" (77), that we acknowledge that women are a diverse group who do not all share the same views, and that we "apply what we learn from women's experiences toward social change and toward the elimination of oppression not only of women but of all marginalized groups" (77–78). In her *HUES* article, Edut's position as a white Jewish woman becomes a site from which she theorizes the intersections of privilege and oppression, notions of "passing," and assimilation.

HUES's intersectional standpoint epistemology is evident in the feature article of its first national issue. Entitled "Red, White, and Clueless?: Republican Women of Color," this article is written from the perspective of Carmela Logroño Gerrero, a Democrat woman of colour, seeking to understand why some women of colour support, even join, the Republican party. The article draws on interviews with five women of colour who are Republicans and discusses the ways in which Republian women of colour are often perceived as sell-outs or "Uncle Toms" to their race. Logroño Guerrero writes, "[W]hen most people picture a conservative of color, someone like Clarence Thomas comes to mind," again highlighting this political, cultural, and media context to which *HUES* was responding, and asks: "But what about the women of color in the Republican Party?" (18). Logroño Guerrero's question seeks to highlight intra-group differences and to make conservative women of colour visible in a political landscape where their voices were/are largely absent. (Condoleezza Rice's service as Secretary of State was still a decade away.) The article, however, also highlights Logroño Guerrero's skepticism of conservative politics; she remains consistently in dialogue with the conservative views presented by those she interviews. Rather than lapsing into relativism, Logroño Guerrero uses the dialogue as a springboard for asking larger questions about the capacity of either the Republican or Democratic parties to represent the interests of people of colour. "Many people of color," Logroño Guerrero concludes, "feel that the entire American system needs to be overturned in order for true revolution to occur" (57). "Red, White, and Clueless?" is representative of the kinds of complex intersectional subjectivities that *HUES* sought to highlight in its pages. *HUES* centred the experiences of women of colour as the base for its magazine. While white women were involved in creating and writing for *HUES* and were represented in its pages, whiteness was fundamentally decentred as the normative identity that constructed the magazine.

REDEFINING SISTERHOOD AND MULTICULTURALISM

HUES consistently decentred whiteness in its pages, foregrounding the experiences of women of colour, while also fostering a politics of cross-racial alliance rather than of identity. One of *HUES*'s early taglines, "for wimmin of non-dominant cultures and everyone else," visible on the cover of the second issue, exemplifies this approach. Privileged subjects, those belonging to "dominant culture," become displaced as the "everyone else" of the sentence but are still figured as potential allies. In using this textual strategy, *HUES* took an inclusive approach that acknowledged power differentials among women, foregrounding differences, and also invited men and privileged women to participate in the dialogue the magazine attempted to open up, but not as central subjects. In using the term "non-dominant," *HUES* also represented itself as a publication that could extend outside of the middle-class and heterosexual audiences usually served by the magazine genre. The spelling of *wimmin* signals the publication's feminist orientation; this spelling is used in some feminist texts as an alternate for *woman*, which etymologically means *wife of man*. As a spelling primarily associated with radical feminisms of the 1970s and 1980s, *HUES* also signals its continuation of a feminist lineage.

HUES's intersectional feminist perspective is signalled in multiple ways, most evidently through the publication's invocation of the words "feminism" and "sisterhood." In the first national issue, contributors to the magazine use the word "feminism" and, in the editorial for the same issue, Logwood and the Eduts sign off their editorial "In Sisterhood" (1995, 3). In my interview with her, Logwood emphasized *HUES*'s dedication to the principle of sisterhood, as well as the magazine's grounding in the second-wave strategy of consciousness-raising. Feminists of colour have frequently critiqued the ways in which some white feminists have used the discourse of sisterhood to homogenize women; elide important differences of race, class, and sexuality; and impose neo-colonialist agendas—see, for example, Gayatri Chakravorty Spivak's (1998) famous line about white women "saving brown women from brown men" (297). In *HUES*, however, sisterhood is valued, even recentred; indeed, the notion of sisterhood is built into the title of *HUES* itself, an acronym for "Hear Us Emerging Sisters."

As an abbreviation of *HUES*, "Hear Us Emerging Sisters" invokes the language of sisterhood, generation, movement, and action. First, it tells people to pay attention and to listen to the voices within the magazine. The phrase frames these voices as emergent: evoking the generational language of youth but also suggesting voices coming out of silence. The phrase suggests that being heard and listened to is not a phenomenon that has always taken place when it comes to women, particularly women of colour. As María C. Lugones and Elizabeth V. Spelman (1995) have argued, "[Privileged] women's voices are more likely to be heard than others" (496). *HUES* invokes this history, while maintaining a focus on sisterhood, enacting what Lugones and Spelman describe as a non-imperialist feminism motivated by friendship (504–7). "Sister" is also used among some communities of colour to refer to the shared connection of race and gender. The phrase "Hear Us Emerging Sisters" enacts a form of feminism that emphasizes the intersections of gender and race, centres women of colour, and signals the magazine as a space for dialogue and critical listening. In these senses, then, *HUES* reimagines the notion of sisterhood, conceptualizing it as a space of alliance and heterogeneity.

HUES imagined itself as a diverse and multicultural magazine, in ways that challenge sanitized state notions of multiculturalism. In the editorial of their first national issue, the three editors state that their goal is to create "a multicultural publication that confronts our differences instead of pretending they don't exist" (1995, 3). This conceptualization of multiculturalism is quite different from the state multiculturalism that constructs nations like Canada, Australia, and to some extent the United States.[4] In her critical work on multiculturalism and the Canadian nation, Himani Bannerji (2000) has demonstrated the ways in which state multiculturalism reifies whiteness as the normative and unmarked centre from which "O/others" are differentiated. In contrast to sanitized, "safe" state multiculturalism that does little to challenge the white supremacist narratives upon which U.S., Australian, and Canadian nationalisms are built, *HUES* envisioned a multiculturalism that would engage difference via critical dialogue rather than the liberal language of "tolerance."

Influenced by womanism and Black feminist thought, *HUES* sought to reconceptualize notions of sisterhood and multiculturalism. Co-founders and co-editors Logwood, Edut, and Edut envisioned "a magazine that gave women of all cultures, shapes, sizes and lifestyles a chance to speak for themselves" (1995, 3). Although *HUES* was not the first feminist magazine to have this vision, it was arguably the first feminist magazine to create this space successfully while also attempting to harness a piece of the mainstream marketplace in the United States.[5] This intersectional approach is evident not only in articles like "Red, White, and Clueless," as I have discussed, but also in the visual politics of the magazine.

ENVISIONING DIVERSITY: A COMPARATIVE APPROACH

Comparing the visual strategies employed by *HUES* to other third- and post-wave magazines enables an analysis of the stories that are told about feminism and diversity in each publication. As Malinda Smith (2010) has argued, storytelling about gender, race, and representation can mean to "tell *about*" and "tell *on*," but that also such stories are *telling* of broader "operations of inequitable power relations and privilege and the ways those are maintained and reproduced" (40–41). Examining the cover images of *BUST, Bitch, Venus Zine, Shameless,* and *ROCKRGRL,* as well as the thumbnail images for *Rookie*'s themed online issues, demonstrates the extent to which some third-wave magazines seem to have retained an allegiance to white supremacy, while others have sought out innovative representational strategies.

As I discussed in Chapter One, one of the inspirations for *HUES* was the experience of Tali Edut working on one of *Sassy* magazine's reader-produced issues: while the readers wished to feature two women of colour on the cover, *Sassy*'s publishers balked. In Kara Jesella and Marisa Meltzer's (2006) homage to *Sassy,* the two authors remark that the magazine industry "has long believed that a black cover model is the death-knell to that month's circulation. But since publications didn't want to appear racist, they would put a black girl on the cover maybe once a year, usually in February, the shortest month and the one that got the smallest circulation numbers, anyway" (98). What is baffling about Jesella and Meltzer's statement is that, in its original context, this comment is placed in parentheses, a fact that further emphasizes the taken-for-grantedness of the systemic racism and tokenistic practices of the magazine industry. As Lauren Berlant (1997) argues, once these kinds of statements "become banal, they are at their most powerful: no longer inciting big feelings and deep rages, these claims about the world seem hardwired into what is taken for granted" (11). The struggle that Edut and her co-producers faced working on the reader-produced issue of *Sassy* points to this larger issue of systemic racism within the magazine industry and the taken-for-grantedness of the notion that only white women's bodies sell units. Whiteness thus operates as normative, as desirable, and as a kind of *tabula rasa* upon which the desires of all subjects may be written.

As an independently published magazine for the majority of its existence, *HUES* was able to visually represent a wide range of women on its covers in ways that directly challenged the systemic racism endemic to the magazine industry. The covers of *HUES* tend to feature groups of two or three women. For example, the first national issue features three women of colour: Anamika Samanta, Margaret Logwood, and Darilis Garcia, posing together for a group headshot, each looking directly into the camera, meeting the viewer's gaze. This design stands in contrast to the industry norm of a headshot of a single (white) woman. While *HUES* did have white women on its covers, they were never featured alone. The construction of *HUES* covers enacted the magazine's vision of feminist friendship across differences.

Comparing *HUES*'s cover images with those of *BUST* (1993–), *ROCKRGRL* (1995–2006), and *Venus Zine* (1994–2010) is telling of the extent to which normative whiteness structured some third-wave feminist representations in the 1990s, 2000s, and—in the case of *BUST*—the 2010s. In its entire run of fifty-seven issues, *ROCKGRL* featured three people of colour on its cover, two of whom were part of group photos of bands. The only woman of colour to receive a stand-alone cover was Yoko Ono (Issue 2). During its first fifteen years of publication and over fifty-five issues, *BUST* featured only seven women of colour on its covers. As early as 1999, *BUST* editors acknowledged that they had received reader responses stating that the periodical was "too white" (Hex, Boob, and Henzel 1999, 4). Nonetheless, *BUST* has remained reticent, when it comes to representing a diversity of women as cover models. As of late 2014, the magazine had not put a woman of colour on its cover for over a year—Janelle Monáe (August/September 2013). Prior to Monáe's appearance on *BUST*'s cover, the last woman of colour featured was Mindy Kaling on their October/November 2011 issue, almost two years earlier. Similarly, examining *Venus Zine*'s cover images reveals that most of the featured people were white. In the publishing years 2000 to 2010, during which *Venus Zine* published thirty-nine issues, the magazine featured nine people of colour on its covers. The number of women of colour as cover models increased following the magazine's sale to publishers Anne Hartnett and Marci Sepulveda in 2006 (six in four years). Both *BUST* and *Venus Zine* design their covers in a style consistent with the genre of women's magazines: that is, a headshot of one (white) woman. This stylistic choice marks the magazines as part of the women's magazine genre, but with a feminist slant. As a result, the visual politics of *BUST* and *Venus Zine* are consistent with the philosophies of self-help, individualism, and improvement via consumption that mark women's magazines.

The normative feminist subject represented on the covers of *BUST*, *ROCKRGRL*, and *Venus Zine* is a white woman. The visual texts that these magazines present shape the kinds of feminist publics that they engender. As Michael Warner argues (2002), texts not only invoke publics but also shape both their character and what is intelligible within them (422). Despite their feminist stances, *BUST*, *ROCKRGRL*, and *Venus Zine* help to reify the notion of whiteness as normative, even constitutive of feminist identity. In this context, racism and white supremacy have a lot to do with who can safely (read: profitably) be ignored, even if they're understood to make up some of the audience for any given product. The potential readers that *BUST* and *Venus Zine* target, and help construct, are primarily hipster white women with progressive politics who would likely decry outward racism. However, the comfort and camaraderie that readers derive from reading these magazines are never linked to the fact that race is rarely discussed within these periodicals and non-white bodies are rarely the subjects of visual representations within them.

Examining the visual politics of *Bitch* and *Shameless* reveals a different representational approach distinct from magazines already examined. *Bitch* eschews photographic images of women completely and opts instead for artistic renderings inspired by the issue's theme. Despite the use of drawings, which could conceivably employ a wide range of representational strategies, *Bitch* covers between 1996 and 2004 all feature images of people, and these tend to either depict solitary white women or groups of women. While this latter group always depicted differently racialized women, it is notable that white women were never in the minority. Thus, in the first eight years of publication, though *Bitch* avoids the generic constraints of traditional women's magazine covers, there is still a quite recognizable discursive pattern that maintains whiteness as the privileged and normative colour of the publication.

Beginning in 2006, *Bitch* changed its representational techniques on its front covers. Since then, the periodical has shown images or artistic renderings of people very rarely, opting instead for more conceptual covers that address the thematic focus of the issue. This technique unhooks the magazine's feminisms from a particular identity-based group, opening up the possibilities for identification based on an interest in feminism and popular culture or in the content of one individually themed issue. Despite this innovative approach, the small handful of *Bitch* covers that have featured images of humans since 2006 are white-skinned folks.

With regard to the content of the magazine, *Bitch*'s articles have focused more on intersectional media analyses and activisms since 2009, when the magazine rebranded itself as a multimedia nonprofit organization, Bitch Media. Throughout *Bitch*'s history, readers have also been key critics of the publication's lack of articles written from the perspectives of women of colour, as well as the lack of their visual representation within the magazine in letters to the editor and in reader surveys. Both published and unpublished letters in *Bitch*'s archives, held at the Sallie Bingham Center, attest to this history. The fact that editors saved these letters and wished to have them included in the archives suggests that these criticisms were taken seriously and considered to be an important record of the magazine's history as a magazine and as an archive of feminism in the late 1990s and early 2000s.

White solipsism in *Bitch* was not unnoticed by readers, nor was it unaddressed by the editors. As I discussed in Chapter One, in 1996, *Bitch* editor Lisa Jervis (1996b) wrote an editorial apologizing for excluding *Essence* and *Today's Black Woman* from an article that compared women's magazines. Jervis referred to the oversight as "absolutely ridiculous—and disturbing and embarrassing" (2). *Bitch*'s approach to issues of race and representation hasn't been perfect, but editors consistently demonstrated accountability to their readers and there has been a clear shift in both the content of *Bitch*'s articles and in how the magazine represents its feminist politics on the newsstand.

Like *Bitch*, *Shameless* uses illustrated rather than photographic images for its covers. Unlike *Bitch*, however, *Shameless* covers almost always include representations of young women and/or teenage girls. Out of the twenty-four *Shameless* magazine covers that feature representations of people, nine of these were of groups of diverse women, six were of single women of colour, four were of single white women, and another three could be read as either white or as a person of colour.[6] In this sense, then, *Shameless*'s cover images often blend *Bitch*'s approach of using illustrations with *HUES*'s technique of picturing groups of women together.

As an online publication, *Rookie* updates its content regularly: the website does not have a "cover" in the same sense that a print publication will. However, its themed monthly "issues" are grouped according to a one-month calendar on which each day is represented with a thumbnail image. These calendar mosaics are capable of being read similarly to the covers of third- and post-wave print magazines. The presence of images side by side allow for a reading of their relationship to each other and to the central theme of the month, while also maintaining their own integrity as individual images. In examining the representation of racial diversity on *Rookie*'s website over three months (July to September 2014), I found that white subjects were pictured almost twice as often as people of colour.

In overly simplistic narratives of feminist progress (Hemmings 2011), third-wave feminism is often described as attentive to the intersectionality of race, class, gender, and sexuality, in contrast to the second wave (Reger 2005, xviii–xxiii). The cover images presented in *BUST, ROCKRGRL,* and *Venus Zine* indicate otherwise. Narratives of feminist progress can foreclose critical discussion on the intersections of gender, race, class, and other identities within contemporary feminisms. Comparing the visual politics of *HUES* to these other publications demonstrates that there is a great deal of variation in the extent to which third-wave feminism has (not) attended to differences among women and to the intersections of identities.

These differences also tell us a lot about the climate of commercial culture more broadly. As for-profit print publications, *BUST, ROCKRGRL,* and *Venus Zine* rely (or relied) more heavily on ad revenue than their not-for-profit counterparts. All three were also able to sustain themselves longer than *HUES*. *HUES*'s co-founders also actively courted larger publishers in a bid to make the magazine more self-sustaining, but were rejected by these same publishers because their magazine did not speak to a narrow enough market niche. As I will show, the intensification of a niche marketing philosophy, in tandem with identity politics in the 1990s, had the result of perpetuating white supremacy within U.S. popular culture representations, which had a direct impact on *HUES*'s ability to survive.

HUES AND NICHE MARKETING IN THE 1990S

The practice of marketing products and services to specialized groups, also known as niche marketing, initially began its growth in popularity during the 1950s. According to Mary Ellen Zuckerman (1998), these segmentation strategies were a response to the crisis in the magazine industry spurred by the growth of television as a popular medium in the mid-twentieth century (xiii). Unlike magazines, which readers generally seek out, choose, and read individually, television programming came directly into the home and could be viewed by multiple household members simultaneously. Because it allowed them to potentially reach such a broad audience, television became a very appealing medium for advertisers. In the face of flagging advertising revenue, women's magazines developed segmentation strategies; that is, in order to draw advertisers back, women's magazines marketed their publications to more specialized groups, with the rationale that advertisers could then target their products toward the specific segment of the marketplace that they wished to capitalize upon. While women's magazines led the shift toward "market segmentation," in light of their success other magazine publications soon followed suit.

Niche marketing intensified in the 1990s in two ways: first, advertisers and publishers attempted to address a wider variety of ethnically or sexually marked groups and, second, niche marketers attempted to target demographics in terms of "lifestyle." Further, Anna Gough-Yates (2003) argues that this period saw the rise of "more pronounced and self-conscious strategies geared to construct not only the identity of the magazines' reader-ships, but also the 'personality' of the text themselves" (20). As I will discuss further in the following chapter on feminism and fashion, BUST was able to adapt to these market conditions quite successfully through its self-branding; as a magazine for "women with something to get off their chests," BUST constructed its readers to advertisers as smart, educated, independent think-ers interested in fashion, crafting, music, and books. It is important to note that "lifestyle" in this context is framed by what readers *buy* and is thus a class-based word based on readers' economic and social capital. While the language of the marketplace suggests a neutral and unmarked space, this is far from the case.

The growth of niche marketing is linked to the rise of identity-based poli-tics in the 1990s within various social movements, such as the feminist and gay and lesbian rights movements. According to Inderpal Grewal (2005), "In the U.S., identity politics have produced strong connections to consumer culture as 'market segments' are categorized by ethnic identities as well as other dimensions including race, class, and sexuality" (95). Critics, such as Alexandra Chasin (2001) and Naomi Klein (2000) have argued that niche mar-keting was a response to calls for greater representation of minority groups within various sectors, including the media, but that this response did not fundamentally disrupt or unsettle whiteness as the normative identity shap-ing media representations. Niche marketing may have resulted in greater representation for some identity-based groups, but only those groups that were upwardly mobile. That is, as some identity-based social movements began to assert themselves within the broader public sphere, they simulta-neously became more recognizable as consumer groups. And, in a reciprocal fashion, as marketers and advertisers began to address minoritized groups, they also constituted them in important ways, by rendering them identifiable and intelligible. Niche marketing offers a proliferation of possible identity categories that consumers can "buy into," as well as an intensified emphasis on identity and individuality as inherent to the self, but also as things that can be demonstrated, propagated, and enhanced through consumer goods.

HUES emerged during this time of intensified niche marketing within the magazine industry, a time when few publications actively sought out a multi-ethnic audience. This market context had a direct impact upon the magazine's ability to garner support from larger publishers and advertisers, which directly affected *HUES*'s ability to survive financially. Because the magazine was committed to reaching all women, because the magazine fostered a politics of alliance rather than identity-based politics, and because the magazine had a pro-woman perspective, *HUES* struggled to attract the larger publishers who could facilitate distribution at a national level. As Logwood recounts:

> When we would go and speak to the larger publishers, they would say, "well, African American women are reading *Essence* and Latinas are reading *Latina*." ... I believe that publishers felt that there were magazines that already filled a particular void, by having magazines specifically for those particular groups, and that one that wanted to integrate all the groups was just not going to be successful. (2007)

Logwood's recollections demonstrate the ways that the popularity of niche marketing during this period stood at odds with *HUES*'s self-positioning as a multicultural magazine for women. While multiculturalism had a place in 1990s popular culture representations (recall: Benetton ads), bell hooks (1992) has argued that such representations are a "commodification of Otherness" through which "ethnicity becomes spice" and dominant power relations change very little (21). *HUES* sought a more profound intervention into the realm of commercial culture: an unsettling of whiteness as a constitutive part of idealized womanhood and real dialogue across difference.

What is also made visible in Logwood's recollection of meetings with publishers is the way in which niche marketing functioned as a form of tokenism within the magazine industry. Because African American women and Latinas are here described as already having their own publications, the logic of niche marketing dictates that the need for publications to speak to racialized women has been "satisfied." In her work on equity talk within academia, Malinda Smith has noted a distinction between "equity as social justice" and "diversity as management" (44–45). While the former is rooted in human rights and anti-discrimination philosophies, the latter emerged in the late twentieth century, Smith argues, as a neo-liberal orthodoxy that "rejects the very idea of social collectivities and, instead, promotes voluntarism and an individualized market-based knowledge" (45). A *diversity as management* philosophy permeates the comments that Logwood recollects from publishers, through the discourse that having one publication for each racialized group of women, rendered here as bounded and homogenous, satisfies the "market need."

The tokenistic and managerial approach to diversity evidenced through a niche marketing approach was most clearly evident in Logwood's recollection in our interview that publishers would say things to the co-founders, such as "Maybe if you didn't have different ethnic women on the cover. Maybe if you put a white woman on the cover, you know, by herself, it would sell more." This bald-faced racism lays bare the normative whiteness and conservatism of the magazine industry: this despite the fact that *HUES* did feature white women on their covers, just not by themselves and not in majority. White women also wrote for the publication and contributed in other ways, but again not in the majority. The equivalence drawn within the industry between white women and sales emerges from within a social context in which whiteness is viewed as the unmarked and normative "text" upon which the desires and aspirations of all others can be written. According to Julian Carter (2007), the rise of "the 'normal' to discursive dominance was a crucial part of the process by which whiteness became not only reticent about its racial meanings but blind to its own struggles to retain racial power" (6). This notion of the "normal" is crucial to understanding the ways that whiteness functions within the magazine industry. Niche marketing does not destabilize whiteness as the invisible *centre* of media representations and in fact contributes to its production and solidification as normative and desirable.

Niche marketing offers the promise of equity through the tokenistic representation of minoritized subjects but ultimately defers equity to a never-to-be-reached future. This temporal logic is readily apparent in Logwood's memories of being told by publishers, "Well, we don't think this country is ready for a multi-cultural women's magazine" and "We think you're a little bit ahead of your time" (2007). By couching the rejection of *HUES* in terms of the "readiness" of the country for the magazine, publishers tacitly inscribed the normative U.S. citizen as white and even as racist. The comments seem to suggest that what *HUES* was doing was too progressive, something not handle-able by the American public. What these comments in fact reveal is a highly conservative approach to diversity within the magazine industry and the ways in which systemic relations of inequality continue to perpetuate themselves through the temporal logic of "someday soon, but not quite yet." White supremacy, as George Lipsitz (2006) argues, "is usually less a matter of direct, referential, and snarling contempt and more a system for protecting the privileges of whites by denying communities of colour opportunities for asset accumulation and upward mobility" (vii). The comments of publishers to Logwood and the Edut sisters make clear the insidiousness of white supremacy, the way in which it holds out the proverbial carrot, promising to someday deliver on its promise of equity. What these comments make clear is that equity will never be attained without struggle and within the capitalist marketplace.

The difficulties that *HUES* had in securing a larger publisher demonstrate the ways in which the discursive and the material work together to perpetuate the normalization of whiteness as the national symbol of U.S. identity, and the ways in which feminist and anti-racist cultural production can be important challenges to these practices. Through its commitment to reaching all women, *HUES* challenged the industry trend of niche marketing, which works in support of racial myths that undergird the notion of white national identity in the United States. Niche marketing essentially proliferates the number of products available to minoritized groups but does not necessarily disturb the normativity of whiteness in media representations.

Niche marketing is highly limited because it is a cosmetic response to the deeper critiques of systemic and structural inequities that could be levelled at corporations. Simply representing racial or sexual minorities can thus become a way of discounting or negating deeper critiques of systemic discrimination. However, the field of mainstream media remains essentially unchanged by the addition of representations of differently sexed, raced, or classed bodies at its *margins*. While different voices and different bodies are seemingly encouraged, their potential to challenge white supremacist and sexist media is simultaneously disabled because their addition does not entail changing or rethinking the dominant and normative position of whiteness within these media. Questions of how different voices might bear on one another, how identity categories are the products of histories, or might be thought about differently, are thus foreclosed and effaced. *HUES* sought to raise these questions through its politics of alliance.

Given that a key facet of identity politics was the battle for greater representation of visible minorities within mainstream media, the proliferation of specialized products and targeted advertising that characterizes niche marketing was an ideal response by corporations because it meant not really having to change business as usual (that is, the structural and economic inequities that benefit white folks and disadvantage visible minorities). Together, niche marketing and identity politics tend to reify a fixed and inherent notion of identity. Identity politics, as Warner (2002) argues, "affirm[s] private identity through public politics and promis[es] to heal divisions in the political world by anchoring them in the authentically personal realm" (26). Likewise, it may be argued that niche marketing affirms a fixed notion of identity and promises to heal inequities through the power of consumerism. Further, as Chasin (2001) points out, the representative "justice" of niche marketing tends to be justice for identity-based groups who are most attractive to advertisers, that is, those who are already economically privileged and thus have the economic means to purchase products and services (6). What this means for feminist magazines is that for-profit publications with a clear, specific, and singular target demographic or lifestyle orientation, through which readers are classed as having some measure of economic means, are in a better position to attract advertisers and publishers. Clearly, this market condition shapes what kind of feminisms can be articulated within the realm of commercial culture and, moreover, who gets to be a feminist within the realm of commercial culture.

Niche marketing and identity politics often foreground only one feature of identity, fragmenting the self into compartmental pieces, and thus cannot be sites from which to build more complex and nuanced understandings of subjectivity. Nonetheless, and despite its limitations, identity politics is important because it allows minoritized groups to assert themselves *as groups*. As Lipsitz (2006) argues, "Different ethnic groups have different histories and experiences; as long as that is the case, organizing along ethnic lines will always make sense ... [but] mobilizing around common group identity does not preclude forming strategic and philosophical alliances with other groups" (68). In contrast to identity politics, the politics of alliance promoted by *HUES* has the potential to acknowledge the complexity of the lived experience of identity and its mutability across contexts, as well as the ways in which people are differently implicated in power relations across different times and places.

Situating *HUES* in relation to the economic context of niche marketing in the 1990s is revealing of a *diversity as management* approach within niche marketing; that is, an approach that seeks to integrate differences of race, gender, class, sexuality, ability, etc., only to the extent to which these differences seemingly provide a rich, colourful, and exotic tapestry of diversity. This approach does little to challenge the normativity of whiteness and perhaps even enhances the extent to which white bodies are seen as the unmarked industry norm. *HUES* sought to challenge these philosophies, through its intersectional politics of alliance that actively decentred whiteness and created space for dialogue across difference.

CONCLUSION

If, as Warner (2002) argues, a public "exists by virtue of being addressed" (67), then what kinds of publics do third-wave magazines call into being? How does the capitalist marketplace shape the kinds of publics that third-wave magazines are capable of addressing? This chapter has argued that *HUES* envisioned a feminist public that engaged in a dynamic dialogue, fostered by friendship and fuelled by a passion for social justice, and that sought to change the world. It is clear that the difficulties *HUES*'s co-founders faced in garnering both advertising revenue and wider distribution from more established publishers demonstrates that the capitalist marketplace was inhospitable to the vision of *HUES*. Logwood (2007) reflected on the fact that other larger publishers wanted to "change the focus of the publication and it would turn it into something that we couldn't stand behind. So, rather than to sell out, even though, trust me, so many people said, 'Well, if you sell out just a little bit, it will help the magazine survive' [we sold the publication to New Moon]." As I discussed in Chapter One, New Moon published a socially progressive periodical for girls ages eight to twelve, but the responsibility of producing two publications was too much for the small company and *HUES* was shelved.

This analysis of *HUES* is not meant to imply that attempts to engage the realm of commercial culture are ultimately futile. Although *HUES* folded after seven years of publication, it is important to point out that many magazines—feminist or not—do not last as long as *HUES* did. In the time that it circulated, *HUES* created a space for readers to engage with intersectional feminist and pro-woman writing. As *HUES* reader Lili Alexander (1996) wrote in a letter to the editor: "You reminded me that there are people in this world who don't bullshit you so deep that you need hip boots to cross the room" (4). In the case of feminist periodicals, particularly, it is not worthwhile to define success or failure solely in economic terms.

The visual politics of *HUES* reflected its intersectional approach. Other third-wave publications that rely more on the conventional visual politics of women's magazine covers, namely *BUST* and *Venus Zine*, do little to challenge normative whiteness through their representational practices. These visual politics run through the complete runs of the magazines, in ways that complicate the discourse of selling out. That is, publications like *BUST* and *Venus Zine* were not inherently unproblematic, utopic bastions of anti-racist feminism before they entered the marketplace, only to become corrupted by the evils of commercialism. The market, a hostile environment for feminist publications of any kind, is generally "friendlier" to feminist publications targeted at a racially unmarked audience through which feminism is marketed as a lifestyle rather than set of political orientations. The following chapter, which critically examines *BUST*'s homage to "fashionable feminists," engages with this idea of "lifestyle feminism."

CHAPTER FOUR

"BE A FEMINIST OR JUST DRESS LIKE ONE": *BUST*, FASHION, AND LIFESTYLE FEMINISM

"Be a Feminist or Just Dress Like One," announced the cover of *BUST* magazine's 2006 fashion issue. Inside, the publication presented looks inspired by Elizabeth Cady Stanton, Gloria Steinem, Bella Abzug, Camille Paglia, Angela Davis, and Kathleen Hannah—feminism's so-called fashionable feminists ("Our Outfits, Ourselves" 2006, 55). The fashion issue of *BUST* serves as an exemplary text from which to unpack a set of broader questions in relation to third-wave feminism in the early 2000s. Given the perceived fraught relationship between feminism and fashion, what happens when feminist media present fashion content? How do readerships, market forces, and editorial demands shape how these magazines present fashion? What are the possibilities and limitations of the "girlie" or "lifestyle feminism" that *BUST* magazine promotes? The intersection of feminism and fashion is an ideal place from which to engage these questions. Given the complex relationship between dress and feminism within the United States, an examination of the dynamics of fashion and feminism, and the *BUST* spread particularly, crystallizes my broader interest in the politics of representation, recuperation, and money within early-twenty-first-century feminisms. At stake in this discussion are the ways that the legacies of "past" feminisms are represented and negotiated in the present and the ways that feminist cultural productions negotiate the terrain of the popular print marketplace; these processes have implications for how people engage with and understand feminism and contribute to shaping the feminisms of the future.

These concerns are addressed in a three-part discussion. In Part One, I argue that *BUST*'s positioning of its own approach to fashion as different from "traditional" feminist approaches to this domain validates, rather than challenges, misrepresentations of feminist perspectives on the politics of dress. Indeed, there are a variety of feminist perspectives on fashion and dress that are glossed by *BUST* in favour of a caricatured representation of feminism and feminists. In Part Two, I discuss the representation of fashion in past issues of *BUST* and in other third- and post-wave magazines. The different ways that each magazine presents fashion suggest that there is no monolithic "third-wave" perspective on fashion any more than there are discrete "second-" or "first-wave" ones. Part Three is a reading of both *BUST*'s fashion spread and its reception. I argue that the *BUST* fashion issue is an ambivalent text: both an ironic, tongue-in-cheek commentary that implicitly critiques negative, backlash versions of feminism and feminists and a presentation of a dehistoricized, decontextualized, and deracialized version of feminism that effaces difference and contestation.

PART ONE: ADDRESSING FEMINIST HISTORY

In her editorial column for the fashion issue, Debbie Stoller (2006) locates *BUST*'s position on fashion in relation to other feminisms. While identifying *BUST*'s own approach to fashion as feminist, the editorial also tacitly reinforces anti-feminist representations of the U.S. feminist movement. Stoller asserts,

> For our fashion issue, we thought we'd take a different approach than might be expected of an outspoken feminist magazine. Rather than criticize fashion, we decided to focus on the aspects of dress that we find embraceable. The culture of clothing has been central to women's lives for centuries, and we think it's as important to find out what could be right with it as it is to pinpoint what's wrong. Consider the alternatives suggested by those who've wanted to save women from the tyranny of fashion: surely we wouldn't be better off with everyone in suits, or in Birkenstocks, or—God forbid—in burkas. (6)

In this passage, the perceived "traditional" feminist approaches to fashion are figured as tyrannical. While certainly these perspectives exist within feminist criticism, they are not the only feminist approaches to the analysis of fashion and dress. The perspectives to which Stoller makes reference are reductive, and her comments about suits and Birkenstocks implicitly invoke a set of stereotypical images of feminists clad as either androgynous, power-suit-wearing working women or, alternatively, Birkenstock-wearing, hippie, "granola" lesbians who, according to popular discourse, feel they occupy a particular moral high ground. To be clear, there are feminists who wear power suits and/or Birkenstocks, but the negative connotations with which these fashion statements are imbued here are influenced by the backlash against feminism that gained strength in the 1980s with the rise of neoconservative movements. Anti-feminists often assert that feminists are ugly and unfeminine, experience neither pleasure nor fun, and judge other women who do. Stoller's comments echo these views, through her characterization of "past" feminist desires to "save" women from the tyranny of fashion while in fact the relationship between feminism and fashion has historically been far more complex.

The *BUST* fashion issue thus encapsulates a much broader and ambivalent relationship between so-called third- and second-wave feminisms, given that elsewhere in the same issue the publication arguably pays homage to the fashion sense of Bella Abzug and Gloria Steinem, two key figures in the U.S. feminist movement in the 1970s. What seems to be at stake in *BUST*'s desire to define its positive perspective on fashion as "different" from the past is a desire to distance themselves from negative mainstream media depictions of the feminist movement. This more ambivalent mode of engagement with feminism exemplifies what cultural studies and feminist media studies theorist Angela McRobbie (2009) calls "postfeminism." In *The Aftermath of Feminism*, McRobbie extends the landmark work of Susan Faludi (1991) on the conservative backlash against feminism that intensified in the 1980s by arguing that what we begin to see in the 1990s is the new phenomenon of post-feminism through which "elements of contemporary popular culture" undo feminism "while simultaneously appearing to be engaging in a well-informed and even well-intended response to feminism" (11). The discursive mode through which Stoller's editorial offers an alternative approach to fashion is consistent with a post-feminist discourse because it reinforces rather than challenges a particular "backlash view" of feminism, even while claiming a feminist stance.[1]

BUST's post-feminist depictions of anti-fashion feminists are the foil against which the magazine's alternative view of feminism and/as fashion is articulated. Within the context of the editorial, the Birkenstock- or suit-wearing feminist is cast as the Other through which *BUST* constructs its implied audience as "hip." But according to *BUST*'s cheeky rhetoric, the Birkenstock and the suit are not the worst possible "solutions" to the "problem" of fashion; rather, it is the burka that garners this distinction. The positing of the burka as a tyrannical imposition does not take into account the complexities of and ambivalent meanings associated with veiling practices among Muslim women or the rise of fundamentalisms as a global issue in which the West is implicated. *BUST* readers are constructed against such symbols of Otherness, here being Islam.

The broader political context in which Stoller is writing is also significant; namely, the continuing U.S.-led "War on Terror" in which the rhetoric of saving burka-clad women from the Taliban was continually deployed as an excuse to invade Afghanistan by politicians who had otherwise shown little interest in issues of women's rights or who had actively participated in the withdrawal of support to women's groups and feminist organizations. Saba Mahmood (2008) argues, "Islam's mistreatment of women is used as diagnosis as well as a strategic point of intervention for restructuring large swaths of the Muslim population if not the religion itself," and "[U]nless feminists rethink their complicity in this project ... feminism runs the risk of becoming more of a handmaiden to empire than a critic of Euro-American imperialist aspirations" (82). The double valence of Stoller's aside, "God forbid," is interesting in this context; on the one hand, this comment is clearly ironic, playful, and tongue-in-cheek; on the other hand, when read "straight," Stoller's aside interpellates her audience as readers who will both identify with a Christian signifier and agree that the burka is the worst clothing item that a woman could possibly wear. In contrast to the promoters of bad fashion (that is, second-wave feminists and the Taliban), BUST readers are constructed as hip feminist women whose consumption of fashion may be read as a symbol of their status as "liberated" and as predominantly non-Muslim women capable of choosing freely the aspects of fashion they wish to either support or eschew.

It's not that I have a problem with discussions of fashion or style within a feminist magazine, even celebratory ones; as Stephen Duncombe (1997) argues, one of BUST's strengths is that "politics is packaged as part of a panoply of women's passions, on par with celebrity and fashion" (119). Indeed, BUST attempts to provide a mix of content that would appeal to both feminists and readers who are in the process of discovering feminism. According to Stoller (2006),

> We know that in the life of today's modern gal, there's room for crafting and sex and music and fashion and politics and, most importantly, that an interest in one doesn't preclude an interest in the others. Of course, we devote space in our pages to typical "feminist issues" such as abortion and equal pay, but we're also determined to create a truly embraceable women's culture, so that reading BUST can help you feel good about being a girl. (6)

Although this statement sets up a problematic dichotomy between "serious feminist issues" and "fun," Stoller's comments nevertheless invoke a "both/and" discourse in regard to BUST's philosophy.

The critique that I make here is thus not about the presence of fashion content in BUST, but rather it is with the normalizing discourse that frequently accompanies such content. Stoller's editorial for the fashion issue sets up a set of troubling dichotomies that both reinforce simplistic, anti-feminist accounts of feminism's relationship to fashion and engage in practices of Othering that work in support of U.S. imperialism, in order to present the public face of feminism—and *BUST* readers—as "normal," unthreatening, and Western. In this sense, the feminist and non-feminist readers that *BUST* might draw in are implicitly constructed as young women with social class and race privilege. While elsewhere the fashion issue seems to pay homage to feminism's past, in the editorial it is used as a simplistic and reductive foil against which *BUST* readers are constructed as hipper, savvier, friendlier, and—ultimately—better feminists. As I argue below, when examined in historical perspective the relationship between feminism, fashion, and style is far more complex and varied.

FEMINIST PERSPECTIVES ON FASHION AND DRESS

In American popular culture, one of the most evocative and enduring signifiers of feminist views on women's fashion is the theatrical protest against the 1968 Miss America beauty pageant during which participants threw "instruments of oppression" like bras and copies of *Cosmopolitan* and *Ladies' Home Journal* into a "freedom trashcan." Although no bras were ever burned at this protest, the women who participated, and those involved in the broader Women's Liberation Movement, were labelled as "bra burners" in mainstream media publications; thus, the protest is remembered not as political theatre but as a literal bra burning (Echols 1997, 456). While the protestors took issue with the ways in which the pageant valued bodies over minds and presented an objectified version of female bodies for a voyeuristic male gaze, their actions have also been memorialized as a statement against fashion. At a glance, this 1968 protest might seem representative of the kind of "Birkenstock" feminism Stoller dismisses in her editorial. Indeed, some feminists have claimed that particular garments, like bras or high-heeled shoes, are both symbolically and literally constraining, restrictive impositions. However, the feminists at the 1968 Miss America pageant were not necessarily anti-fashion. Rather, these women advocated a different kind of aesthetic, which was influenced by countercultural trends in the United States during the 1960s.

In her account of the Miss America protest, Candace Savage (1998) argues that the perspectives on the relationship between feminism and fashion were ambivalent in this period. For example, Carol Hanisch, who had participated in the Miss America protest, wrote one year later that their protest had failed to take into account their own investment in the culture of beauty, as well as the way that the criticism of women who participated in the pageant could not foster sisterhood (Savage 1998, 8). Hanisch's writing demonstrates that at the time of the Miss America protest, feminists were already discussing critically the differences between critiquing institutions themselves and the women who participated in them. Both the Miss America protest and the contemporary debates about it demonstrate that fashion is an overdetermined site through which feminists have debated the significance of different modes of dress, as well as—more broadly—the relationships between feminist and non-feminist women and the politics of conventional femininity.

The differing perspectives on the Miss America protest include what Elizabeth Wilson (1985) has identified as two early feminist approaches to fashion: one was a condemnation of fashion as an oppressive tool of the patriarchy; the other, a kind of populist liberalism, suggested that it would be elitist to criticize a pastime enjoyed by so many women (230). In *Adorned in Dreams*, Wilson criticizes both these approaches to fashion. The first, she asserts, is a puritanical argument relying on the logic of utility, which does not acknowledge either the pleasure or creativity of fashion. Further, "those who see fashion as one form of capitalist 'consumerism' ... fail to understand that women and men may use the 'unworthiest' items of capitalist culture to criticize and transcend that culture" (244). According to Wilson, the second argument, that women should be free to wear whatever they wish, contains an implicit assumption about "free choice," which fails to acknowledge the way in which choice occurs within contexts that are socially constructed and are thus always already constrained and limited through that context. Fashion, Wilson argues, "is ambivalent—for when we dress we wear inscribed upon our bodies the often obscure relationship of art, personal psychology, and the social order" (247). Wilson thus advocates a theory of fashion that takes "play" into account. That is, through fashion, we fashion ourselves and have the opportunity to create and explore alternative ways of being in the world (245).

The notion of fashion as play is adapted most prominently by Judith Butler (1990) in her discussion of drag, which incorporates dress into the parodic performance of gender identity. According to Butler, drag functions to reveal the constructedness and contingency of gender. That is, through the hyperbolic iteration of conventional gender codes, "drag fully subverts the distinction between inner and outer psychic space and effectively mocks both the expressive model of gender and the notion of a true gender identity" (174). For Butler, drag is one example of the potential ways in which dress can play a role in broader projects of resistance and/or subversion.[2] Similarly, Dick Hebdige's (1979) landmark study, *Subculture: The Meaning of Style,* demonstrates the ways in which style can be an important signifier of being out of step with dominant culture. Samantha Holland's (2004) ethnographic study of punk women's sense of their own style further bears out Hebdige's claim, although Holland argues that most participants did not view their style of dress as a kind of political statement.

Like Butler, Hebdige, and Holland, Nan Enstad's (1999) work discusses the potentially subversive aspects of style, but her focus is on the fashion of women garment workers in the 1910s. Due to technological developments at the end of the nineteenth century, it became easier to reproduce mechanically clothing styles that were traditionally made by a tailor and hence were only available to more upper-class women. As a result, women workers began to adopt the clothing of more upper-class women, a move that threatened class boundaries; Enstad argues, "[L]abour leaders in the International Ladies Garment Workers Union (ILGWU) and the Women's Trade Union League (WTIL) routinely chastised working women for their ceaseless pursuit of fashion" (3). Enstad's study finds that "working women drew upon the resources and identities that they had formed in relationship to commodities when they created themselves as strikers" fighting for better working conditions (15). One striker, Clara Lemlich, for example, argued during the shirtwaist strike in 1909 that women workers needed a place to put their hats so that they did not get trampled over the course of the workday: hats, Enstad argues, here serve both as important signals that these women were workers who earned money and as signifiers of Americanness (8–9).

There are continuities between the workers of Enstad's historical study and those working within the contemporary garment industry. Feminist scholars have addressed the working conditions within the garment industry, as well as the struggle for women workers to unionize; these analyses are exemplified in studies such as Annie Phizacklea's *Unpacking the Fashion Industry* (1990), Angela Hale and Jane Willis's *Threads of Labour* (2005), and Edna Bonacich, et al.'s *Global Production: The Apparel Industry in the Pacific Rim* (1994). Lucie Cheng and Gary Gereffi (1994) note in their discussion of U.S. retailers and Asian garment production, "There is a link between U.S. women consumers and Asian women workers in the garment industry" (77). Fashion is a feminist issue at the global level, in terms of the broad economic systems that shape how clothes are made, in what conditions, and by whom. Fashion is a feminist issue at the institutional level, in terms of the gendered norms that regulate "appropriate" dress in educational and workplace environments. And fashion is a feminist issue at the individual level, in terms of how subjects deal with clothing as it intersects with gender, race, and class. These different interrelated spheres shape the politics of fashion in contemporary contexts and are also visible in the long history of feminist engagements with the politics of clothes.

In her study of the relationship between consumer culture and nineteenth- and early-twentieth-century suffragists, Margaret Finnegan (1999) examines the relations between feminism, fashion, and power and argues that there was a multiplicity of feminist views on fashion. Some suffragists embraced the fashion of their time as a sign of gentility. As Finnegan puts it, "Accounts of woman suffrage conventions repeatedly describe women 'elaborately gowned in the height of the fashion,' and some suffragists obsessively followed the latest styles" (18). Others advocated various forms of dress reform, such as bloomers, which are perhaps the most well-known example of "rational dress." These bifurcated garments allowed women more freedom of movement than the crinolines of the mid-nineteenth century.

The motivations for dress reform were varied and, according to Gayle Fischer (2001), to call dress reform a "movement" is misleading, insofar as there were a variety of reforms that occurred at different times and for different reasons (4). In her discussion of feminist dress reformers, Linda M. Scott (2006) argues that the Puritan or aristocratic roots of these feminists shaped their views on fashion, leading them to treat any sign of luxury as either a symbol of moral corruption or a threat to class status.[3] In this sense, dress reform was both "a form of social control and a reaction against such control" (Fischer, 5); that is, while bifurcated garments allowed for greater physical mobility, some rational dress reformers were also motivated by a desire to shore up class boundaries because, according to these reformers, fashionable dress contributed to a lower birthrate and hence threatened the white middle class. As Fischer argues, "[D]ress reform had less to do with fashionable clothing and more to do with perceptions about woman's place in society, who would determine that place, and how it would be maintained" (17).

Early women's rights periodicals, such as New York State–based *The Sibyl* (1856–64), began as dress reform publications but soon expanded their scope beyond a single-issue focus. In addition to dress reform, these periodicals discussed a variety of topics, including suffrage, women's education, divorce, property rights, and domesticity. Later nineteenth-century publications, such as *The Woman's Tribune* (1883–1909) and *The New Northwest* (1871–87), regularly included columns on fashion.[4] In some respects, *BUST* shares more similarities with these nineteenth-century women's rights periodicals than with their more immediate second-wave precursors. The context out of which *BUST* publishes is, of course, very different from these early women's rights periodicals; what we now know as mass market or commercial culture did not exist during mid-nineteenth century and did not begin to develop until the 1890s (Ohmann 1996, vii).

An additional continuity between *BUST* and these early women's rights periodicals is in the attempt of both to distinguish themselves from non-feminist- or non-women's-rights-based magazines. As Amy Aronson (2002) argues, nineteenth-century feminists often made a distinction between feminist "women" and sentimental-domestic "ladies" and used this discursive strategy as a means to mark their publications as belonging to the suffrage movement. For example, Paulina Wright Davis wrote in *The Una* that "women have been too well, and too long satisfied with Ladies' Books and Ladies' Magazines and Miscellanies; it is time they should have stronger nourishment; and with a work so peculiarly their own" (quoted in Butcher 1989, 4). Davis's writing demonstrates that for at least one early feminist editor, it was expedient to construct "ladies' magazines" as intellectually inadequate, in order to persuade readers of the more substantive importance of women's rights.[5] This distinction between "women's rights" and "ladies'" publications continued to structure feminist magazine discourse throughout the nineteenth and twentieth centuries (arguably reaching its highest intensity during the 1960s and 1970s). The mobilization of sentimental discourse demonstrates that a "women's rights magazine" and a "ladies' magazine" are not necessarily discrete genres with no overlap. Indeed, like "ladies' magazines," many early women's rights publications included fashion and household hints, and provided a mixture of political, practical, education, and entertaining items (Butcher 1989, 10). In many ways, this format is consistent with what *BUST* attempts to do with its content. However, while there is no evidence to suggest that the contemporary readers of women's rights periodicals viewed the inclusion of entertaining material as contradictory to the ideals of the movement, over time the generic association of fashion and household advice with ladies' magazines has become more entrenched and politicized, and thus the inclusion of these kinds of materials within feminist publications now has a different resonance.

While some suffragists embraced fashion and others worked to reform it, in both cases the broader issues at stake involved the relationship between consumerism and politics; the relationship between feminism and femininity; the relationship between women of different class statuses; and how to represent feminism to the broader public. These issues continue to shape contemporary debates about feminism and fashion. Indeed, rather than being a break with the past, as the *BUST* editorial would suggest, the *BUST* fashion issue shares some interesting continuities with the history of feminist relationships to fashion, including the notion of play as well as—more problematically—the yoking of style to class and race. However, the editorial for *BUST*'s fashion issue oversimplifies the history of feminists' relationships to fashion. Indeed, there are a variety of feminist approaches to fashion, which demonstrate that feminists have used style and dress as important signifiers of political affiliation and identity construction.

PART TWO: FASHION IN THIRD-WAVE PERIODICALS

Examining fashion coverage in *HUES*, *Bitch*, *Shameless*, *Venus Zine*, and *BUST* demonstrates that there are varied ways in which third-wave feminist publications have approached feminism and/as fashion. These different perspectives on fashion also shed light on broader relationships and tensions between third-wave periodicals and other women's magazines, readerships, and the marketplace. For example, while the inclusion of fashion spreads that present clothes available for purchase can bring in valuable revenue for a magazine publication, as evidenced below, the use of these kinds of fashion spreads has the potential to anger readers steeped in feminist critiques of the beauty industry, seen as a capitalist enterprise designed to encourage the unbridled consumption of beauty products by making women feel that their bodies are in perpetual need of being "fixed." Since some critiques of the fashion industry accuse women's fashion magazines of indoctrinating readers into the "cult of femininity" (Ferguson 1983), the inclusion of fashion content in feminist publications might be viewed as tantamount to "sleeping with the enemy," because of the ways in which, critics argue, the fashion and beauty industries engage in practices that oppress women. Certainly, periodicals established mid-century, such as *Chrysalis*, *off our backs*, and *Ms.*, did not include fashion spreads, a decision due in part to the feminist critique of beauty standards as well as the influence of New Left politics that saw selling products as fuel for an oppressive capitalist system. It is thus not surprising that fashion in contemporary feminist magazines is such fraught terrain, given that the inclusion of fashion content may raise questions of how the magazine is different from the "traditional women's fashion rag." While Nancy Walker (2000) and Ros Ballaster, Margaret Beetham, Elizabeth Fraser, and Sandra Hebron (1991) have argued that "traditional" women's magazines are themselves multivalent texts, which contain complex and contradictory discourses regarding expectations of femininity and beauty ideals, the discursive distinction between "women's magazines" and "feminist magazines" remains an important one for third-wave magazines to maintain, politically, despite some of the similarities between them, particularly in the case of *BUST* and *Venus Zine*.

In contrast to its mid-twentieth-century forerunners, *HUES* magazine regularly published fashion pages; however, its spreads usually featured women wearing and discussing their own clothes and rarely featured items available for purchase. *HUES*'s coverage of fashion was also not presented in an entirely celebratory manner; for example, in their second issue (1994), the editors introduce their two-page, black-and-white fashion spread, "Out-of-Barbie Experience," by stating: "We don't know about y'all, but we have had it up to here with trying to squeeze our ethnic proportions into clothes tailored to fit our Aryan childhood playmate. If today's sizes aren't cuttin' it for you either, heed the words of the *HUES* fashion deities, as we tell how we dress ourselves" (Out-of-Barbie Experience 1993, 14). The magazine celebrates the fashion styles of individual women who represent a range of racial and sexual identities, while also critiquing conventional beauty standards that posit Barbie as the idealized female figure, the fashion industries that make clothes for a limited number of body types, and the solipsism inherent in both.

As *HUES* expanded, the format of its fashion coverage remained relatively consistent. In their first national issue (Spring/Summer 1995), the editors ran an ethnically diverse fashion spread called "Closet Politics" in which they stated, "Every woman's style makes a statement.... our clothes tell the world who we are" ("Closet Politics" 1995, 34). Overall, the coverage of fashion is here presented in a quite ambivalent manner: while the editorial suggests that clothing has a potentially positive function through its ability to convey visual cues about a person's personality or politics, the department in which the spread appeared, "Fash-isms," alludes to the negative relationship many women have with clothing. The women themselves who are featured in the spread discuss the assumptions made by others on the basis of how they dress, while also celebrating their own particular styles.

HUES's fashion spread in its Winter 1996 issue is, paradoxically, most similar to and most unlike a traditional fashion spread. On the one hand, the publication adopted a more conventional visual layout for its spread, featuring glossy photographs and editorial commentary, which was a departure from *HUES*'s use of direct quotes from the models themselves. On the other hand, the spread also parodies fashion coverage in other women's magazines. Entitled "PMS Fashions," this tongue-in-cheek spread is filled with juxtapositions: text boxes in the shapes of tampons and panty-liners accompany the fashion photography; "PMS" is spelled with tampons, while "Fashions" is rendered in red cursive writing. The fashion spread thus contrasts the idealized representation of women's bodies in fashion magazines (as coherent and "clean") with an aspect of women's bodies, menstruation, which is frequently constructed as abject. HUES acknowledges that fashion plays in an important role in the construction of subjectivities, at the same time as it recognizes the ways in which representations of fashion have the potential to foster body shame.

As a journal-style, not-for-profit publication, *Bitch* does not inhabit the same generic category of magazines that traditionally contain fashion spreads and style pages.[6] Thus, *Bitch* has never published fashion spreads. The periodical has, however, featured critical articles relating to fashion and style, particularly in its 2006 "Style and Substance" issue, which appeared on newsstands simultaneously with *BUST*'s controversial fashion issue. The editors write, "[Fashion] provides endless fodder for our feminist critiques—and we criticize because we love" (Zeisler and Fudge 2006, 5). In this context, *Bitch* extends its ambivalent "love/hate relationship" with popular culture to the fashion industry; that is, the enjoyment of fashion need not, and should not, exempt it from scrutiny. The approaches of both *Bitch* and *HUES* demonstrate the ambivalent relationship between some third-wave feminisms and fashion. Echoing Pamela Church-Gibson's call for a feminist theory of fashion that "position[s] itself somewhere between what Jameson calls celebration and repudiation—or in an oscillation between them," these publications suggest that being fashionable or stylish is not necessarily incommensurable with feminist politics, but that the enjoyment of fashion be coupled with a critique of the more distasteful aspects of the industry (361).

Like *Bitch*, *Shameless* does not publish fashion spreads. Positioning itself as a direct alternative to teen-girl publications that promote consumption of fashion, *Shameless* encourages youth to express their style through handmade goods. *Shameless*'s DIY sensibility is certainly neither anti-style nor even anti-consumption per se; rather the magazine encourages its readers to produce their own creations. Like *Shameless*, *Venus Zine* also emphasizes DIY culture for producing one's own style. However, the magazine, like *BUST*, also publishes fashion spreads in every issue. Interestingly, since *Venus Zine*'s stated mandate is less overtly feminist, the inclusion of fashion content seems less politicized than *BUST*'s coverage, and the debates on fashion found in the pages of *BUST* are not replicated within *Venus Zine*. Indeed, *BUST*'s move from discussing clothes to selling clothes has met with some resistance from its readers; each increase in *BUST*'s fashion content has been coupled with an editorial describing financial hardships faced by the publication. While it is impossible to draw a direct line between *BUST*'s bottom line and the amount of fashion for sale in the magazine, the intersection between increases in fashion content and editorial commentary on finances is suggestive.

BUST FASHION: "BECAUSE WHY SHOULD TRANSVESTITES HAVE ALL THE FUN?"

After five years of publishing, *BUST* introduced fashion pages in its 1998 sex issue (Issue 10), which featured a two-page black-and-white spread ("The Season of the Witch: Comfy Clothes for Modern-Day Mystics"). In the following issue, the magazine published a letter to the editor in which one reader complained about both the presence of fashion itself in *BUST* and the magazine's use of "real" models: "What's up with the fuckin' Vogue models on the pages of the sex issue—in fact, what is up with the fashion. Come on now women, are you going to become Sassy or Jane? ... I hope I am not alone in this complaint for then I shall feel not only ugly, but stupid also" (Kate 1998, 7). This writer iterates a common critique of fashion magazines, which is that their fashion pages make women feel ugly and inadequate through their use of conventionally attractive, thin models. Interestingly, rather than targeting fashion-based publications like *Glamour* or *Elle* as exemplars of what *BUST* risks "becoming," the letter writer identifies *Sassy* and *Jane*. Indeed, it is more plausible that *BUST*'s introduction of fashion pages would render it more similar to *Jane* or later issues of *Sassy*, given the fact that these publications present (or presented, in *Sassy*'s case) both fashion spreads and feminist-inflected content. However, there may be an additional reason for naming *Sassy* and *Jane* in this context: many readers of *Sassy* and *Jane* felt terribly betrayed by both publications. As I discussed in Chapter One, when *Sassy* was sold to Petersen Publishing in 1994, it became a much more conservative publication, and when founding *Sassy* editor Jane Pratt went on to launch *Jane*, many readers were disappointed by its lack of feminist edge. The effect of including references to *Sassy* and *Jane* in this letter is that it signals the affective dimensions of magazine reading, and the feelings of betrayal and broken trust that can be produced by changes in content and/or editorial perspective.[7] This letter to the editor demonstrates that there was some resistance to the introduction of fashion content into *BUST*, and more broadly that there can be tension between what readers want and what brings in money for a magazine.

In keeping with the dialoguing spirit typical of many early issues, BUST's editors responded directly to the reader's letter: "[W]e agree with you about the models—and we promise never again to use them in BUST. However, we're not going to stop doing fashion, because, well, why should transvestites have all the fun? Check out 'Fashion Nation' on pages 65–68 of this issue, where we have only 100% real girls, and let us know what you think" (Stoller and Karp, 4). BUST's tongue-in-cheek justification for its fashion pages suggests, through the figure of the transvestite, a kind of masquerade element to fashion that has some grounding in early feminist theorizations of gender and the body.[8] In these arguments, the figure of the transvestite has the potential to foreground the constructed nature of gendered identity categories through taking on the dress of the "opposite" sex. Nowadays, the term is considered derogatory, when used to refer to trans folks because it assumes that gender is simply about the clothes that one wears. Within the context of BUST's editorial response, the figure of the transvestite functions as the Other through which BUST's readership is constructed as "authentically" female/girly. BUST's use of the phrase "100% real girls" indicates the magazine's shift back to featuring women wearing their own clothes, accompanied by a short profile piece. But, moreover, when juxtaposed to the figure of the transvestite-as-Other, BUST readers and the profiled subjects of Fashion Nation are constructed as gender normative.

As of 2016, BUST continued to publish Fashion Nation in each issue: each profile featured a woman wearing clothes from her own wardrobe; the accompanying text described, in the profiled subject's own words, how or where she came to acquire each piece of the outfit; and finally, the subject of Fashion Nation was asked to summarize her "look." While the earliest iterations of Fashion Nation invited readers to submit pictures of themselves for the column, in later issues the subjects of Fashion Nation tended toward women who had already attained some measure of celebrity status. For example, band members from *Broadcast* were featured in a 2006 issue of Fashion Nation. Initially appearing as a "standalone" column, Fashion Nation currently belongs to BUST's "Looks" department, which has grown to include in every issue a profile of a fashion designer, product testing, tips on how to produce a given hairstyle, and stories on new and second-hand goods. Further, the initial number of profiles (five) has been reduced to one per issue: content that discusses clothes has been reduced, while content that sells clothes has been increased.

Although BUST ran Fashion Nation as its only fashion-minded article for the 1998 "Girlfriends Issue" (Issue 11), in the subsequent "Money Issue"

(1999), *BUST* expanded its offerings by featuring both Fashion Nation (two pages in black-and-white) and a five-page colour fashion spread. While Fashion Nation profiles women wearing their own clothes, *BUST*'s fashion spread features clothing the readers can purchase. In their accompanying editorial for the "Money Issue," the editors reiterate their promise to use only "real women" (i.e., not professional models) in their future issues, although this promise was broken by 2004, when the periodical began using agency models in its fashion pages. According to the co-editors of the 1999 Money Issue, "We're growing as businesswomen, trying to figure out how to put *BUST* in the black rather than in the red ... and still do it our way.... If we sound defensive, well, maybe we are. We're having growing pains, too" (Hex, Boob, and Henzel, 4). This editorial highlights the multiple—and even conflicting—demands placed on *BUST* from their readers, their own editorial vision, and their bottom line. Given the reintroduction of fashion pages in this particular issue and the revenue offered by them, *BUST*'s decision to include fashion spreads may be read as, at least in part, a decision to improve the publication's financial viability within the marketplace.

Indeed, *BUST*'s expansion of its fashion offerings in the "Money Issue" is not the only time that expansion of the publication's coverage of fashion has coincided with financial difficulties. In the Spring 2002 "Fight Like a Girl" issue, the editors recount that they temporarily went out of business following the attack on the World Trade Center on September 11, 2001. As Stoller explains in her editorial for the issue, the magazine industry was struggling in the months preceding the events of September 11 and continued to flounder in the months following. *BUST*'s publisher at the time, BUST Company, Inc. (a division of Razorfish Studios), decided to discontinue publication of the magazine (4). The following spring, Stoller and art director Laurie Henzel relaunched *BUST* as an independently produced publication; they also introduced the "Looks" department (described above) and increased the number of pages for their fashion spreads (from five to eight pages). These editorials in the Money (1999) and Fight Like a Girl (2002) issues suggest a link between *BUST*'s financial situation and the amount of content that features clothing for sale.

Examining the different amounts of fashion coverage in third-wave periodicals demonstrates that these publications have a variety of approaches to fashion and style, which may be attributed to both the generic differences and the political positions of these magazines, and it further suggests that the generic categories these magazines inhabit are also not politically neutral. For example, *Bitch*'s lack of fashion spreads because it happens to be a not-for-profit journal is not coincidental; rather, the decision to be a not-for-profit journal is a political one that allows the periodical to avoid marketing its readers as consumers to clothing advertisers. As a for-profit publication, *BUST*'s inclusion of fashion content is related to the need to maintain financial stability, but it is also related to *BUST*'s philosophy of making feminism appealing to readers who might also purchase conventional women's magazines and be attracted to the magazine on the newsstand. However, as I have demonstrated above, part of *BUST*'s strategy in creating a version of feminism that is perceived as "more fun" relies on the Othering of both non-Western women and second-wave feminists (in the case of Stoller's fashion editorial) and trans identities and drag cultures (in the case of the editorial response to the introduction of fashion spreads). As my reading of *BUST*'s spread devoted to "fashionable feminists" demonstrates below, the desire to make feminism appealing and "safe" to readers comes at the expense of a dehistoricized and deracialized version of feminism.

PART THREE: *BUST*'S FASHIONABLE FEMINISTS

BUST's "fashionable feminists" spread opens with a single page containing small labelled photographs of Elizabeth Cady Stanton, Gloria Steinem, Bella Abzug, Camille Paglia, Angela Davis, and Kathleen Hanna. The accompanying headline announces that the fashion spread consists of looks inspired by these "fashionable feminists." The subsequent six-page spread devotes one page each to models that physically resemble the profiled women (with the possible exception of Stanton) and wear new clothes (available for purchase) that are updated versions of the period dress worn by each of the women. Every fashion photograph is accompanied by a short quotation attributed to the feminist whose look is represented.

BUST's selection of U.S. feminists indicates an attempt to be somewhat representative of a range of time periods, ethnicities, and sexual orientations. Iconic feminists from each major wave are depicted, as well as other figures, such as Camille Paglia, who does not fit so easily into the wave structure (or into particular definitions of feminism). Both the inclusion of a quotation from each of the represented women and the use of labelled, archival photographs on the opening page of the spread suggest that *BUST*'s fashion spread functions not only to present fashion but also to document feminist history. That is, the spread works to introduce readers to particular iconic figures within U.S. feminism and suggests that fashion and feminism need not be viewed as antithetical to each other. In this sense, the spread may effectively work as an entry point into feminism, for readers who may not otherwise be acquainted with the history of the U.S. movement.

If the *BUST* fashion spread serves as a document of feminist history, then it is important to ask what version of feminist history is being presented. Indeed, the question of how we remember our histories is always also a political question, one that is particularly germane to the lives of women and other marginalized groups whose histories have been systemically and systematically erased and/or undervalued and who have experienced first-hand the consequences of not knowing our own histories.

The version of "feminism" presented in *BUST*'s fashion spread is quite limited. This becomes particularly apparent when examining as a group the quotations that accompany the fashion pictures: from Kathleen Hanna, "While sexism hurts women most intimately, it also damages men severely"; from Gloria Steinem, "I have yet to hear a man ask for advice on how to combine marriage and a career"; from Bella Abzug, "The test for whether or not you can hold a job should not be the arrangement of your chromosomes"; from Elizabeth Cady Stanton, "We hold these truths to be self-evident: that all men and women are created equal"; from Angela Davis, "To understand how any society functions, you must first understand the relationship between men and women"; and from Camille Paglia, "Woman is the dominant sex. Men have to do all sorts of stuff to prove they are worthy of woman's attention." While generational and ethnic difference may be evoked visually within the spread, the quotations from each of the feminist figures efface these differences. Each of the above quotations offers a version of feminism in which gender—and more specifically the relationships between men and women—is the only consideration. As a group, the quotations present the categories of "men" and "women" as coherent, unmarked groups (which thus implicitly marks these categories as white and heterosexual). Historical specificities and analyses that consider, for example, class and race subjectivities are effaced in a version of feminism that seems based on a notion of universal sisterhood that transcends time, locality, and difference.

The photographic image inspired by Angela Davis's "look" is exemplary in this regard (Figure 2). Davis has written about a host of subjects, including prison abolition; the intersections of Marxism, feminism, and anti-racism; and notably, for the purposes of this chapter, the ways in which photographic images of herself from the 1970s have been mobilized in contemporary fashion magazines.[9] According to Davis (Autumn 1994), "[I]t is both humiliating and humbling to discover that a single generation after the events that constructed me as a public personality, I am remembered as a hairdo" (37).

The *BUST* image inspired by Davis conjures up a particular moment in American history while simultaneously emptying the image of its political

FIG. 2 Angela Davis, fashion plate, *BUST* (2006)

significance. That is, the image of Davis, with afro, leather jacket, and raised fist, evokes her involvement with the Black Panthers. Yet these visual traces meant to evoke the past seem hopelessly decontextualized here, as the political significance of the model's hairstyle, wardrobe, and pose are codified solely in terms of fashion. The use of black-and-white photography for this image suggests a newspaper clipping or her "wanted" poster. But since all the other fashion photographs, with the exception of Stanton, are in colour, this particular image and the political period it invokes are also coded as "past." The accompanying quotation ("To understand how any society functions, you must first understand the relationship between men and women") diminishes the historical specificities of the time period represented in the visual image and deracializes its connotative meanings.

The representation of feminism through fashion allows *BUST* to present a particular version of what constitutes "feminism" to its readers. This iteration of the movement reduces it to a story that is only about gender difference. Intersectional perspectives on the ways in which systemic forms of oppression often work together are not part of the picture, so to speak. This single-axis narrative elides important contestations and dynamic exchanges that have made feminist movements exciting, mutable, and not always "safe" for those in power.

JOURNALISTIC CRAFT TRADITIONS AND FEMINIST POLITICS

BUST's fashion spread draws on two journalistic conventions within the magazine industry: the use of individuals to stand in for collective identities and the use of the "quip" (the written equivalent of the sound bite) to represent a broader set of social sentiments or political positions. One of the benefits of the former strategy is that it encourages readers to identify personally with the represented figures, to read themselves into alignment with a particular person and their views. *BUST* achieves this through its use of "Our" in its headline "Our Outfits, Ourselves," which evokes a kind of collectivity that includes the editors, the readers, and the represented feminists in the spread. The phrase also references the Boston Women's Health Collective's groundbreaking *Our Bodies, Ourselves* and invites comparison, particularly with regard to agency. The *Our Bodies, Ourselves* project was an example of radical collective work that attempted to demystify health and medicine for the purpose of empowering women to have more agency when it came to their bodies.[10] In *BUST*, however, agency is here conceptualized as being ultimately about consumerism.

While the use of individual feminist figures has the potential to invoke sympathetic identification in the reader, it also has certain limitations as a feminist strategy. From the perspective of some critics, the positing of particular feminists as "leaders" is a problem in itself, given that this strategy inscribes a hierarchical structure through which the opinions of certain figures are imbued with more authority than those of others. Moreover, the use of individual figures has the potential to elide notions of collective struggle entirely. To return to Davis's discussion of the ways in which her image has been mobilized in fashion photography, she argues,

What is also lost in this nostalgic surrogate for historical memory—in these "arrested moments," to use John Berger's words—is the activist involvement of vast numbers of Black women in movements that are now represented with even greater masculinist contours than they actually exhibited at the time. (43)

Although Davis is referring here specifically to the ways through which Black women have collectively been written out of the histories of, for example, the Black Power and Communist movements in the United States, her comments are also pertinent for the consideration of how the use of "celebrity" feminists erases the everyday work of countless women and men for activist causes and how Black women's and women of colour's activisms are often written out of histories of the feminist movement.

The generic convention of the quip raises a set of similar concerns. The inclusion of aphoristic quotations allows BUST to link the fashion sense of individual feminists with the political views of those same figures. In this sense, BUST is not presenting "just fashion." But the use of these quips also inevitably results in a simplification of the political views of these figures and an elision of their own views on fashion. For example, Elizabeth Cady Stanton had happily taken up bloomers in the mid-nineteenth century but eventually abandoned them. She wrote of her decision, "Yet such is the tyranny of custom, that to escape constant observation, criticism, ridicule, persecution, mobs, one after another gladly went back to old slavery and sacrificed freedom to repose" (quoted in Scott 1972, 54). It is interesting that Stanton's represented "look" in BUST features her not in bloomers, but in a ruffled dress, clothing reminiscent of a style she may have found, to some extent, "oppressive."

Although the selection of quotations does not present a homogenous view of feminism, the parameters of difference among the represented positions are quite narrow, given that gender difference is the only axis through which feminist politics is considered. In her discussion of the elision of radical politics from newsmagazines, Carolyn Kitch (2005) argues that the absence of alternative stories that trouble unified understandings of history demonstrates the ways in which magazines shape both collective memory and collective amnesia. She asserts that "[w]hile these errors have political implications, they most likely have narrative causes: it is not the unpopular but rather the incongruous that gets left out" (29). BUST's use of quips functions similarly, in that they erase important contestations and debates within feminist movements. This erasure becomes of a form of whitewashing, when the intersections of gender and race get left out of discussions about feminism.

FEMINIST REPONSES TO THE FASHION ISSUE

The release of *BUST*'s fashion issue generated controversy among various feminist readers. Although no critical letters on the issue were printed in *BUST* itself (and it is possible that none were submitted), a debate ensued online on several blogs and websites. Following the release of the fashion issue, Twisty Faster (2006)—who writes the radical feminist blog, "I Blame the Patriarchy"—asserted that "*BUST*, a young women's indie-hip lifestyle magazine with a purported feminist slant, merely re-brands materialism as 'feminism'; that for all its empowerful sass, it's really just another philosophically empty fashion rag hawking 'girly stuff' in the traditional style." *Salon .com*'s Paige Rockwell (2006), writer of the column *Broadsheet*, responded to Faster's claim, by arguing that

> the *BUST* approach may not hit all the right notes—the promise that it'll help me "feel good about being a girl" does make me recoil a little—but its genuinely pro-woman approach still makes it a smarter read than many major mags. Even the fashion and beauty features, which run without emaciated models, thousand-dollar shoes and plastic surgery advocacy, represent a small step in the right direction. And, like it or not, there are still women who are on the fence about feminism; *BUST*'s light hand and inclusive stance may be a useful introduction to the great world of patriarchy blaming.

Both Faster and Rockwell make persuasive arguments that demonstrate the ways in which the same issue of *BUST* may be read as alternately "radical" or "not radical enough," depending on its reading audience and reading context. That is, read alongside other women's fashion magazines, *BUST*'s fashion spread certainly makes available more socially progressive messages about women's bodies and feminism than those offered within higher circulation magazines for women. Within this context, it is at least an unusual if not a radical statement to deem feminism "fashionable." When examined in relation to other feminist periodicals, however, it is evident that, while *BUST*'s perspective on fashion shares some overlap with third-wave publications, such as *Bitch* and *HUES*, it also diverges from them in significant ways.

Bitch and *HUES* have respectively presented more critical articles on fashion and reworked the magazine "fashion spread" in an innovative manner. Thus, when examining these magazines comparatively, it is important to consider their relationship to the marketplace and to readers. While *Bitch* assumes an audience of women who already identify as feminist, or are sympathetic to feminism, and *HUES* targets a readership who is rarely represented in mainstream fashion spreads, BUST attempts to reach young women who may not necessarily identify with feminism. In this sense, BUST's use of the feminist fashion spread may be read as a way of making feminism "accessible" to a particular (read: white cis-gendered women) demographic group.

In a sphere in which there exist few positive representations of feminists and feminism, the issue of how feminisms are represented is for some critics, such as Faster and Rockwell, one in which a great deal is at stake. Implicit in the arguments of both Faster and Rockwell is an assumption that the realm of commercial culture—and how feminisms are represented within it—is important, and that the representations generated therein have at least some potential influence on readers.

LIFESTYLE FEMINISM AND THE POLITICS OF FEAR

In an article for *Briarpatch* magazine, Becky Ellis (2007) concludes, "Instead of focusing so much energy on recasting feminism as non-threatening, we should reclaim our right to be angry about sexism and other forms of oppression" (3). The development of non-threatening or what I call "lifestyle" feminism in the 1990s and 2000s emerges out of a conjunction of forces, whose epicentre is the United States, including the 1980s Reagan/Bush era, the movement to defeat the Equal Rights Amendment, and the growth and increasing influence of the Christian Right. Given the impact of these forces, I argue that the development of lifestyle feminism is motivated by, at least in part, fear of the power of this "backlash" against feminism. As a consequence, in the case of BUST's fashion spread, the re-presentation of feminism through both fashion and relatively benign quotations casts feminism as unthreatening and minimizes some of its "uglier"—yet important—dimensions: anger, criticality, and dissent. While some argue that this strategy makes feminism more accessible to a broader demographic, I suggest that this strategy only makes feminism palatable to a specific demographic that may be characterized by a certain measure of privilege. While this strategy sidesteps standard backlash criticisms against feminism and feminists, it also limits the possibilities for critiques of systemic and institutionalized forms of discrimination.

I use the term "lifestyle feminism" in relation to BUST in order to invoke a body of work on lifestyle and consumption. Lifestyle media, as David Bell and Joanne Hollows (2005) argue, "are forms through which we work through our ideas about taste, status, and identity" (1). BUST, therefore, is far more than a feminist print magazine about trends and fashion for "hipster girls"; rather, it is a medium through which readers refine their senses of what being cool and being feminist mean. In *BUST*, as the publication's fashion issue makes clear, emphasis is placed on both the reclamation of feminism as stylish and sexy and the representation of feminist politics as a set of individual lifestyle choices expressed through consumption. However, as Bell and Hollows assert, "we need to consider how an investment in lifestyle, far from being about individual choice, may still be closely related to class relations and positions" (6). Given the classed and racialized dimensions of lifestyle, the discourses on feminism within *BUST* merit critical attention, especially with regard to their implications for how people understand, and engage with, feminist politics.

As I have argued above, the headline "Our Outfits, Ourselves" suggests a notion of agency linked to consumption. Similarly, the cover line of *BUST*'s fashion issue, "Be a feminist or just dress like one," draws upon the notion of agency by highlighting the notion of choice. This cover line is, of course, an ironic commentary on both perceived feminist attitudes toward fashion and the reputation of feminists as "unfashionable." *BUST*'s tagline inverts these stereotypes, through its suggestion that dressing like a feminist is fashionable and desirable. As a rhetorical device, however, irony always carries both primary and secondary meanings, suggesting "both complicity and distance" (Hutcheon 1985, 67). It is thus important to read through the double vocality of *BUST*'s cover line.

When stripped of its ironic connotations, the phrase "Be a feminist or just dress like one" delivers a message that is consistent with the neoliberal discourse of "choice" that pervades the magazine. With its cover line, *BUST*'s editorial slant seems to shift toward an "either/or" discursive mode through which the magazine invites the reader to pick and choose which aspects of the magazine she wishes to embrace, which may involve ignoring or rejecting the magazine's feminist elements entirely. In this sense, *BUST* seems to suggest the possibility of claiming a feminism that is almost devoid of politics.

BUST's presentation of fashion content might be best viewed, in Nan Enstad's (1999) words, as a "creative space of cultural contradiction" (50), given that the publication balances its bottom line, readers' demands, and feminist mandate, which are, at times, competing interests. *BUST*'s representation of feminism as friendly, fun, and sexy, and its integration of fashion content, has helped to maintain the financial success of the publication. Yet this financial success comes with a price; ultimately, in *BUST*, notions of agency are constructed mainly in terms of the consumption of products, in ways that seem to cheapen the history of feminism to which many fashionable feminists have contributed.

CONCLUSION

In critically examining *BUST*'s presentation of feminism as style, I do not wish to suggest that there is no room for a feminism that uses fashion or style to convey a political position. As the work of cultural theorists has demonstrated, there are ways that fashion and dress can be subversive. The notion of choosing particular aspects of fashion culture, and not others, seems compatible with ideas of ambivalence and play discussed within the work of Judith Butler and Elizabeth Wilson. However, the move from discussing clothes to selling clothes in *BUST* has provoked some troubling discursive practices, which involve presenting a version of feminism that is both Westernized and gender normative, and—moreover—a version of feminism that promotes imperialist practices and discounts its own history. Consequently, this analysis raises the question of how we are to envision the formation of feminist publics through print culture, if the most widely circulating texts construct readers in such a narrow manner. While certainly these texts do have an implied reader who inhabits a relatively privileged set of identity categories, this fact does not necessarily account for the ways in which actual readers can interact with these texts in challenging and dynamic ways. As the online exchange between Faster and Paige Rockwell demonstrates, readers do play an active role in interpretation and may challenge or reject what they encounter. In the next chapter, I further explore the active role of readers within the context of feminist craft cultures.

"JOIN THE KNITTING REVOLUTION": REPRESENTATIONS OF CRAFTING IN FEMINIST MAGAZINES

In its Spring 2002 issue, *BUST* magazine (1993–) invited readers to "join the knitting revolution" (Stoller 2002, 15). In the early 2000s, *BUST* was at the forefront of a trend among third- and post-wave publications that involves the promotion of reclaiming and, in some cases, repoliticizing activities traditionally associated with the domestic sphere, particularly knitting. But the language of revolution and recuperation necessarily invites the questions of why knitting needs to be reclaimed in the first place. For whom is domesticity being refigured? From whom is domesticity being reclaimed? This chapter explores these questions through an analysis of the ways that the entwined discourses of reinvention and revolution are mobilized in the promotion of crafting within the letters to the editor, editorials, articles, and advertisements of third-wave magazines. These discourses often help to shore up generational boundaries between younger knitters and older practitioners, generic boundaries between "feminist" and "women's" magazines, and political boundaries between third-wave feminists and their forerunners. By historicizing third-wave periodicals' promotion of knitting, this chapter sheds light on the changing ways in which the domestic sphere has figured within the broader history of U.S. feminism and suggests that, despite their appeals to "the new," these periodicals are actually in conversation with, what is to some extent, an imagined feminist past. Moreover, rather than serving as a radical break from their precursors, feminist periodicals that promote crafting carry on an engagement with do-it-yourself (DIY) principles that runs through the long history of feminist publishing. Historicizing the promotion of craft within feminist magazines demonstrates the ways in which feminisms do not follow easy, linear progress narratives but are rather shaped by, and feed back into, multiple contexts.

While there are continuities between second- and third-wave feminism, these two categories are frequently set up in opposition to each other and figured as sites of inter-generational tension. Third-wave magazines are often used as evidence of the alleged turn away from more recognizably "political" feminist work of the second wave, in ways that elide the points of alliance between the waves and that place rigid boundaries on what can and should count as appropriately "political" work. Thus, when in the mid-1990s and intensifying in the early 2000s, many of these publications feminist periodicals began discussing and—in many cases—promoting the reclamation and repoliticization of crafting activities, this turn to craft could be read as a sign of this wave's difference from the second wave, positioned as a selling out of feminist principles or cited as further evidence of the political apathy of young women. *BUST* and other feminist periodicals, including *Bitch* (1996–), *Venus Zine* (1994–2010), *Shameless* (2004–), and *Rookie* (2010–), frequently cast knitting, sewing, and crocheting as new and fun ways of being hip and feminist. Despite the frequent discursive appeals to the political potential of knitting, it is worth asking these questions about the use of reclaiming craft as political and as feminist, linking them to broader concerns regarding the productiveness of so-called third-wave feminism. Following Lora Romero's (1997) work on domesticity, in which she argues that "we need not call domesticity 'feminist' in order to appreciate its antipatriarchal motivations" (20), this chapter examines the articles and readers' letters to the editor on crafting within feminist magazines in ways that help to move us beyond simplistic and binary modes of conceptualizing cultural production as either radical or complicit or as either political or apolitical.

The chapter begins with a discussion of the rise of crafting within third-wave feminism in the early 2000s and its development in third- and post-wave magazines. It analyzes the reciprocal relationship between production and consumption within third-wave crafting and of the ways in which the promotion of crafting has facilitated the expansion of third-wave magazines, *BUST* particularly, into the realms of other media. I then turn to the generational discourse that shapes feminist crafting, arguing that this discourse highlights the ambivalent relationship that third-wave feminism has to its forerunners. I consider the political implications of crafting practices and the specific ways in which crafting projects are promoted within third-wave magazines. The final section historicizes feminism's relationship to crafting, seeking to provide a counter-narrative to the discourse of craft as new to feminism. In its broadest sense, this chapter both puts into relief the shifting relationship between feminism and domesticity within the context of the third wave and beyond, and examines the role that feminist magazines play in shaping craft cultures.

THE RISE OF FEMINIST CRAFTING

The first craft project to appear in a third-wave magazine was *BUST*'s 1997 introduction of a do-it-yourself (DIY) department. *BUST* was on the cutting edge of a veritable explosion of interest in crafting that occurred in the early 2000s. As Celina Hex (*BUST* editor Debbie Stoller's *nom de plume*) and Amanda Ray noted in a 2000 issue of *BUST*, "girls of all stripes" were becoming addicted to knitting (17). According to the Craft Yarn Council of America (CYCA), between 1997 and 2002 the "proportion of women under the age of 45 who [knew] how to knit doubled" from 9 to 18 percent (Minahan and Cox 2007, 7). And between 2002 and 2004, the CYCA reported that "the number of knitters and crocheters between the ages of 25 and 34 jumped 150 percent ... attracting 5.7 million people" (Waickman 2008). Indeed, by 2000, knitting had become so popular that it drew the attention of the mainstream press: *The New York Times*, *Time* magazine, and *The Washington Post* all ran articles devoted to the renewed interest in knitting among young women that year. Feminist magazines were clearly trend-setting, with regard to crafting, helping to shape a larger cultural shift toward revaluing certain kinds of domestic leisure activities.

All third- and post-wave magazines that published in the 2000s made activities traditionally associated with the domestic sphere an integral part of their content.[1] *Shameless*, *Venus Zine*, and *BUST* feature a DIY section in every issue that contains instructions on how to craft, bake, or repair an item on one's own. Similarly, the online post-wave magazine *Rookie* has a dedicated category—called fun—that frequently features DIY crafting, repurposing, and cooking projects. Unlike its sister publications, *Bitch* does not feature how-to articles. However, the magazine has featured coverage of and discussion about feminist crafting and its interface with other topics frequently discussed within the magazine, such as motherhood and domesticity. *Venus Zine* began publishing how-to articles in the early 2000s, and *Shameless* has published such articles since its inception. Past projects in *Venus Zine* include instructions for how to make perfume, concoct sourdough bread, sew a laptop cozy, and make fabric alterations. Similarly, *Shameless* has encouraged readers to make their own paper, stencils, and silkscreens, and to reinvent old vinyl records as decorative bowls and old T-shirts as underpants. Perhaps because *Shameless* targets a younger, less financially independent teen audience, the publication tends to promote crafts more frequently for their affordability and their ability to be used as gifts. For the most part, the how-to craft projects included within these publications tend to have a decorative purpose, and the emphasis is as much on the enjoyable

TABLE 3 Growth of DIY Business Advertising in *BUST*, 2001–2002

Year	Average # total ads per issue	Average # DIY-related ads per issue	Average % DIY ads to total ads	Average total pages of magazine	Average % ad pages per issue
2001	44	9	20.4%	100	20%
2002	79	39	50%	114	18%

process of making a craft as the finished product itself. But beyond the craft departments of these publications, the aesthetics of DIY crafting often infuse feminist magazines throughout: for example, although *Rookie* is a completely online magazine, its title font is created to look like handwriting.

Third- and post-wave magazines not only promote projects that readers can do themselves, they also profile artisans who make their own goods. Further, advertisements for goods that are produced independently (or, in some cases, for items that *appear* independently produced) make up a large proportion of the total ads in the magazines. Since 2002, DIY products have made up approximately half the total ads in *BUST* magazine, a significant jump from its 2001 numbers, when independently produced products comprised approximately 20% of the total ads (see Table 3). This increase may be attributed to *BUST*'s development of a classified section for the final pages of the magazine in the early 2000s, which allowed smaller businesses to purchase ad space for a relatively low cost.[2] Further, the increased popularity of the Internet facilitated the ability of crafters to turn their creative pastimes into full-fledged businesses. Online stores, such as etsy.com, function as a kind of virtual craft fair, showcasing handmade goods from all over the world: Etsy reported $88 million in sales for 2008 (Tiffany 2009). The company has run full-page ads in *BUST* and *Venus Zine* and has embedded advertising in *Rookie* via clickable links. The world of homemade goods has clearly become a thriving business.

The rise of crafting as a feminist pastime—and potential business—has helped extend third-wave magazines beyond their primary iterations as print periodicals. That is, the promotion of crafting and the industry it has spawned have allowed feminist periodicals to adapt to and negotiate the changing demands of the capitalist marketplace, which is an increasingly difficult sphere for print periodicals—and has always been a difficult sphere for feminist periodicals—to operate within. The forays of third-wave magazines onto the Internet are arguably the most important innovations undertaken by these publications, which have now developed their own online blogs, stores, and discussion forums. That is, the websites associated with the magazines have extended the possibilities for increasing the levels of audience, interactivity, and commerce. *BUST*'s online store, the Boobtique, features items that are independently made and that usually promote a pro-girl philosophy. As a complement to the online store, the *BUST* company also introduced advertorials in its magazine about independently made crafts, many of which are available for sale through the website. *Bitch* has also diversified its media delivery through the development of a radio show, website, blog, book (*Bitchfest*), and Facebook group. *Bitch* has also developed itself into a not-for-profit organization, which means that it is less reliant than *BUST* on the commerce DIY craft culture provides. Similarly, *Shameless* has diversified its media to include the print magazine, a blog, a website, and a YouTube channel; *Shameless* also has a Web presence on Facebook, YouTube, Tumblr, Twitter, and Instagram. And, as noted above, *Rookie* straddles the imbricated worlds of crafting, advertising, and feminism through embedded links to saleable items. As the cost of producing print magazines rises, these periodicals have adapted to the changing environment with new, hybrid forms of publication—and the rise of craft culture has facilitated this move. Contrary to the argument that print is under threat by virtual culture, feminist magazines' use of the Internet, and the use of the print magazine as an advertising venue for online DIY companies, suggests a more reciprocal relationship, in this context, between print and virtual cultures. This relationship has been facilitated by the surge of interest in DIY products, an interest that has been nurtured by these new media and marketing modes.

Both writing about crafting and advertising crafts shape the content and aesthetic of third-wave magazines. In *BUST*, particularly, content about crafts is a central feature of each facet of the publication, both within and beyond the print magazine at the core of the company. For example, editor Debbie Stoller has written six books in her *Stitch 'n Bitch* series, which commenced in 2003 with *Stitch 'n Bitch: The Knitter's Handbook*. *BUST* is associated with the popular social practice of stitch-'n'-bitch knitting circles, the namesakes of Stoller's books, which are knitting-centred gatherings, usually held in a café or knitting store, during which knitters socialize and work on their projects. Stoller's books helped inspire a worldwide knitting circle craze: Stitch 'n Bitch circles can be found in thirty-seven countries on all the continents (excluding Antarctica). The name Stitch n' Bitch itself has been the subject of a copyright dispute between Stoller and the company Sew Fast/Sew Easy (settled in 2008) over who legally owns the name. This dispute highlights the monetary stakes of the move to reclaim crafting and the way in which this world is thoroughly imbricated in consumer culture. Interestingly, as Anne MacDonald (1998) notes, the term *stitch 'n' bitch* has been used to describe knitting circles since the Second World War, a point that speaks to a kind of historical amnesia about the lineages within which these crafting discourses are, or could be, located (302). As I will discuss, this historical amnesia is also evidenced in the discourse of knitting as "new."

CHALLENGING THE "LURE OF THE NEW": FEMINIST HISTORICAL CONTINUITIES

One of the most consistent aspects of craft discourse that appears in both feminist magazines and mainstream news media is the figuring of crafting hobbies as "new." Although there has been an intensification of crafting in recent years, what is at stake in continually figuring crafting practices in this way? This discourse allows media texts to self-construct as cutting edge and trend setting, a journalistic craft tradition that Patricia Bradley (2003) dubs "the lure of the new" (91).[3] However, one effect of this persistent discourse of newness is that it also results in a distancing from the history of craft practices, eliding the important alliances—familial, political, aesthetic, and cultural—that might be forged in making these historical continuities more visible.

Domestic activities like crafting were politicized long before 2002 and the perception that all feminists looked down upon domestic work is inaccurate. For example, Minahan and Cox (2007) argue that there was a "resurgence of interest in crafts in the 1960s and 1970s [that] was clearly aligned with the anti–Vietnam War protesters [...]. Women in the western world took up their needles and threads during this era. Spinning wheels were in full flight producing yarns for hand knits and looms threaded to produce textiles for wear and domestic use" (13). Contrary to the assumption that cultural production does not align with political activism, Minahan and Cox's research demonstrates that crafting and progressive political stances have been aligned in the past. The DIY spirit of contemporary crafting clearly shares continuities with the establishment of independent feminist presses and feminist periodicals in the second wave.[4] Publications like the *Whole Earth Catalog* (1968–72), for example, emphasized a do-it-yourself approach to living more simply for environmental and ethical purposes. Further, an examination of *Ms.* magazine classifieds turns up several ads for handmade feminist shirts, jewellery, and buttons. Although advertisements for handmade goods appear fairly infrequently in second-wave periodicals, their presence in *Ms.* suggests a view of handmade crafted goods as not incompatible with the goals of the women's movement in the 1970s.

Certainly, there were radical feminist critiques of domestic arrangements, and among these critiques were varied perspectives on what the problems were and how they might be addressed. Barbara Crow's (2000) collection of radical feminist writings from the 1960s and 1970s documents some of these views, which tend to focus on the problems and politics of housework. Betsy Warrior (2000) and Vivien Leone (2000) both advocate paid housework, in order to revalue the activity through bringing it into the public economy. Warrior's writing challenges the notion that all second-wave feminists advocated that women should leave the home for the workforce en masse in order to achieve liberation, suggesting that the realities of oppression are far less easily solved (see Warrior 530). Warrior and Leone's contemporary, Pat Mainardi (2000), did not advocate for paid housework, but rather advised her readers on strategies to help share the burden of housework more equitably since "[p]articipatory democracy begins at home" (527). Far from trivial, housework, for Mainardi, serves as an important site for women to implement their politics, perhaps for the first time. The perspectives represented in Crow's text, while not exhaustive, represent well the multiple perspectives on domesticity among radical feminists.

The inaccurate claim that all second-wave feminists advocated wholesale rejection of the domestic in favour of entering the public world of work is likely shaped by a text that is widely considered foundational for feminism's second wave: Betty Friedan's 1963 classic, *The Feminine Mystique*. In it, Friedan identified a "problem with no name" facing women who felt unsatisfied with their undervalued status as housewives, an important claim that resonated with many women although it betrayed a thoroughly middle- and upper-class bias, given that working-class women had long worked outside the home in order to help support their families. Friedan charged that women's magazines were responsible for perpetuating the problem through their articles promoting good housekeeping practices. Although magazine scholar Nancy Walker (2000) has since challenged the notion that women's magazines indoctrinate their readers into a "cult of femininity" (Ferguson 1983), Friedan's widely read book—often credited with sparking the second wave of liberal feminism—clearly shaped the ongoing relationship between feminism and domesticity in the decades that followed.

Feminist periodicals from the 1970s similarly contained critical articles on domesticity, which politicized and made of public concern the "private" problems and struggles faced by women. In ways that are revealing of the implicit white feminist subject of much radical feminist writing, housework is often likened to a kind of slavery, as in the editor of *Aphra*'s claim that "we [women] have all been house niggers in the mansion of man" (Fisher 1970, 6). This distancing from the domestic sphere is also reflected in the absence of "household hint" departments, in contrast to the women's magazines that were contemporary with these feminist periodicals. The more liberal approach of *Ms.* is reflected in an article on housework that ran in the magazine's inaugural issue. In it, Anne Crittenden Scott (1972) argued that "'Occupation: Houseworker' is a viable and respectable choice for anyone, male or female, provided it is treated as such, socially and economically" (59). *Ms.*'s perspective anticipates what Linda Hirshman (2006) later identified as the phenomenon of "choice feminism." It is significant that Hirshman's work focuses on the choices women make with regard to working outside or within the home. It is clear from these earlier writings that feminists held a range of perspectives on the realm of domesticity and its place within feminist politics and that in many ways the more liberal strands of feminist thought from this era helped set the stage for the reclamation of domestic pastimes, such as knitting, in the decades that followed.

Although second- and third-wave feminisms are often presented as having quite divergent perspectives, when it comes to domesticity, both generational brackets recognize that domestic activities are devalued and largely unrecognized. However, the contexts from which these groups are writing are very different. While indeed many second-wave feminists were critical of domesticity, the kinds of domesticity being reclaimed in third-wave magazines are quite different from the domesticity critiqued by second-wave feminists, who were also not homogenous in their positions on this matter. The domestic activities promoted in BUST, *Venus Zine*, and *Shameless* are potentially pleasurable because they are figured as leisure activities. One would be hard-pressed to find an article in a third-wave periodical advocating for the reclamation of toilet cleaning, vacuuming, window washing, dish drying, or floor mopping. Activities that are being promoted include knitting, sewing, and soap-, lamp-, and jewellery-making. Thus it is domesticity as *leisure* and *pleasure* that is being advocated, the activities that allow most easily for creativity and the creation of a tangible product, rather than quotidian household tasks. In this sense, it is reductive and inaccurate to place these two waves in opposition to each other, when it comes to the matter of craft, because the imagined spaces of the private sphere are markedly different across these feminist waves.

The ways in which domestic activities are figured differently across temporal and cultural spaces demonstrate the relationality and historical and cultural contingency of terms such as "private" and "public." This shift from quotidian to luxury also entails further commodification of these domestic practices. For example, specialty wools for decorative clothing are far more expensive than the more economical acrylic blends that typify more utilitarian garments. The failure of third-wave periodicals to acknowledge the class dynamics inherent to crafting cultures is stunning, to say the least, and suggests a broader lapse within some branches of third-wave feminism, when it comes to critically engaging with the intersectionality of race, class, age, ability, and gender. Because third-wave feminism is often set in strict opposition to the second, it is crucial to attend to the continuities across these two feminist waves, with regard to both their inclusions and their elisions. Looking further back in feminist magazine history to nineteenth-century suffrage periodicals similarly reveals a rich history of feminist discussions of domestic life that sheds light on the phenomenon of reclaiming domesticity at the turn of the twentieth century.

Many suffrage magazines included household hints and discussed concerns associated with the private sphere, and they likely did so for multiple purposes. First, the editors of these periodicals wanted to make the magazines appealing and interesting to their readers. That is, when they took a broad perspective and covered a variety of topics, suffrage magazines seemed to attract more readers; the *Woman's Tribune* (1883–1909), for example, was able to maintain publication once it adopted this strategy and, in so doing, demonstrated the importance of suffrage through its relation to a variety of other topics. Other feminist publications like *The Lily* (1849–58), *The New Northwest* (1871–87), and *The Woman's Journal* (1870–1931) all attempted to provide an entertaining mixture of articles (Smith 1996, 176; Spencer 1996, 473; Steiner 1996, 234). Second, coverage of domestic concerns also served a strategic purpose within suffrage periodicals: suffragists adapted the separate spheres discourse that saw women as paragons of domesticity—angels in the house—to their own advantage, by arguing that their exemplary household skills and virtuous "natures" would help clean up the "dirtiness" and corruption of the public sphere. This discourse was often troublingly aligned with racist attitudes toward newly enfranchised racialized immigrants and African Americans, who were seen by dominant whites as threats to power. Finally, the promotion of the domestic sphere helped counter attacks on the femininity of suffragists in the mainstream press, such as the accusations that prominent suffragists Elizabeth Cady Stanton and Susan B. Anthony were bad mothers and bad housekeepers. In response, Stanton asserted that Anthony's and her magazine, *The Revolution* (1868–1870), would discuss both "bread and babies" (quoted in Gottleib 1996a, 340). Arguably, the contemporary accusation that feminists reject the domestic sphere is just a continuation of this initial attack on Stanton and Anthony for being bad wives and mothers. The varied content of these publications indicates that suffragists did not necessarily view articles associated with domesticity or entertainment as "taking away from" or diluting their primary concern with women's rights.

The presence of domestic content in suffrage magazines clearly served a variety of entertainment, informative, and political purposes. The history of U.S. suffrage periodicals demonstrates that domestic concerns have figured prominently within feminist discourse and have not been eschewed to the extent that some feminists and anti-feminists believe. However, there are marked differences between the ways in which domesticity is politicized across the "waves"; for example, third-wave feminists who pursue crafting do not write about this interest as a "natural" inclination, as some of their first-wave sisters did. Rather, the "new" crafting may be read, as Minahan and Cox (2007) suggest, as a campy performance of, and ironic commentary upon, a fictionalized version of domestic womanhood. However, the element of ridicule involved in ironic reclamations is also tempered by the quite earnest cross-generational connections some crafters have found with others.

"NOT JUST FOR GRANNIES": THE GENERATIONAL DISCOURSE OF NEO-CRAFT

As noted above, the growth of interest in craft, and knitting particularly, did not go unnoticed by the mainstream press. Beginning in the early 2000s, a spate of articles was published on the "new knitting," featuring titles such as "Not Your Grandmother's Hobby" (Greider 2001), "A Pastime of Grandma and the 'Golden Girls' Evolves into a Hip New Hobby" (Lee 2005), "Knitting: The New Yoga" (Marer 2002), "Rock-and-Roll Knitters: They May Have Blue Hair, but They're No Grannies" (Scelfo 2004), and "That Clicking Sound: Grandma's Favorite Hobby Hooks a New Generation of Young, Urban Go-Getters" (Tartakovsky 2000). As these titles demonstrate, the ways in which the resurgence of knitting was covered in the mainstream press emphasized the discourse of "newness" and trendiness, frequently at the expense of grannies (the "old knitters") who are constructed as the antithesis of cool, a demographic figured here more in terms of hip replacements than as just plain "hip." However, in examining the discursive construction of crafting within periodicals like

BUST, Bitch, Shameless, and *Venus Zine,* what can be found in these feminist texts is a richer and more complex relationship between different generations.

In comparison to more mainstream media publications, the relationship between younger and older generations is generally constructed more positively within feminist magazines. For example, in *BUST,* the author of one how-to article on rag rugs encourages readers to put "their own twists on old-school skills and crafts," with a pattern "inspired by one my grandmother made many years ago" (Worick 2007, 25). Within the letters to *BUST,* the potential for craft to link practitioners, particularly women, of different generations is emphasized. In letters to the editor about *BUST*'s craft content—and contrary to mainstream media accounts of "new" knitting—readers discuss the ways in which knitting has helped them connect to older family members. One letter writer claims to "love the warm, inclusive feminism of *BUST* and I think you have done brilliant work reclaiming knitting as a respected craft. My Grandma, who taught me to knit, is highly amused by the name Stitch 'n Bitch—her group is called Knit and Natter!" (Wise 2006, 8). Another letter writer tells the editors that her friend's aunt borrowed the magazine after seeing the crafts her niece had made (Wing 2006, 7). The potential of craft to link different generations is also discussed in *Bitch.* Wendy Somerson's (2007) article on the reclamation of knitting, for example, takes to task those discursive constructions of craft that rely on "distance from the previous generations, and thus from knitters' own histories" (39). These contributions to feminist magazines emphasize the intergenerational aspects of craft and figure older women as sources of inspiration and knowledge rather than as figures from whom distance needs to be kept.

While the relationships between knitters of different generations are generally constructed more positively, as multivocal publications, this representation of knitting is not always consistent within feminist magazines. Indeed, there are articles in feminist magazines that come closer to the ageist rhetoric of the "not just for grannies" knitting headlines in the mainstream press. For example, Hex and Ray encourage *BUST* readers to knit by stating that "knitting's not just for grannies anymore" and "don't let the old-lady aesthetic frighten you away," before adding parenthetically, "unless you find yourself drawn to things associated with old ladies" (2000, 17). This ambivalent statement about the association of craft with old ladies and grannies acknowledges the more mainstream construction of "new" knitting and upholds its ageist rhetoric, while simultaneously claiming to enjoy this same pastime *because* of its association with old ladies. The parentheses around this latter statement, however, minimize the value of this aspect of crafting, in this instance, likening the claim to more of a guilty admission than an embrace. While the generational language in feminist magazines often speaks to crafting's capacity to bring older and younger folks together, an ambivalence toward older women also characterizes some third-wave discourse. Nonetheless, the capacity for craft to build connections among practitioners is frequently emphasized in articles and reader letters within turn-of-the-century feminist magazines.

THE POLITICS OF CONTEMPORARY CRAFTING

Some mainstream media accounts have framed the resurgence of knitting as a return to conservatism and the private sphere; a *Washington Post* opinion piece by Emily Matachar (2011) asks, for example, if the "new domesticity" is fun and empowering or "a step back for American women." However, as Somerson (2007) argues, another way to look at the reclamation of craft is in "its potential for building community, rejecting consumerist sweatshop culture, and encouraging creativity" (39). This emphasis is also found within the ways that feminist magazine readers describe their own crafting practices. For example, one letter writer to *BUST* remarks that "[w]ithin the first week of being loaned a few of your back issues, I made no less than three snow globes, two rock T-shirt handbags, and two showy rings. I then proceeded to rave about you to all of my crafty homegirls who were not already informed" (McClellan Derr 2006, 8). In this response, third-wave magazines' promotion of crafting is celebrated for its generative and creative qualities and for its capacity to build feminist community.

The collective, community-based potential of craft resonates with consciousness raising (CR) groups established by radical feminists in the 1960s and within Riot Grrrl chapters in the 1990s. Similarly, Stitch 'n Bitch groups offer sites for crafters to get together and discuss their lives, potentially linking their personal experiences with more structural and systemic problems. Although crafting is a pastime that can be practised individually, within feminist magazines the potential of crafting to foster friendship and community is frequently highlighted. The simple act of making connections and creating community is, as Alison Piepmeier (2009) puts it, "meaningful for girls and women in a culture in which they are often figured as each others' competition rather than as allies" (79). Contemporary craft practices have the potential to unsettle conventionally held beliefs about what constitutes "the political" and how one engages in political practices.[5]

Crafting practices foster small-scale acts of friendship, care, and love not only among individuals—third-wave magazines also cultivate strong bonds with their readers by valuing crafting and showcasing readers' own crafts. *Venus Zine*, for instance, regularly printed photographs of mail art and crafted items sent in by readers inspired by the magazine (see Figure 3) and BUST has published photographs that readers have submitted of their completed craft projects. This practice of sharing cultivates a particular kind of relationship to texts, to crafts, and to community, creating a sense of discursive solidarity that has long been a hallmark of what Lauren Berlant (2008) calls "women's culture" (5). According to Berlant, "one of the main jobs of minoritized arts that circulate through mass culture is to tell identifying consumers that 'you are not alone (in your struggles, desires, pleasures)': this is something we know but never tire of hearing confirmed, because aloneness is one of the affective experiences of being collectively, structurally unprivileged" (ix). In addition to the photographs of readers' own craft projects, third-wave magazines often print letters that demonstrate the affective relationships between readers and texts, relationships often as intense, as personal, and as fraught as interpersonal ones. Writes one reader, "You give me hope that the world isn't all right-wingers, and that there is a community for us 'indies.' I look to you for so many resources, and I can't thank you enough" (Clark 2004, 7). This affection for texts is often figured through their personification, as readers frequently liken magazines to a friend or sister. Another letter writer, for example, likens BUST to "an authentic, crafty, interesting friend" (Lenn, 2007, 7). As the above examples make clear, third-wave magazines help to produce particular kinds of affects, such as care, love, creativity, and thrift, through the act of reading.

When feminist magazine readers celebrate crafting, they tend to do so with awareness of the perception that a feminist has "sold out" if she has dropped her burning bra and is knitting one, instead.[6] For example, Sally Melville (2001), herself the author of multiple knitting books, wrote a letter to BUST that said: "Congratulations on your discovery of knitting.... I find it fascinating that while many of us 'get it'—the intrinsic value of handmade things, the soothing nature of the activity, the community it engenders—there is still, so often, a note of apology surrounding the admission that one knits" (6). The apologetic tone cited by Melville references the broader discussions on the politics of crafting debated within feminist print communities. However, the rhetoric of these debates is often framed through a false dichotomy of politics (the bra-burning feminist) vs. culture (the knitting feminist). Of course, these two positions are not incommensurable with each other. One does not need to forsake feminist activisms, such as volunteering at a women's shelter, marching in a protest, or advocating for equal pay if

6 letters & whatnot

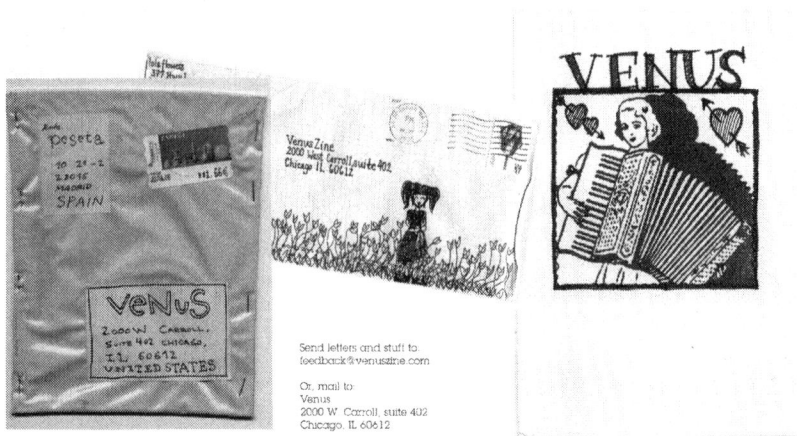

FIG. 3 Letters page, *Venus Zine* (2005)

one is also a knitter. As Ann Cvetkovich (2012) argues, "[C]rafting is not the homology or first step or raw material for some form of political change.... It is already a form of self-transformation, although it can also be a way to build the spiritual warrior self necessary for doing other kinds of work in the world, including organized political activism" (169). The "politics versus culture" dichotomy misrecognizes the political potential of craft.

The feeling of guilt that accompanies the admission that one is a feminist who knits is signalled not only in readers' letters but in the ways in which crafting is framed in some how-to articles in third-wave magazines. For example, a *BUST* how-to article on knitting advises readers to "put aside socio-feminist conflicts and work it on the homefront" (Bardot 1997, 10). "Working it on the homefront," with its dual connotations of both labour and (sexualized) fun, is constructed at odds with a particular version of feminism. The perceived conflict between feminism and domesticity is upheld, and knitting, as a feminist activity, is constructed as a form of sassy, tongue-in-cheek rebellion against norms, including feminist ones. *BUST*'s rhetoric in the above passage is resonant with its more ambivalent relationship with radical feminisms, generally, as I have detailed in Chapter Four. The rec-lamation of knitting, and other forms of craft, in this context relies upon a certain distancing of third-wave feminist practices from more recognizably "political" feminisms. As Cvetkovich asserts, crafting should not be seen as outside of "previous generations of feminism but rather as another moment in a long-standing set of constitutive tensions about the relation between ... women's culture and feminism" (172). While women's and feminist cultures overlap, the debates about what it might mean to "reclaim" activities associated with domesticity foreground these larger tensions on what counts as feminist politics and highlight the ways in which so-called women's culture is still broadly conceived as devoid of politics. The pleasurable political possibilities of knitting, however, are coded in third-wave magazines in ways that have implicit middle-/upwardly mobile class dynamics; these dynamics are not unpacked or even remarked upon within third-wave magazines but clearly help construct the subjectivity of the crafter.

WHO'S CRAFTY?: THE ECONOMIES OF FEMINIST CRAFTING

As I have discussed, there are differences between how crafting is presented within mainstream media texts and how it is depicted within feminist periodicals. What is found in feminist periodicals is a broader discourse on craft that discusses it in terms of business, community, friendship, thrift, love, and care. *Shameless*, for example, frequently appeals to the creative and productive aspects of crafting, and also constructs its readers as smart and thrifty for making handmade goods. This discourse also circulates within *BUST* through its repeated salutation of readers as "crafty." The word "crafting" suggests a skilled activity that requires time and thought and that has value as a potential art form. In this sense, applying the word to particular kinds of domestic activities recasts them as leisure activities, rather than everyday menial work. For instance, *BUST* contributor Jean Railla (1999) argues that "being crafty isn't just about the activity itself, it's about crafting your life and living in an artistic way," suggesting the crafting is as much about cultivating a particular kind of lifestyle as it is about producing a fuzzy sweater (quoted in McGhee 2004, 109). Crafting is thus a "taste culture" (Bourdieu 1984, 1–7) coded in a way that has middle- or aspiring-middle-class dynamics and a kind of hipster cultural capital.

The description of readers as *crafty* suggests that they are astute, cunning, and quite possibly "up to something" when they get together—a framing that implies a politically subversive element to craft activities. Indeed, the longtime title of *BUST*'s craft column, "She's Crafty," constructs readers as smart and subversive; further, as a reference to a Beastie Boys song with the same title, the periodical figures female readers who craft as savvy about independent ("Indie") culture and, given the song's lyrics, as attractive and sexually available to heterosexual men (perhaps particularly hipster "bad boys").[7] While much contemporary craft is explicitly queer in its focus and while much encourages the participation of all genders,[8] in BUST, the ways in which crafting is framed tends toward heteronormativity, which is in keeping with the overall flavour of the magazine—a tendency that has also been flagged by readers. In this sense, acts of reading should not be viewed as simply consuming information, but rather as processes yoked, as Pamela Butler and Jigna Desai (2008) put it, to subject formation and "(dis)identification" (27). Making the crafts described in feminist magazines, reading these magazines, discussing them, or even just having them lying around the house, therefore, become performances of feminism and of a particular kind of white hipster feminist identity.

Crafting activities that have a certain appeal to punk or hipster girls figure prominently within third- and post-wave magazines. Young women with tattoos, piercings, or deliberately messy haircuts are shown either engaging in the promoted craft or enjoying the finished product in the photographs that accompany the featured projects. Playful written copy also helps elevate crafting's cultural cachet and its appeal as a fun, urban, slightly ironic, but sexy, hobby: soap-making instructions, for example, result in "dope homemade soap"; a summary of the knitting craze becomes the "shiz-knit"; and another article playfully asks: "Voulez vous decoupage avec moi?" ("Contents" 2008, 4; Stoller 2002, 15; Bardot 1997, 10). These kinds of do-it-yourself projects have long been a generic staple of for-profit women's magazines, a trend that intensified with the rise to fame of "domestic goddess" figures like Martha Stewart and Nigella Lawson.[9] BUST, Shameless, Rookie, and Venus Zine continue in this generic vein. Indeed, in a Bitch magazine article on domesticity, Justine Sharrock (2003) writes that the advertising for household products appearing in "Bust, Venus, and, yes, Bitch, sometimes [makes] these magazines look more like Martha Stewart Living than Ms" (60). Although there is overlap between them, third-wave periodicals differentiate themselves from women's magazines through the punk/indie aesthetics of their craft projects, a sense of irony about the gendered dimensions of craft, and emphasizing crafting as politically progressive.

There is a link between the rise of crafting within feminist indie culture and the rise of neo-domestic celebrity figures. However, the reclamation of domestic arts is frequently figured in third-wave magazines, at least aesthetically, as a more critical appropriation. For example, in the pages of BUST and Venus Zine, there is a reworking of images of women from the 1950s and 1960s, ironically recontextualized so that while the aesthetic elements of the 1950s housewife may be retained, her reframing within indie subculture creates an "as if-ness" to the image, as in, "as if it were really like this." As Minahan and Cox (2007) argue, the renewed interest in crafting "may signify an ironic mimicry or melancholia for a past that never was rather than a romantic nostalgia or desire for return" (6). The myth of the happy housewife is implicitly acknowledged as a myth, and yet, while the hard work and primarily invisible and always unpaid work performed by the housewife is not being reclaimed, the aesthetic stylings of this figure as retro kitsch are maintained.

In contrast to what the 1950s housewife represents—a selfless, tirelessly working figure dedicated to home, husband, and children—the ways in which crafts, linked as they are to the realm of domesticity, are being reclaimed have key differences with this figure. That is, within third-wave magazines, crafting is often figured as a leisure activity and as a way to unwind from the busy world of paid work rather than figuring domesticity as the centre of one's life. What these continuities and differences between feminist craft cultures and celebrity domestic goddess figures indicate is that—despite the ways in which feminism is often figured as at odds with, or outside of, mainstream culture—feminist and women's cultures exist in a relationship of exchange and negotiation. Broadly speaking, contemporary feminist crafting is much more closely tied to the public sphere, in the kinds of political interventions performed by crafters, such as "yarn bombing" (a knitted version of graffiti in which urban objects are "warmed" with handmade cozies). The political dimensions of crafting are often foregrounded in third-wave magazines, as well as other contemporary feminist publications.

Crafting's political cachet is signalled most clearly through BUST's invocation of the word "revolution" to describe the popularity of knitting. This way of describing crafting is reflected in other writing from the early 2000s, such as Justine Sharrock's "The Revolution Will Not Be Sanitized" (2003), Kim Werker's Crochet Me: Designs to Fuel the Crochet Revolution (2007), and Lisa B. Rundle's "Subversive Stitchery" (2005). The mobilization of the word "revolution" particularly suggests a recasting of what counts as politics within third- and post-wave feminisms. However, the politicization of knitting in third-wave magazines also works as a way of making crafting cool to readers, differentiating these activities from the not-explicitly-politicized crafting of women's culture, and can thus also be understood as a strategy of differentiation.

In third-wave magazines, the discourses of community, political progressiveness, and economy are coded in ways that produce a privileged semi-bohemian subject from a middle-class background whose economic precarity, if any, may be temporary. Like their not-explicitly feminist counterparts, third- and post-wave magazines promote crafting as trendy and economical, as well as providing "balance" to daily life. In an early 1997 issue of *BUST*, for example, knitting is conceptualized as an economical way to say "I'm broke but I love you" (Bardot 1997, 10). Given the growing prominence of specialty yarns and boutique knitting stores and cafés, and the decreasing price of mass-produced garments, this hobby has arguably become a less and less economical way to produce garments. Nonetheless, the discourse of economy persists in helping to construct knitting, and other forms of craft, as a positive pastime.

In third-wave magazines, crafting is also coded as a leisure activity. For example, in *BUST*'s Spring 2002 issue, Sally Melville explains, "New Knitters know that it is possible and, in fact, preferable to 'have it all'—a life that embraces both computer engineering and knitting. Their knitting provides a necessary balance from their hours in front of computer terminals, phones, consumers" (quoted in Stoller 2002, 15). Melville's statement highlights the pursuit of knitting as a leisure activity, a way to unwind from the stresses of daily life. Crafting, in this sense, remains closely associated with the private, feminized sphere—the complement to the busy, public world of computer terminals and consumers. The "have it all" approach to knitting taps into a wider discourse that assumes that women have missed out on the enjoyable aspects of domesticity for the sake of their careers. Working-class and poor women have always needed to work outside the home, and the "have it all" discourse does not speak to this reality. As Somerson (2007) argues, "There seems to be a stunning failure—among feminists and antifeminists alike—to acknowledge that our so-called choices regarding working inside or outside the home are not made on a level playing field" (38). In this sense, the subject of feminist crafting is an implicitly middle-class one.

The classed dimensions of the crafter in feminist magazines emerge primarily through the written copy that describes appeal of making one's own products. For example, one how-to article in *BUST* asks, "Do you envy your wealthy friends as they fly off to week-long spa retreats?" (Railla 1999, 22)—a question that suggests a reader who can relate. Although feminist crafting emerged out of the DIY ethos of punk, particularly Riot Grrrl, which has an implicit—and frequently explicit—anti-capitalist stance, the appeal of crafting in this instance relies on its approximation of a luxurious lifestyle, rather than a rejection of it. Here, crafting is a temporary stopgap on the road to being able to afford, to misquote Virginia Woolf, "a week-long spa retreat of one's own." While magazines are generally a middle-class genre because the advertising they rely upon requires readers with some disposable income, the unremarked and uncritical nature of these class dynamics in feminist magazines like *BUST* is surprising, to say the least.

Rather than a rejection of market culture, the promotion of crafting in feminist magazines creates what Cvetkovich (2012) calls "an alternative market culture" that is about both production *and* consumption (171). Within feminist DIY periodical culture the distinction between production and consumption becomes blurred, and the two practices come to exist in a reciprocal relationship with each other. DIY, as Clive Edwards (2006) puts it, is "both a producing and a consuming culture," and this relationality is made more visible within, and capitalized upon, within feminist periodicals (11). *BUST*'s regular column, "Buy or DIY," through which readers can learn how to make a handcrafted item or where to purchase a similar one made by someone else, is emblematic in this regard. In this sense, the relationship between feminist crafting and the marketplace is situated at a politically ambivalent crossroads of privilege, complicity, and resistance.

The alternative market economy that craft generates is particularly emphasized within the discursive construction of craft in *Venus Zine*. Many of *Venus Zine*'s articles on crafting are written with an eye toward how handmade craft projects might be converted into small businesses. While certainly not radically challenging to capitalist consumer culture, this discourse represents an important intervention into the realm of commercial culture. *Venus Zine* encourages women to establish small businesses, in a cultural context where corporate multinationals have the greatest stake in the marketplace. It provides information to its readers on how to start and maintain a business in a cultural context in which such information is frequently less accessible to women. Finally, *Venus Zine* actively encourages its readers to develop critical skills in and knowledge of finance. This framing of craft shifts its meaning from a leisure activity to a potential business activity. While crafting can connote pre-industrial cultural practices seen as devoid of the "passive" consumerism that characterizes the late-capitalist marketplace, in third- and post-wave magazines, readers are encouraged to both craft and buy independently produced crafts. Crafting, therefore, is not a pure space that exists outside the logic of capital. On the contrary, the practices of production and consumption are thoroughly enmeshed in third-wave crafting practices.

CONCLUSION

The rise in the visibility and popularity of feminist crafting at the turn of the century is part of a longer history of feminist engagements with the realm of domesticity. This latest iteration redefines feminist politics and domesticity through the practice of crafting. That is, the reclamation of crafting promotes a more expansive definition of what counts as "feminist politics," seeking to integrate more traditional forms of political protest (e.g., knitted anti-war banners; knit-ins) with understandings of the ways in which fostering community and friendship are also political acts. To talk about "crafting as political," therefore, is not a contradiction in terms. Feminist crafting also redefines domesticity through making visible the ways in which domesticity is a politicized sphere in which certain forms of pleasure might be cultivated. In this way, the representation of feminist crafting within third- and post-wave periodicals troubles easy binary distinctions between what is political and what is not, and between what is radical and what is complicit. Rather than taking an "either/or" position, when it comes to these categories, these texts demonstrate the inherently "both/and"-ness of political activism.

While contemporary feminist crafting redefines domesticity in terms of its pleasures, it does so through figuring traditionally domestic pastimes as new forms of leisure. The promotion of craft-as-leisure fails to acknowledge the (aspiring) middle-class dynamics of feminist crafting as promoted within third-wave magazines, particularly in *BUST*. Alexandra Chasin (2001) has argued that *consumption* "mediates the production of social identities," but the promotion of crafting in feminist magazines demonstrates that *production* also mediates identity (12). In third- and post-wave magazines, producing and consuming are interrelated and help construct subject positions emphasizing youth and hipness in ways that are undergirded by assumptions about class status. While third- and post-wave feminisms are often discussed as having moved beyond classism and racism, the ways in which crafting is promoted in these publications suggest that classism and racism remain under-discussed or invisible within some feminisms. The question of who has the privilege to reclaim crafting touches on much broader issues of privilege and access. Despite the ways in which feminist crafting is often described as "new," the questions that feminist craft brings to the surface are much longer-standing ones.

The multiple contexts out of which feminist craft cultures emerge—women's cultures, DIY zine and Riot Grrrl scenes, second-wave feminisms—challenge more straightforwardly linear histories of feminism, as well as the overdetermined wave categories. These multiple contexts demonstrate the need for more complex ways of accounting for feminist histories, ones that acknowledge, for example, the ways in which feminism is not a pure space untouched by capital. However, crafting does open a space for alternative economies. As I have discussed, crafting practices offer an alternative to mass-produced products sold by multinational corporations and revalue the art of making one's own goods. Third- and post-wave magazines emphasize this aspect of craft. They offer readers a space to enunciate and negotiate their relationships to crafting, in dialogue with each other, with older generations of crafters, with the periodical texts, and with their broader cultural milieu. In this sense, these periodicals serve as important media for the fostering of feminist craft communities and the many activisms generated within and through them.

CHAPTER SIX

DILDO DEBACLE: ADVERTISING FEMINIST SEXUALITIES IN *BITCH* MAGAZINE

In the Fall 2002 issue of *Bitch*, a full-page advertisement for a purple vibrating dildo appeared on the publication's back cover (Figure 4). The advertisement, for the Seattle-based sex store Toys in Babeland, and the location of the image on the magazine's outer cover, provoked a letter from the postal service alleging distribution of potentially obscene and lewd material (Jervis and Zeisler 2003, 6). The advertisement also generated controversy among *Bitch* readers, spurring an exchange of letters to the editor with accompanying editorial responses that spanned multiple pages of the following three issues of the magazine. Some readers even cancelled their subscriptions because of the ad. With readers still weighing in on the politics of the advertisement nearly one year later, in their Summer 2003 issue, *Bitch* editors Lisa Jervis and Andi Zeisler announced that they were ending the debate and changing their advertising policy. The controversy was so significant that it is mentioned in BitchMedia's timeline of important events in its development (History 2015). This advertisement, featuring the slogan "Pet your bunny" (2002b) acted as a lightning rod that concentrated a set of much longer-standing arguments about the relationship between sex and feminism. Although the editors of *Bitch* ended the debate, these arguments were—and remain—unresolved.

This chapter uses the *Bitch* magazine vibrator controversy as a case study for examining these underlying concerns and assumptions about the relationship between sex and feminism. Primarily, I argue that the vibrator ad controversy is revealing of a preoccupation with *what feminism should look like in public*. The ad presents a sexualized feminist identity that became a source of (dis-)identification for readers (Muñoz 1999). As I will explain, the ad offers an image of a queered feminist sexuality. The most immediate forerunners of this debate within *Bitch* are the feminist sex wars and the so-called lavender menace. The controversy is thus a site that crystallizes a set

FIG. 4 Pet Your Bunny advertisement for Toys in Babeland, *Bitch* (2002).
Photograph by Debra St. John.

of much broader concerns within feminist thought regarding the politics of representation, sex, and publicity. *Bitch* was the site for this argument; the magazine mediated the debate and served as a forum for readers to present their thoughts and feelings about the advertisement.

This chapter analyzes the Pet Your Bunny (PYB) advertisement, in comparison to similar Toys in Babeland ads previously run on the back cover of *Bitch*, to demonstrate the ways in which this particular ad presented an unapologetically queer feminist sexuality that diverged from prior representations of sex and sexuality seen in the magazine. As I will discuss, this version of feminist sexuality both converges with and diverges from the sexual politics of the feminist identities that are presented in other third-wave magazines. The chapter then contextualizes the controversy within the history of the 1980s sex wars and one of their main outcomes, sex-positive feminism. The final section of the chapter turns to the reader responses to both the ad and its location within the magazine. At stake in the vibrator controversy is the question of how feminism represents itself to a broader "unmarked" public (Phelan 1993) that is unsympathetic to feminist concerns and is supportive of only hetero- and homonormative social relations (Berlant and Warner 1998; Puar 2007).

MAGAZINES, ADVERTISING, AND ALTERNATIVE MARKET CULTURES

Advertisements are a crucial element of modern magazines, and they inform the ways in which magazines "read" to consumers. As Sean Latham and Robert Scholes (2006) have argued, advertisements are a key part of what makes periodicals "unique cultural and material objects" (521). Historically, advertising has been one of the defining features of women's magazines, particularly. According to Mary Ellen Zuckerman (1998), early-twentieth-century publications such as *Delineator* (1869–1937) and *McCall's* (1873–2002) were established for the sole purpose of advertising clothing patterns for the Butterick and McCall's companies respectively. Other major women's magazines, such as *Ladies' Home Journal* (1883–) and *Women's Home Companion* (1873–1957), had ongoing relationships with advertisers, offering them free copy. These early relationships set the stage for other magazine publications and continue to influence the magazine industry. The controversial ad on the back cover of *Bitch* is thus integral to, rather than separate from, the magazine text and influences reader perceptions of the publication's feminist politics.

Bitch is a not-for-profit magazine and thus relies less heavily on ad revenue. As I discussed in Chapter One, the magazine is sensitive to the politics of advertising commercial products that might undermine feminist goals. The magazine rejected an advertisement in 2000, shared this decision with readers, and invited them to weigh in on their choice. *Bitch*'s website now moves away from the language of advertising to *sponsorship* "because what we promote is just as important to us as what we don't" (Advertise with *Bitch* 2015). In making its advertising policies and key decisions visible, *Bitch* cultivates transparency and dialogue with its readers—a practice that is clearly evidenced in the magazine's handling of the dildo debacle.

Like other third- and post-wave magazines, *Bitch* cultivates alternative market economies that are engaged with, not outside of, the politics of production and consumption.[1] *Bitch*'s ad space is mainly devoted to advertising other media, such as CDs and zines by independent artists, as well as clothing, crafting, and ecologically sound feminine hygiene products. As a women-owned sex store, Toys in Babeland (now known simply as Babeland) was a fairly typical advertiser in *Bitch* that ran an ad in every issue up until 2007. Babeland's mission statement is "to promote and celebrate sexual vitality by providing an honest, open, and fun environment; encouraging personal empowerment, community education, and support for a more passionate world" (History of Toys in Babeland 2015). The relationships between *Bitch*, its advertisers, and its readers thus foster a mutually beneficial feminist marketplace within the broader sphere of capitalist market culture. The PYB ad controversy put tension on these relationships, demonstrating a limit point of what is capable of being articulated within a commercial environment.

PET YOUR BUNNY: A COMPARATIVE QUEER READING

The advertisement that was the source of so much controversy features a photograph of a model wearing a black leather bodysuit or mini-dress. The buckles on the side of the garment and its shiny, silver built-in underwear suggest it is a kind of fetishwear. In one hand, the model is gripping a dildo, held at crotch level, while the other hand is pulling up the bottom of the leather garment. The image suggests movement and action, as though the model is about to begin pleasuring themself.[2] The figure's hands are veined and contain tension as they grip both the sex toy and the garment with purpose, suggesting sexual arousal. The model faces the camera squarely and exceeds the frame of the advertisement, so that the viewer sees a body pictured from the lower ribcage to the mid-thigh. The imperative phrase "Pet your bunny" accompanies the image. (One part of the sex toy resembles a rabbit.) The company logo for Toys in Babeland and its slogan, "Sex Toys for a Passionate World," appear just below this command.

I argue that the PYB presents a version of queer feminist sexuality. I use the term "queer" in this context not as a synonym or umbrella term for the "alphabet" of GLBTIQ2-S identities (Smith and Jaffer 2012, 7).[3] Rather, I use the term to denote identities, behaviours, practices, etc., that are resistant to hetero- and homonormative structures. I use Lauren Berlant and Michael

Warner's (1998) definition of heteronormativity, which they argue is "the institutions, structures of understanding, and practical orientations that make heterosexuality seem not only coherent—that is, organized as a sexuality—but also privileged" (548). With the intensification of gay and lesbian rights advocacy in the United States and Canada, which are often framed by a politics of respectability (in contrast to radical queer politics), it has become now possible to also speak of homonormativity. Jasbir Puar (2007) argues that homonormativity does not undermine heteronormativity, and may in some ways reinforce it, "and the class, racial, and citizenship privilege" heteronormative subjects require (9). I thus mobilize the word "queer" as an intersectional term that acknowledges the differential capacities of belonging/not-belonging that shape the relationships of individual subjects to dominant culture.[4] In this usage, *queer* retains its sense of *making or being strange* (Smith 1996, 277; Johnson 2001, 1). Because PYB features a model whose gender, race, and sexuality are indeterminate, there is a queerness to the image that is not reducible to sexuality alone.

The combination of signifiers in this ad was unprecedented in *Bitch* magazine. Toys in Babeland advertised in every issue from 2001 to 2007—a total of twenty-two issues—discontinuing its advertising after Issue 35 (2007). Twenty ads ran on the inside back cover of *Bitch*, while two, including PYB, ran on the outer back cover. Since several ads ran more than once during this time period, a total of seventeen different advertisements for Toys in Babeland products ran in *Bitch*. Of these ads, the majority (twelve) did not contain photographic representations of people. Given that Toys in Babeland ads almost exclusively ran on the inner covers of the magazine and that the majority of ads did not contain photographic representations, it is already clear that PYB was an exceptional advertisement for both *Bitch* and the Toys in Babeland. Of the remaining five advertisements that feature images of people, two of these do not show people holding sex toys. Of the remaining three images, one photo is of the fully clothed founders, each holding the same purple rabbit vibrators seen in PYB (Issue 15; Winter 2002), presumably at work and reminiscent of a candid company photo. The two remaining ads are PYB and another ad that features the slogan "I Started My Own Sexual Revolution." A comparative analysis of these two advertisements is further revealing of the queerness of PYB.

The only other advertisement for Toys in Babeland that featured a person holding a sex toy ran on the inside back cover of Issue 21 in the summer of 2003 (Figure 5). In this advertisement, a smiling full-figured Black woman lies on her side in bed holding her Hitachi Magic wand. As mentioned, the image is accompanied by the slogan "I started my own sexual revolution" and a testimonial detailing her journey to sexual self-discovery. The testimonial is temporally framed by a move from youth ("I never masturbated when I was younger") to adulthood, and from sexual doubt ("I was never sure I was having orgasms") to certainty (describing her first orgasm with a vibrator as "definitely the real thing!"). The testimonial is attributed to Thea, a Toys in Babeland customer and, we are to presume, the woman in the picture. Thea masturbates often, she tells the reader, "in celebration of her own sexual revolution." Here, the ad links sexual satisfaction with sexual politics. The advertisement reinforces this connection through a framing narrative that sits alongside Thea's story. In bold lettering, above the Toys in Babeland logo, written copy asserts, "We hear stories like this from our customers everyday." In this sense, Thea's personal narrative is linked with a broader cohort of women, suggesting that Thea's personal sexual uncertainty is part of a wider social phenomenon. Toys in Babeland's identification as a woman-owned store in this written copy further reinforces the connections between feminism, empowerment, and sexual pleasure. The experience of shopping for sex toys is here described as "comfortable and fun," and as part of the journey toward sexual self-discovery. The setting of the photograph, a sunshine-filled bedroom with pink linens and a blanket, reinforces this notion of comfort, as sexual pleasure is associated with privacy, safety, and the domestic space of the home.

This background stands in sharp contrast with the stark blank background of the PYB ad. Unlike the warm domestic space of Thea's bedroom, PYB's background connotes a commercial or studio space, if anything at all. PYB strips away the physical background space of intimacy and comfort. Instead, the stark blank background signals to readers what they are actually looking at: an image produced for commercial purposes. Since "normal" sex acts are usually considered to belong to the private (and noncommercial) realm of intimacy, the PYB ad challenges normative constructions of a healthy sexuality. These normative models are bound up in what Lauren Berlant (1997) calls "sexual citizenship" and are thus linked to ideas of nationalized belonging (80). In contrast to the ad featuring Thea, PYB is not at all invested "protecting the heterosexual privacy zones of 'adult' national culture" (60). In addition to the location of the photograph, the location of the PYB ad itself on the outer back cover of *Bitch* further contributes to the violation of these privacy zones.

The studio space of the PYB ad highlights this particular representation of sex not as intimate and private, but commercial and public. In her famous

FIG. 5 "Thea" advertisement for Toys in Babeland, *Bitch* (2003).
Photograph by Debra St. John.

essay on the politics of sexuality, Gayle Rubin (1984) argues that modern Western societies are permeated with a "hierarchical system of sexual value" (158). According to Rubin, within this system, "sexuality that is 'good,' 'normal,' and 'natural' should ideally be heterosexual, marital, monogamous, reproductive, and non-commercial. It should be coupled, relational, within the same generation, and occur at home. It should not involve pornography, fetish objects, sex toys of any sort, or roles other than male and female. Any sex that violates these rules is 'bad,' 'abnormal,' or 'unnatural'" (152). In every way, PYB violates the characteristics of good, normal, and natural sexuality described in Rubin's hierarchy. The advertisement presents solo rather than marital, coupled, or relational sex. PYB suggests non-reproductive commercial sex that involves sex toys rather than reproductive sex that occurs within the home. While the ad does not involve pornography, the U.S. postal service and some *Bitch* readers suggested that the ad itself was pornography.

Rubin's identification of heterosexuality as constitutive of "good" sexuality is notable for thinking through the queerness of the PYB ad. I have presented versions of this chapter at two separate conferences, and, at each event, during the Q & A period, a different audience member has asserted that the figure in the PYB ad is *obviously* lesbian, citing the clipped thumbnail of the model as *clear evidence*. While the model's clipped thumbnail and very capable-looking hands may suggest lesbianness, the image is not reducible to "a picture of a lesbian," in any kind of simple, straightforward manner. Trimmed fingernails can also represent, for example, a working-class identity, a point to which I return in my discussion of the ways in which negative reader responses to the ad were often coded according to class-based notions of respectability. In this sense, the ad exceeds the conventional categories of lesbian, gay, or straight. One reason PYB resists any easy interpretations is that the ad is cropped so that conventional cultural signifiers of masculinity, femininity, straightness, or lesbianness are not pictured. In this sense, it is less that the model in the PYB ad is not intelligible as heterosexual, but rather that they are not intelligible as having any kind of easily identifiable sexuality.

The queerness of the PYB advertisement is also racialized, since the model is not identifiable as white or of colour in any straightforward way. The hue of their skin suggests a number of possible racial identifications.[5] In his theorizing of racialized sexualities, Patrick Johnson (2001) argues that the notion of *excess* is integral to the construction of *quareness*, specifically Black quare identity: "something that might philosophically translate into an excess of discursive and epistemological meanings grounded in African American cultural rituals and lived experience" (2). While the model in the PYB ad is not recognizably or necessarily Black, Johnson's analysis of how racialized sexualities are defined by a kind of excess resonates with the visual politics of this advertisement. Specifically, the fact of the image being a cropped photograph enhances the indeterminacy of the model's identity. This is not to imply that seeing the model's face, or more of their body, would be somehow revealing of the "truth" of identity. Rather, the absence of many conventional identity signifiers, due to the cropping of the image, increases the effect of indeterminacy. This technique also contributes to the "excess" of the image: the ad gives us a "larger than life" version of feminist sexuality. This effect is enhanced by the medium, photography, which is often perceived as a less mediated (or more "real" or "direct") form of representation.

Cropping photographs of women in advertising is a technique that has long been critiqued by feminist media critics (see Franklin, Lury, and Stacey 1991, 10, 12; Gallagher 2001, 95; van Zoonen 1994, 103) for its objectification of the body. Seen as "cutting up women's bodies," cropping images of women is often interpreted as performing a kind of symbolic violence to women's bodies. To see this style of advertising in a feminist magazine is unusual, to say the least. While there is nothing inherently oppressive about a particular camera angle or technique, it is through the context of the image and its history of previous iterations that meanings are developed. Indeed, it is possible to read the PYB ad as a queer feminist take on the pornographic crotch shot. Given the location of the image on a feminist magazine and the use of appropriation as a tool of third-wave feminism, this advertisement recontextualizes the kind of sexualized imagery traditionally associated with non-feminist advertisers and the mainstream porn industry. As Jacques Derrida (1977) argues, "Every sign, linguistic or non-linguistic ... in a small or large unit, can be *cited*, put between quotation marks; in so doing it can break with every given context, engendering an infinity of new contexts in a manner which is absolutely illimitable" (185). Of course, this new iteration can never be fully "owned"; it will carry with it the history of its past citations. As Judith Butler (1993) argues in her discussion of the reclamation of the word *queer*, "discourse has a history" (227). In this sense, the PYB advertisement is not "oppressive" or "pro-woman" in any kind of straightforward way. The controversy surrounding the ad may thus be attributed *both* to the queerness of the image *and* to its location on the outer back cover.

Only one other advertisement for Toys in Babeland had previously run on the outer back cover of the magazine (Figure 6). This ad ran in Issue 17 (Summer 2002), just one issue prior to the controversial PYB, but did not generate any published letters to the editor. This ad, it seems, raised the eyebrows of neither readers nor the U.S. postal service. Issue 17's advertisement is a visual adaptation of the famous nineteenth-century Japanese woodblock print "The Great Wave off Kanagawa" (*Kanagawa Oki Nami Ura*). In Toys in Babeland's (2002a) reimagining of this iconic image, a curved double-ended glass dildo is superimposed upon the print, riding the great wave that threatens to overcome a canoe-like boat. The image metaphorically signifies sexual pleasure, and the written copy of the advertisement accentuates this point. Accompanied by the slogan "Make a Splash," the written copy encourages readers to "Dive into G-spot pleasure with the Artful Archer Wand" (Toys in Babeland

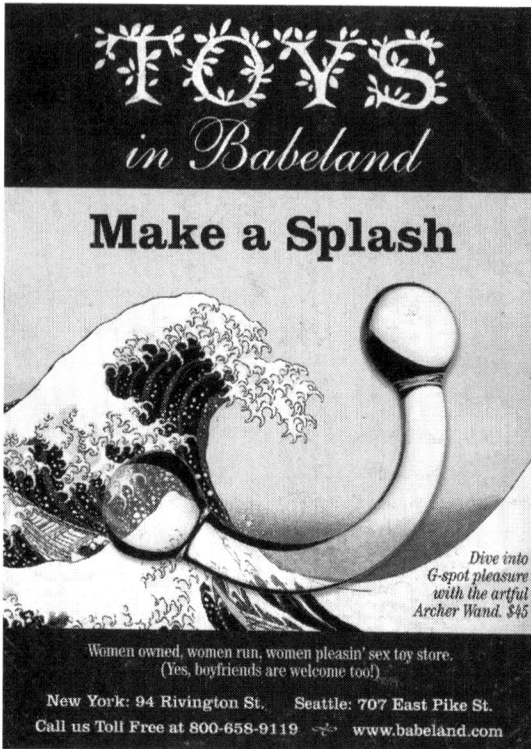

FIG. 6 Make a Splash advertisement for Toys in Babeland, *Bitch* (2002)

2002a). The description of the dildo as *artful* emphasizes the associations between the pleasing visual aesthetics of both toy and art, an association that also invokes discursive codes of respectability, beauty, and value that are usually associated with high art. The ad thus assumes a readership with a certain degree of cultural capital.

Unlike the controversial Pet Your Bunny ad, bodies are absent from this image, and, at first glance, it is not as immediately apparent what is being marketed. It might be easy, for example, to mistake the sex toy for a piece of jewellery. While the PYB ad contains an imperative command, the written copy for "Make a Splash" takes the tone of friendly introductory exploration. Additionally, while one might typically associate a double-ended dildo designed for G-spot stimulation with women who have sex with other women, the written ad copy mentions that "boyfriends are welcome too!" in its description of the Toys in Babeland store. The PYB advertisement contains no such assurances. In fact, while masturbation is stated or implied as the primary activity for which such products would be used, the print copy of both "Make a Splash" and the ad featuring Thea mentions partners, in a way that constructs a normalizing discourse for sex toys as being part of more conventional dyadic partnerships. In PYB, the imperative phrase "Pet your bunny" (a euphemism for masturbation), focuses only on the individual's pleasure and thus leaves open the question of same- or differently-sexed partners, if any. The *your* of the slogan also speaks to readers directly, interpellating them into conversation with the model.[6] As I will discuss, some readers responded to this call with hostility.

The purpose of analyzing the Toys in Babeland advertisement is not to judge whether the ad, and its location on *Bitch*'s back cover, is either "good" or "bad" or either "feminist" or "anti-feminist," for such a reading would assume that images arrive to readers fully formed. Further, as Amy Erdman Farrell (1998) argues, such a reading would assume that "there is one static meaning rather than multiple meanings and perspectives constructed within the text and in relation to the readers and the context" (9). As the letters to *Bitch* editors responding to PYB demonstrate, there were a range of responses to this particular advertisement. What these responses have in common is their engagement with the complex interrelations of feminism, femininity, and sexuality.

READER RESPONSES TO "PET YOUR BUNNY"

Letters to the editor published in *Bitch* represented a range of responses to the PYB advertisement. A total of twelve letters were printed in the magazine in the next three issues. Five letters responded directly to the advertisement; these were printed in Issue 19. In Issues 20 and 21, *Bitch* published five letters responding to and critiquing this initial round of letters, as well as two responses to the editors' decision to change their advertising policy. When examining these letters, three distinct perspectives emerge. The magazine printed one letter that voiced unambiguous approval of the advertisement. Another group of readers found the image offensive. *Bitch* editors published only two of these letters. Rather than devote space to these voices, the editors chose to paraphrase some these responses in their initial editorial response to the controversy in Issue 19, stating that these readers found the image "masculine and dominating" (Jervis and Zeisler 2003, 6). The final group of readers, and the largest, did not find the image offensive per se but raised questions about the visibility of the ad on the magazine's outer cover.

The published letter that represented the perspective of a *Bitch* reader who did not find the ad offensive argued that the ad "celebrates the divine female ownership of feminine pleasure" (Siegal 2003, 6). That this letter appeared in Issue 19, which immediately followed the PYB ad's publication, suggests anticipation of negative responses to the ad and a desire to preemptively frame the ad as a positive representation of feminist sexuality. That is, that the ad would prompt positive commentary at all reveals some form of recognition that the ad would be controversial. For this letter writer, the feminist sexuality of the ad emphasizes agency. The model's gender is also emphasized in this letter: the words "female" and "feminine" appear in the short sentence cited above. In contrast to the negative responses to the ad, which characterized the figure as *masculine*, this letter emphasizes the femininity of the ad. It is indeed possible to read this ad as redefining femininity: as athletic, sexual, and assertive. What interests me here, however, is that both the positive and negative letters about PYB attempt to locate the visual politics of the ad within the gender binary, claiming the image as either *good* based on its representation of femininity or *bad* based on its representation of masculinity. In the former instance, the goodness of the image relies on its *consistency* with the assumption of the model's femaleness, while in the latter instance the badness of the image relies on its *inconsistency* with the model's assumed femaleness. That it seems necessary to define the model's body as masculine or feminine at all is revealing of the indeterminacy of the image.

As mentioned above, *Bitch* editors declined to publish the negative responses to the PYB ad that characterized the image as "masculine and dominating." However, the editors did print one letter that opposed the ad on the basis of its content, rather than its location. In it, *Bitch* reader Heather McGee (2003) characterized PYB as a "low class sex ad" (8). This class-based discourse invokes a kind of respectability politics that sees sexual representations as detracting from the credibility of the movement. Feminism, here, is thus implicitly coded as middle-class and "respectable," in contrast with the vulgar "low-class" sex of queers. McGee asks: "Am I mistaken in my notion that real sex is a good thing? Self-sex is safe; I'll grant that. But self-sex as a lifestyle? Not progressive" (8–9). Here, the letter writer invokes a "hierarchical system of sexual value" wherein coupled (heterosexual) sex is more real—and thus more natural, authentic, healthy, and superior—than solo sex (Rubin 1984, 158). The idea that the PYB ad sells not only a vibrator but a *lifestyle* is resonant with homophobic discourses that seek to construct queerness as contagion, as decadence, and as unseemly. For the letter writer, PYB is not simply an advertisement, but a larger statement about what feminism is and what a feminist looks like.

McGee's (2003) concern with what feminism ought to look like in public infuses the letter. Ads like PYB, she argues, "make feminists seem obsessed with toys and trappings, ignoring men altogether" (8–9). The letter writer's objection to the Toys in Babeland advertisement is rooted in how the ad will *make feminists seem*, which is revealing of the writer's concern with how feminism represents itself to the larger public sphere. The feminist subject who haunts this writer's letter is sexually non-normative, a likely lesbian, disturbingly self-sufficient, and perhaps even mentally unstable (i.e., not interested in toys, but *obsessed*). Enabling her to completely ignore men, the rabbit vibrator perhaps stimulates not only the model's genitals but also a lesbian separatist agenda. Clare Hemmings (2011) has argued that the post-feminist subject of the present is often pitted against a caricatured lesbian separatist figure who is seen as anachronistic, out of place, and masculine, an embarrassing and even shameful reminder of feminism's "past" (8). The good feminist subject is thus implicitly coded here as heteronormative, middle class, and neuronormative. While McGee's concerns about PYB could be easily dismissed as anomalous, they are part of a larger conversation within the pages of *Bitch* at the intersections of feminism, lesbianism, and publicity.

A RABBIT-SHAPED LAVENDER MENACE

Discussions about lesbianism, and its relationship to feminism, are new neither to third-wave magazines nor to feminist print culture more broadly. Indeed, the subject of lesbianism was directly addressed by *Bitch* editors in their editorial in (coincidentally?) the same issue that featured the PYB ad on the outer back cover. Titled "I Thought This Was a Feminist Magazine, Not a Lesbian Magazine," Jervis and Zeisler's (2002) editorial discussed their frustration with the amount of letters they received from readers complaining about an over-representation of "lesbian issues" in the publication. "Just to clear things up," Jervis and Zeisler write, "lesbian issues are feminist issues" (5). Jervis and Zeisler used the editorial to call out these kinds of responses, arguing, "[F]olks who claim that they 'just don't relate' to articles about lesbians and thus don't want to read a magazine that might contain some are exhibiting a kind of closed-mindedness that's almost worse than up-front bigotry" (5). That is, to simply claim disinterest in the subject of lesbianism elides the lesbophobia that codes such responses.

Bitch did not publish full letters from homophobic readers. In their editorial, however, Jervis and Zeisler quote selected passages from these reader responses. One reader, as the editors describe, "saw fit to identify proof of our insidious Sapphic agenda by scribbling 'See? You put this article [focusing on lesbian identity] first!'" next to a description of upcoming articles in the magazine (2003, 6). Similar reader responses are archived in the *Bitch* magazine archives at the Sallie Bingham Center. In one letter, a reader calls for the magazine to "stop hiding in the closet" and acknowledge that it is a magazine "for lesbians." Another letter writer suggests that "*BUTCH*" might be a more apt title for the magazine, adding, "If you are a gay magazine, why don't you admit it and Be [*sic*] what you are instead of including a few heterosexual articles" (Bitch Magazine Records 2003). For these readers, the inclusion of content about or related to lesbians and queer cultures rendered the entire magazine *lesbian*. The metaphor of the closet is a common theme in all these letters, suggesting that the problem lies not in the letter writers' own lesbophobia, but in the magazine's gay shame and refusal to "come out." These examples, coupled with Jervis and Zeisler's editorial, reveal a wider perception among some of *Bitch*'s readership that lesbians and feminists are, or should be, mutually exclusive groups, and that concerns specific to lesbians are not of interest or relevance to heterosexual feminists. The discourse of coming out, like McGee's letter, also demonstrates a preoccupation with how *Bitch*, and feminism more broadly, represents itself to a larger public made up of both feminist and non-feminist folks.

Reader concerns about the association between feminism and lesbianism have been less visible within third-wave publications *BUST* (1993–) and *Venus Zine* (1994–2010). However, both of these magazines construct their readers as primarily heterosexual, with little representation of queer sexualities. For example, in an inversion of the Sunshine Girl glamour shot, *BUST* features a "boy du jour" in every issue, while *Venus Zine* contained a similar profile of a man in every issue in a department called "Penus." *BUST* also contains a "one-handed read" at the end of every issue. The climax of (and for the female characters in) these erotic short stories is almost always heterosexual, penetrative sex. The version of sex-positive feminism espoused in *BUST*, particularly, is thus heteronormative, standing in marked contrast with *Bitch*'s attempt to represent diverse sexualities. Nonetheless, the perception that feminist magazines exist solely for lesbian readers was not isolated to *Bitch* alone.

Like *Bitch*, the third-wave publication *ROCKRGRL* (1995–2005) also dealt with claims that the magazine was first and foremost a lesbian magazine. In an editorial, editor Carla DeSantis (1995) spoke to this perception arguing that "the lesbian contingent is a very large and critical part of *ROCKRGRL*'s audience, [but] it is not by any means the only audience, nor the only voice echoed within these pages" (2). That editors need to speak to these concerns at all are revealing of the homophobia that codes some reader responses to magazines that include lesbian representation. These concerns about lesbianism are sadly part of feminism's long history.

In 1969, Betty Friedan, then president of the National Organization of Women (NOW), referred to the participation of lesbians in NOW as a "lavender menace" that threatened the credibility of the organization and would taint the broader public's perception of feminism. A group of lesbian feminists who were members of NOW (and some who weren't) staged a creative intervention into this troubling aspect of the organization's politics at the 1970 Second Congress to Unite Women in New York City. Calling themselves the Lavender Menace, members of this group disrupted the conference first by turning off the lights. As Lavender Menace member Karla Jay (2010) recounts, when the lights came back on, the audience found themselves surrounded by women all wearing T-shirts that said "lavender menace." The women took to the stage and demanded that lesbians and lesbian issues be seen as central to NOW. This legendary action by the Lavender Menace did not eradicate lesbophobia from the women's movement, however, and feminist magazines in the 1970s and beyond have continued to struggle with readers who reject lesbians within the movement.[7]

The challenges third-wave magazines have faced regarding the representation of lesbians and lesbian issues resonate with their historical precursors. For example, in 1979, the editors of *Chrysalis: A Magazine of Women's Culture* (1977–80) wrote in an editorial statement that is quite similar to *Bitch*'s editorial statement twenty-five years later: "When lesbianism comes up in *Chrysalis*, in whatever way, letters come in saying 'Cancel my subscription; I'm not one of them.' Sadly, this issue continues to divide us from each other and from our selves on the deepest level" (quoted in Johnson 1996, 61). The editorial response within *Chrysalis* highlights the broader tensions within the women's movement concerning lesbianism, and it also demonstrates the publication's commitment to presenting content that represented a spectrum of lived experience. Given that most feminist magazines have subsisted primarily on subscription revenue, maintaining readership levels was—and is—a crucial factor in continuing publication. This relationship between readers and text becomes complicated when the representational commitments of feminist magazines are put into conflict with the politics of some readers.

These responses to the representation of lesbian and queer issues can be traced back to the turn of the last century. In the 1890s, the "New Woman" figure was often denigrated in popular publications, such as *Punch*, as being too mannish, a stereotype that was partially based on the New Woman's public-ness. That is, among other activities, such as riding bicycles, the New

Woman dared to speak at public events, a domain traditionally gendered as masculine and the province of men. The association between the so-called mannish woman and lesbianism became entwined with the publication of Radcliffe Hall's novel *The Well of Loneliness* in 1929, a fictionalized account of the life of a "female invert." The media coverage of the novel's obscenity trial focused on Hall's self-presentation as a masculine woman. As Joanne Winning (2002) argues, "Hall herself became a cultural signifier, mapping signifiers of class, dress and corporeal appearance on to the previously invisible category of 'the lesbian'" in a manner that is similar to the ways in which Oscar Wilde's trial for sodomy in the 1890s bound together the disparate signifiers of decadence and sodomy (378). In this sense, the letters to the editors of *Bitch* that called the advertisement "masculine and dominating" are bound up in and resonate with this much longer history of relationships between masculinity, femininity, publicity, and feminism. What these examples seem to have in common is that they are each concerned with lesbianism's perceived capacity to taint the feminist movement and how that movement represents itself to a broader public.

SEX ON THE SUBWAY; OR, WHEN FEMINISTS READ IN PUBLIC

The bulk of the letters to the editor responding to PYB were centrally concerned with the location of the advertisement on the outer back cover of the magazine. In Issue 19, the first published after the Pet Your Bunny advertisement, four of the five published letters were centrally concerned with the location of the ad. While these readers had a range of positions on the ad itself, all expressed their unease with the potential for children or teenagers to inadvertently see the image. One reader detailed her process of thinking through her feelings toward the ad: "[W]hat do I say if 6-year-old Daisy sees this? I found myself turning the magazine face up in case she came across it. Wait a second. What kind of sex-positive mother am I? If she asks, I'll just tell her it's an ad for things people like to masturbate with" (Canaan 2003, 6). Although this particular reader ultimately decided that the advertisement was acceptable for her daughter to see, another letter writer came to a different conclusion: "I have a teenager who does not need this exposure" (Schafer 2003, 6). In her writing on U.S. citizenship, Lauren Berlant (1997) argues it is through the figure of the little girl (real or imagined) "that state and federal governments have long policed morality around sex and other transgressive representations" dating back to the 1873 Comstock Law against obscenity (58–59). Like U.S. obscenity law, the little (white) girl codes these letters to the editor as a figure of innocence. Responses to the ad's presence on the outer back cover clearly varied among readers, with at least one reader opting to take the ad as a potential educational opportunity and another choosing to threaten subscription cancellation. What these responses have in common, however, is their consciousness of the ways in which the magazine's outer cover has a publicity that makes the text accessible to a wider audience than the intended reader.

The outer cover of a magazine shows, literally, its public face. Magazines are texts with social lives: people leave them lying around their houses; they are read on the subway; they exist in public spaces. This important element of publicity is highlighted in Laura Crickett's (2003) letter, published in Issue 19. In it, Crickett wrote of her qualms about displaying the advertisement on public transit:

> With the current vibrator/dildo life-size and in color on the back page, I don't feel comfortable reading the magazine in public. I usually enjoy reading it on the sub-way or bus; however, there are several schools on the route that I take between work and home. Because of this ad, I don't feel that this issue would be appropriate reading for a bus crowded with children. I'm disappointed that I'll have to save *Bitch* for reading at home and read something else on my commute. (6)

Echoing the concerns of the other letter writers regarding the potential inadvertent exposure of children to PYB, this letter also highlights a limit point of what is capable of being articulated within public spaces, as well as the intimacy of those spaces.

Despite the ways in which intimacy and sexuality are considered part of the realm of privacy, Berlant (2000) argues, "collective scenes [are also] intimate spaces" (8). The public space of the bus thus represents a potential site of connection, of intimacy. However, these spaces are not hospitable to any form of expression. In general, public spaces are hostile to the articulation of non-normative sexualities; the very fact that the letter writer to *Bitch* is uncomfortable reading Issue 18 on the bus indicates the heteronormative climate of this public space. In "Sex in Public," Berlant and Michael Warner (1998) discuss recent political reforms and amendments in the United States that perpetuate socially conservative family values and develop an increasingly privatized "hegemonic national public around sex" (314). Berlant and Warner assert, "[B]ecause this sex public claims to act only in order to protect the zone of heterosexual privacy, the institutions of economic privilege and social reproduction informing its practices and organizing its ideal world are protected by the demonization of any represented sex" (314). The *Bitch* reader's concern about displaying the Toys in Babeland advertisement on the bus should be read in the context of this broader political climate.

While commonly associated with domestic spaces, reading is an act that also occurs in public. In his history of reading practices in antebellum New York, David Henkin (1998) asserts that "acts of reading may have been silent and functional, but to call them private is to ignore the way they function on the stage of public life" an observation that troubles any easy distinctions between "public" and "private" acts (7). Henkin's use of the word "stage" in describing public life is particularly apt, since it alludes to the ways in which reading in public can function as part of an identity performance. Although the relationship between reader and text may be an intimate one, it is not necessarily private. Reading in public can announce to others the reader's likes, dislikes, literacy level, political and ideological commitments, and so on. Thus, the reading of *Bitch* in public may be interpreted as an expression of feminist politics. Hence, in a realm that is typically hostile to feminism, reading in public spaces can be a form of activism. What PYB demonstrates, however, is that there are limits on the kinds of feminism that may be articulated within certain public spaces.

It is not simply that the space of public transit is coded as heteronormative, however. If that were the case, would not the Babeland ads featuring Thea or the *artful* archer wand have produced similar letters to the editor? According to Puar (2002), "[W]hile it is predictable that the claiming of queer space is lauded as the disruption of heterosexual space, rarely is this disruption seen as a disruption of racialized, gendered, and classed spaces, nor is it seen in tandem with a claiming of class, gender, and racial privilege as well" (112). Puar's argument raises provocative questions about who can claim queer space, and in what ways (see also Cohen 2005). It also encourages a reading of the PYB ad's disruptiveness as a product of both its excess and its indeterminacy. It seems that a Black woman in bed holding a non-penetrative sex toy or a large, but stylized, double-ended dildo do not produce the same unease with regard to public display. Rather, the ambiguously gendered, raced, and classed figure that wears fetish-wear is the *sine qua non* of obscenity.

At the heart of the PYB ad controversy are larger questions concerning publicity, excess, and indeterminacy. It is notable that the PYB ad ran a second time in *Bitch* magazine, this time in the Summer 2004 issue, and this time on the inside of the back cover. In this iteration of the advertisement, the frame of the photograph is enlarged. While the model's head is still cropped from the photograph, more of their body is visible, and their body literally takes up less space in the advertisement. As a result, the vibrator is also less "present" in the image. Perhaps by design, or perhaps by effect of the photographic enlargement, the skin of the model is also noticeably lighter. The ad did not solicit any printed letters to the editor.

THE SEX WARS

The publication of the PYB ad on *Bitch*'s outer cover solicited not only letters from readers, but a letter from the U.S. postal service (USPS), which viewed the back cover as potentially in violation of federal obscenity laws, which prohibit the distribution of "obscene, lewd, lascivious ... filthy, vile, or indecent" material by mail (USPS, quoted in Jervis and Zeisler, 2003, 6). USPS ordered *Bitch* to conceal its magazine in an opaque wrapper or envelope, should the publication wish to continue placing such ads on the outer back cover of its publication, in order to remain compliant with the law. In this instance, the ability of *Bitch* to print controversial visual materials was curtailed by the threat of losing distribution by USPS or the potential additional expense of packaging the magazine in an opaque envelope, not to mention the cancelled subscriptions of readers who did not approve of the advertisement and/or the placement of sex-related ads. In light of these combined pressures, it is not surprising that *Bitch* adapted its advertising policy.

Issue 20 primarily contained letters that responded to *Bitch*'s policy change. One reader called the decision "a Christian-right response" (Spivey 2004, 89). In framing *Bitch*'s policy change as an act of censorship, this letter recalls a set of earlier debates between feminists on pornography, which were particularly intense during the 1980s. These discussions produced a curious alignment between anti-pornography feminist and morally conservative positions, which both sought censorship of sexually explicit materials. These feminist arguments about pornography are part of a larger set of debates known as the sex wars, which were centrally concerned with the political implications of sexual practices, such as BDSM, pornography, and group sex.

One of the major flashpoints in the sex wars was the 1982 Barnard Conference on Women and Sexuality, an event that, like the PYB ad controversy, crystallized around a set of concerns regarding feminism's relationship to S/M and sexually explicit (e.g., pornographic) media representations. The ninth in a series called "The Feminist and the Scholar," the 1982 Barnard conference focused on the theme "pleasure and danger." Anti-pornography feminists were angered by their exclusion from the conference planning committee. They protested the event by distributing leaflets that profiled certain speakers based on their assumed sexual practices. As Lisa Duggan and Nan Hunter (1995) recount, members of Women Against Pornography (WAP) protested the Barnard conference by wearing T-shirts that said "For Feminist Sexuality" on the front and "Against S/M" on the back (24). These slogans attempt to counter the assumption that anti-pornography feminists were anti-sex; however, they also work to police what should and should not count as "good" feminist sexuality. Indeed, the slogans imply that feminism and S/M should be seen as mutually exclusive. According to Andrew McBride (2008), the Barnard Conference served to "harden the battle lines that had been drawn by each side during the Sex Wars," perhaps due particularly to the targeted, personalized nature of WAP's protest. The conference proved so controversial and divisive that the series lost its funding and was discontinued.

Following the conference, debate raged on for months in the pages of feminist periodicals, like *off our backs* (*oob*) and *Feminist Studies*, providing a forum for a discussion of the conference and its broader implications.[8] The lesbian porn magazine *On Our Backs* was launched in 1984; its title responded to what some felt was biased coverage in *oob* favouring the perspectives of WAP (Latham 2015, 231). That the bulk of these debates took place within magazines is indicative of the ways in which periodicals have played a vital role in shaping the terms of feminist discourse. In assessing the role of print culture in the feminist sex wars, Kathleen Martindale (1997) argues that "this highly cerebral and ironically disembodied struggle set the terms and agenda for contemporary feminist and lesbian discourses on sexuality and representation" (7). Indeed, one of the major consequences of the sex wars was the emergence of what is now known as sex-positive feminism.

The PYB advertisement references sexual practices that were particularly controversial during the 1980s sex wars; that is, the model's leather outfit and its buckles have an association with S/M. Additionally, the politics of dildo usage among lesbians was also a point of some debate in the 1980s. In her essay "Lesbianism: A Country That Has No Language," Mariana Valverde (1985) takes up representations of lesbianism intended for a heterosexual male audience, and she makes reference to one story appearing in *Penthouse* involving two women and a double-headed dildo. While she argues persuasively that this particular scene perpetuates a male-centred fantasy that women cannot live without the phallus, the extrapolations that Valverde makes from this analysis are indicative of the kinds of tensions surrounding the place of sex within lesbian feminist cultures. She assures the reader that dildos "are virtually unknown among lesbians, though vibrators are certainly becoming popular" (98). Although I do not know whether this claim is an accurate one within the context of the 1980s (and the author does not provide any evidence to support it), one of the implications of Valverde's argument is that "real" lesbians don't use dildos. She concludes, "Lesbianism is thus robbed of its radical potential because it is portrayed as compatible with heterosexuality, or rather as part of heterosexuality itself.... It is autonomy and self-determination, not kinky sex, which characterizes our growing lesbian culture" (99). Here, there seems to be a conflation of penetration with heterosexuality; further, Valverde's argument is quite dismissive of the role of sex (kinky sex, specifically) within lesbian publics. At stake in these older debates were people's credentials as both "good feminists" and "good lesbians" if they admitted to enjoying practices that were considered by others to be associated with violence, heterosexuality, and/or masculinity.

These discussions resonate through the various reader responses to the Toys in Babeland advertisement, particularly from those readers who called the ad "masculine" and "dominating." The debate over the sex toy ad in *Bitch* can thus be read as one of the latest skirmishes of the sex wars, demonstrating that feminism does not operate in the linear, discreetly bounded ways suggested by the first-, second- and third-wave categories used in conventional histories of feminist movements. Rather, the sex wars debates are more diffuse, flaring up in often unexpected places. The dispute among readers and editors over the politics of sex toy advertisements in a feminist popular print publication and, indeed, the sex wars as a whole, may seem like rather insignificant infighting among a relatively small group of participants. However, like Martindale (1997), I read the sex wars, and this debate in *Bitch* magazine, as an iteration of a much larger and often divisive battle among feminists over the politics of sex and sexuality (8). The sex toy ad and its ensuing controversy serve as rupture points through which these "forgotten" tensions resurface.[9]

CONCLUSION

The Pet Your Bunny advertisement presents a photographic version of feminist sexuality in which the female subject is active, in control, self-sufficient, and seeking pleasure on her own terms. Moreover, the Toys in Babeland ad constructs a subject position for the Bitch reader as one who unapologetically enjoys leather and sex toys. Clearly, not all readers were willing to embrace this form of feminist subjectivity. As Lynne Pearce (1997) argues,

> an interpretive community does not represent a set of fixed, and shared values, values with which the reader mindlessly agrees, or to whom s/he defers. Rather,

it should be thought of as its own site of struggle: a group whose "position" is constantly being renegotiated and re-legitimated by its constituent members. (212)

The *Bitch* vibrator controversy highlights the diversity of its reading community and is evidence of the ways in which print culture has provided a crucial site for hashing out feminist positions on both the politics of sexuality and the politics of visibility. In this sense, the print Letters to the Editor section of *Bitch* anticipates, or perhaps helped engender, the vibrant and dynamic debates within feminist communities online.

The Toys in Babeland controversy was not an isolated incident. While feminist perspectives on sexuality have shifted, reader responses to the PYB ad recall earlier moments within feminism, such as the sex wars and the Lavender Menace intervention. The similar concerns within these moments, about "acceptable" and "unacceptable" articulations of feminist sexualities, are linked with larger questions about what feminism ought to look like in public. Thinking about how class-based discourses shaped the PYB controversy, or its preoccupation with what feminisms ought to look like in public, gives us insight into how the idea of a "Lavender Menace" in NOW or sex war-era debates about feminists who like S/M and porn might also have been classed and related to a kind of feminist respectability politics.

In light of not only negative letters to the editor, but a letter alleging distribution of obscene material by the U.S. postal service, the PYB advertisement's location on the outer back cover of *Bitch* highlights a limit point for the forms of sexuality that are capable of being articulated within the public sphere. While the PYB ad highlights *Bitch*'s engaged community of readers, a community that is enabled by *Bitch*'s dissemination within the literary marketplace, the ad also highlights the ways in which this marketplace constrains the forms of feminism that may be articulated on the pages of the publication. These material conditions challenge the ability of publications to present queer images of feminist sexualities. This finding has consequences for both feminist publications and other oppositional texts that wish to enter the commercial realm. Amy Erdman Farrell (1998) argues, "In late-twentieth century culture, the realm of popular culture—of commercial culture—is the most powerful arena in which ideas are circulated. To abdicate this space means that feminists will not have access to this important terrain" (197). While I agree with Farrell, I think it is also important to amplify the cultural production of feminists whose work may sit less easily within the framework of capitalist production and consumption.

CONCLUSION

In the early and mid-1990s, third-wave zines and magazines began appearing in mailboxes and feminist independent bookstores across the United States and Canada, filling the hands of eager readers excited to tap into larger feminist conversations on fashion, domesticity, identity, sexuality, and more. Now, in the mid-2010s, most feminist bookstores have closed their doors, due in large part to the ascendancy of online bookseller Amazon and ebooks. In a related vein, feminists are increasingly finding reading communities online. Dynamic discussions on the politics of contemporary feminism are found on a range of online media platforms. On Twitter, we see feminist hashtag activism, such as #SolidarityIsForWhiteWomen, which calls out white feminism for its blindness to privilege. On Tumblr, discussions of Gloría Anzaldúa and Cherríe Moraga's *This Bridge Called My Back: Radical Writings by Women of Color* have contributed to its republication, after having been out of print for decades (Nakamura 2015). Blogging platforms like Wordpress enable feminist blogs like Crunk Feminist Collective and Black Girl Dangerous to publish insightful Black feminist critique. On YouTube, Anita Sarkeesian skewers gendered tropes in video games, while Laci Green offers sex-positive advice on sex and sexuality. BUST and *Bitch*—the only magazines in the original cohort of third-wave publications in this study still publishing—now exist as magazines that offer both print and online subscriptions, as well as free blog content. Post-wave magazines, like GUTS, *Rookie*, and *Shameless*, exist as either entirely online publications or, like BUST and *Bitch*, are hybrids. Clearly, there has been a major shift from print to digital culture over the course of the last two decades, and feminist media has been part of that change.

Making Feminist Media has sought to imagine new and more complex ways to think about feminism. Specifically, this book has been concerned with how we write about feminist histories, the politics of feminism in the

1990s and early 2000s, and how print culture has helped sustain feminist communities. Each case study has shown that feminism does not work in a linear progressive fashion. Third-wave magazines, like their forerunners, play a crucial role in defining, developing, and shaping the discursive and material contours of feminism. Despite their frequent appeals to the "new," as I have argued, third-wave magazines are very much in conversation with the past and have interesting historical resonances with their forerunners. It behooves feminists to look for the commonalities as well as the differences across both generational and political boundaries, and to not sell their own histories short for the sake of expediency or an easy narrative.

This insight is clearly indebted to Clare Hemmings's (2011) examination of the narratives of progress, loss, and return that structure feminist theory. This book applies Hemmings's analysis to the realm of feminist independent publishing. As the case studies demonstrate, it is simply not the case that feminism "learns its lessons" and then moves on, better and stronger than ever. Rather, it might be more accurate to assert that feminism, what it is and who it includes and excludes, is highly contested through these magazines. Feminism is an unstable and dynamic force. Rather than reify what feminism is, third-wave magazines and their readers are often involved in challenging accepted notions of what feminism is or should be. These ideas do not supersede the past, as a progress narrative might imply, but rather are often in conversation or negotiation with that past.

This book also complicates feminist narratives of loss. Specifically, the case studies in this book demonstrate that the move from zines to more widely circulating magazines has not resulted in a simplistic loss of a publication's critical edge. Rather, it might be more accurate to say that the marketplace is more amenable to certain forms of feminism than others, and that feminist publications that were able to sustain themselves in the for-profit sphere were more amenable to capitalism from the start. A second loss narrative this book complicates is the move away from print and toward online media. Although it is undeniable that there has been massive growth in online media, print publication remains a valued and attractive medium for many feminists. It is how these print publications come to signify differently in an age of online media that is worth noting. A zine in 1990s signifies differently from a zine made in 2015. To see the move from print to online formats as a loss also fails to recognize the ways that feminist print and online media often feed into each other. One of the most straightforward extensions of this book would be to explore further these reciprocal relationships between print and online media. A second might be to examine the ways in which online communities are similar to or different from the kinds of feminist cultures we see in print publications.

This book has brought together discourse analysis, interviews with editors, and archival research. While *Making Feminist Media* pays attention to reader responses to third-wave magazines, an extension of this work would be to conduct interviews with readers. Letters to the editor give us some sense of readership, but they cannot account for readers who did not write in or whose letters were not published. This kind of work could help make further sense of the affects of readership, as well as the shift from print to online media.

These magazines hold an important place in the lives of many feminists. Indeed, my own initial interactions with them were not as an academic, but as a fan and avid reader of their sharp-witted and sarcastic feminist critique. Despite my ultimate support for, and enjoyment of, these magazines, it's important and worthwhile to ask questions about the limit points of these popular print publications. As this book has shown, third-wave magazines that stand outside of the narrowly defined niche of "lifestyle publications for straight white hipster girls" tend to have a difficult time garnering the financial support of advertisers and publishers. These limits tell us as much about the magazines as they do about the climate of the popular print marketplace and contemporary U.S. and Canadian culture. For example, *Bitch*, which has published non-normative, queer images of feminist sexualities, has had its livelihood threatened not only by cancelled subscriptions, but by the U.S. postal service. While it might be easy to dismiss these publications out of hand because of their perceived appeal to a relatively narrow demographic, they do play a vital role in shaping feminist practice, establishing a forum for debating feminist politics, and even providing a lifeline for readers who need a feminist friend.

PUBLICATION HISTORIES OF THIRD-WAVE MAGAZINES

BITCH (1996-)

Periodical Title and Title Changes: *Bitch: Feminist Response to Popular Culture* (1996-)

Volume and Issue Data: Vols. 1.1–3.3; 10–. Tri-annually (1996–98); Bi-annually (1999–2000); Quarterly (2001–8); Summer 2009 issue cancelled; Quarterly (2009–)

Founders: Lisa Jervis, Andi Zeisler, and Ben Shaykin

Publishing Companies: Amazon Girl Publishing (1996); Bitch Publications (1996–2000); B-Word Worldwide (2001–2009); Bitch Media (2010–)

Publisher: Lisa Jervis (1996–2005); Debbie Rasmussen (2006–9); Julie Falk (executive director) (2009–)

Place of Publication: Oakland, California (1996–2007); Portland, Oregon (2007–)

Editors: Lisa Jervis and Andi Zeisler (1996–2001); Lisa Jervis, Andi Zeisler, and Rachel Fudge (2001–2); Andi Zeisler and Rachel Fudge (2002–7); Andi Zeisler and Miriam Wolf (2007–8); Andi Zeisler (2009–); Kjerstin Johnson, editor in chief (2011–)

Circulation: 6,000–7,000 (1998); 8,000–10,000 (1999); 37,000–40,000 (2001, based on estimate requests to printers in *Bitch* magazine archives); 80,000 (2014, self-reported online)

BUST (1993-)

Periodical Title and Title Changes: *BUST* (1993–99); *BUST: The Voice of the New Girl Order* (1999); *BUST: For Women with Something to Get Off Their Chests* (2000–)

Volume and Issue Data: Vols. 1.1–1.4; 5–. Bi-annually (1993–99); Tri-annually (2000–1); Winter 2001 issue cancelled; Quarterly (2002 5); Bi monthly (2005–)

Publishing Companies: BUST Magazine (1993–96); BUST Magazine Enterprises (1996–2000); The BUST Company, Inc., A Division of Razorfish Studios (2000–1); BUST, Inc. (2002–)

Publishers: Betty Boob [Marcelle Karp] and Celina Hex [Debbie Stoller] (1996–2002); Laurie Henzel and Debbie Stoller (2002–)

Place of Publication: New York City

Founders: Debbie Stoller and Marcelle Karp

Editors: Celina Hex [Debbie Stoller] and Betty Boob [Marcelle Karp], (1993–2001); Debbie Stoller (2001–)
Circulation: 6,000 copies printed in 1995; 7,000, self-reported in 1997; 32,000, self-reported in 1999; 81,000, self-reported in 2007; 90,000, reported in 2014

HUES (1992–99)

Periodical Title and Title Changes: HUES: *Hear Us Emerging Sisters* (1992–99)
Volume and Issue Data: Issues 1–4; Vols. 1.5– . Sporadic (1992–95); Bi-annually (1995–99)
Publishing Companies: Self-Published (1992–94); HUES, Inc. (1995–1996); New Moon (1997–99)
Publisher: Ophira Edut, Tali Edut, and Dyann Logwood
Place of Publication: Ann Arbor, Michigan (1992–97); Duluth, Minnesota (1997–99)
Founders: Tali Edut, Ophira Edut, and Dyann Logwood
Editors: Dyann Logwood, Tali Edut, and Ophira Edut (1992–95); Tali Edut (1995–97)
Circulation: Largest print run 40,000 copies

ROCKRGRL (1995–2005)

Periodical Title and Title Changes: ROCKRGRL (1995); ROCKRGRL: *For Women in the Music Business* (1995–96); ROCKRGRL: *Information and Inspiration for Women in the Music Business* (1996); ROCKRGRL (1997); ROCKRGRL: *No Beauty Tips or Guilt Trips* (1997–2001); ROCKRGRL (2001–3); ROCKRGRL: *Supporting a Woman's Right to Rock* (2003–5)
Volume and Issue Data: Vols. 1.1–2.2; 9–57. Bi-monthly (1995–2001); Tri-annually (2002); Quarterly (2003–4); Bi-monthly (2005)
Publishing Company: ROCKRGRL (1996–2005)
Publisher: Carla DeSantis (1995–2005)
Place of Publication: San Mateo, California (1995–96); Mercer Island, Washington (1996–2005); Seattle, Washington (2005)
Editor: Carla DeSantis

SHAMELESS (2004–)

Periodical Title and Title Changes: *Shameless: For Girls Who Get It* (2004–2010); *Shameless : Talking Back since 2004* (2011–)
Volume and Issue Data: Issues 1–12. Bi-annually (2004); Tri-annually (2005–2006); Bi-annually (2007–2008); Tri-annually (2009–)
Publisher: Nicole Cohen and Melina Mattos (2001–2007); Stacey May Fowles (2007–2010); Nicole Cohen (Winter 2010); Nicole Cohen and Jo Snyder (2011–2014); Julia Horel (2014–)
Place of Publication: Toronto, Ontario
Founders: Nicole Cohen and Melinda Mattos

Editors: Nicole Cohen and Melinda Mattos (2001–2007); Megan Griffith-Greene (2007–2010); Sheila Sampath (2010-)
Circulation: Unknown

VENUS ZINE (1994–2010)

Periodical Title and Title Changes: *Venus* (1994–); *Venus Zine* (2006–2007); *Venus Zine: Emerging Creativity* (2007–)
Volume and Issue Data: Vols. 1–. Sporadic (1996–2000); Quarterly (2000–10)
Publisher: Amy Schroeder (1996–2006); Anne Brindle and Marci Sepulveda (2006–10); Sarah Beardsley (2010)
Place of Publication: East Lansing, Michigan (1996–2000); Self-published, Valejo, California (2000–4); Chicago, Illinois (2005–)
Publishing Company: Self-published (1996–2006); Venus Media LLC (2006–)
Founder: Amy Schroeder
Editor: Amy Schroeder (1996–2008); K. Tighe (2008–10); Jill Russell (2010)
Circulation: 60,000, self-reported in 2007; 60,000, reported in 2010.

NOTES

INTRODUCTION

1. For analyses of zines made by girls and women, see Bleyer (2004), Freedman (2009), Harris (2003), Kearney (2006), Leonard (1998), Piepmeier (2009), Radway (2001), Schilt (2003), Sinor (2003), and Zobl (2009). For further readings on zine culture, generally, see Duncombe (1997) and Todd and Watson (2006).

2. My claims about the importance of print culture's materiality is indebted to Alison Piepmeier's (2009) study of girl zine cultures, particularly her argument that zines help instigate *embodied* communities (58).

3. Likewise, in her analysis of mainstream print media coverage of third-wave feminism, Carolyn Bronstein (2005) found that "positive portrayal of third wave feminism was frequently accomplished through negative comparison to the second wave" (790).

4. In the early years of *BUST* magazine, co-founders Debbie Stoller and Marcelle Karp wrote under the names of Celina Hex and Betty Boob. I reference these articles with the names the authors used in the original publication. For example, work that Debbie Stoller published as Celina Hex may be found referenced under "Hex" rather than "Stoller."

5. Marital rape was not outlawed in all fifty U.S. states until 1993 and there are still differences in how marital and non-marital rape is treated under some state laws.

6. Similarly, in the period between the first and second waves of U.S. feminism, we see the continuation or development of women's rights advocacy, with some feminists actively working within pacifist, communist, and anarchist movements. Feminist periodicals that began or continued to publish during the "inter-wave" period included Margaret Sanger's *Birth Control Review* (1917–1939), which raised awareness of the injustice of the birth control laws; a newsletter called *Equal Rights* (1923–1953) that advocated an equal rights amendment (ERA) in the United States and was published by the National Woman's Party (NWP); *National Business Woman*, the official voice of the federation that is now called Business and Professional Women/USA, which began publication in 1919 and continued to publish in the 1990s; and *Toveritar [Comradess]*, a small-scale, Finnish-language

socialist women's paper founded by Selma Jokela McCone, Maiji Nurmi, and Helmi Mattson, which was published from 1911 into the 1980s and, according to Mari-Jo Buhle (1983), advocated woman suffrage, temperance, and the well-being and education of children (110). When feminist histories are confined to the wave model, the contributions of these periodicals may be neglected.

7. Indeed, there are also few comprehensive studies of second-wave feminist print culture. The works of Flannery (2005), Endres and Lueck (1996), and Chambers, Steiner, and Fleming (2004) are important contributions to this field.

CHAPTER 1

1. For a full account of the history of *Sassy*, see Kara Jesella and Marisa Meltzer's (2007) *How Sassy Changed My Life.*

2. *BUST* highlighted *Sassy* once again in 2004, when the publication ran an article on the demise of the magazine (Simms).

3. Amy Adele Hasinoff's (2015) analysis of sexting discourses provides a more recent example of the ways that girls are positioned as victims of their own sexuality.

4. For a full account of Tali Edut's experience at *Sassy* and her role in the making of *HUES*, see Edut (1997).

5. For book-length histories of Riot Grrrl, see Marcus (2010) and Monem (2007). For collections of Riot Grrrl essays and art from the 1990s, see Darms (2013). For historiographic critiques of Riot Grrrl histories, see Eichhorn (2013) and Nguyen (2012).

6. The reclamation of derogatory language was not unique to third-wave feminism, however. Take, for instance, the name of the first feminist press in the United States, *Shameless Hussy*, established in 1969 or Joreen Freeman's "Bitch Manifesto" (1969).

CHAPTER 2

1. There are also, of course, significant contextual differences among feminist periodicals from different years and from different places. For studies of early periodical cultures, see Lorinda B. Cohoon (2006); Delap and DiCenzo (2008); Mott (1970); Russo and Kramarae (1991).

2. It also forecloses more complex accounts of continuities between "feminist" magazines and "women's" magazines, when the latter is constructed as irredeemably apolitical.

3. Third-wave publications maintain subscription rates in the tens of thousands.

4. Similarly, *The Una*, a mid-nineteenth-century women's rights periodical, folded shortly after the national suffrage association rejected a proposal that the periodical be adopted as the organization's official organ.

5. As Olympia Willis asserted in her 1917 biography of *The Woman's Tribune* editor Clara Bewick Colby, "Undoubtedly this very versatility and variety unfitted the *Tribune* to be an organ of the National-American Association [*sic*] while it made

it a most interesting and profitable family paper in which Woman's Suffrage [*sic*] was commended to many by the very fact that it was made interesting by being associated with other subjects" (quoted in Endres 1996e, 483).

6. Margaret Finnegan (1999) provides a detailed and insightful analysis of the tensions between Blackwell and the NAWSA in *Selling Suffrage* (153–57).

7. See also Collins's (1993) "Toward a New Vision: Race, Class, and Gender as Categories of Analysis and Connection" (240–57).

8. In calculating the number and percentage of advertisements, I did not include the publications' own appeals for subscriptions or advertisements to purchase back issues of their magazine (which appear in both ROCKRGRL and *Bitch* but not in BUST). I did include the publications' own advertisements to shop at their online stores for T-shirts, mugs, and the like, which appeared in both BUST and *Bitch* but not in ROCKRGRL.

9. The statistical breakdown was as follows: 82.4% of readers unequivocally supported *Bitch*'s decision to not print the ad; 7.8% thought *Bitch* should have printed it; 3.9% were glad the magazine didn't print it but thought *Bitch* should have excluded a second ad featuring a scantily clad woman that had run in the same issue; another 3.9% were glad the magazine didn't run the ad but disagreed with the rationale; and 2% thought the magazine was run by "fat bitter dike[s]" [*sic*] (Pie Chart 2001, 7).

CHAPTER 3

1. I thank Amy Erdman Farrell for telling me about the promotion of HUES at the NWSA conferences in the 1990s.

2. Other events that received similar levels of spectacular media coverage included the 1995 trial of O. J. Simpson for the murder of Nicole Brown Simpson and the 1992 beating of Rodney King by members of the Los Angeles police, which precipitated a civil uprising in the city.

3. Anna Carastathis (2013) provides a contrasting analysis from Nash on identity politics and Crenshaw's analysis of them, through her conceptualization of identity categories as potential coalitions.

4. Canada and Australia both have official policies of multiculturalism that have helped construct the "imagined community" (Anderson 1996) of the nation in both countries. U.S. national identity has relied more on the "melting pot" model.

5. While *Ms.* magazine arguably tried to present a multicultural perspective, as Amy Erdman Farrell (1998) points out, the publication's "attempt at diversity and inclusivity were limited by a somewhat tokenistic approach" (168). At the staff level of *Ms.*, there were analogous problems, in that some writers of colour felt that their employment provided a way for white feminists to feel less implicated in processes of oppression that they might have a hand in perpetuating (see Thom 1997, 156). While mid-century publications did contain discussions of racism, and sometimes dedicated space to minoritized groups, they neither fundamentally decentred

whiteness within the publications nor did they enter the mainstream marketplace in the same way as *Ms.* and later *HUES* did (see Flannery 2005, 57; Johnson 1996, 58; Lafky 1996, 89; and Lesher 1996, 415).

6. This ambiguity points towards the larger fact of the social construction of "race," as well as the ways in which who is read as white or "non-white" can shift. As Sherene Razack (1998) points out, "[T]he way we talk currently about differences is most assuredly socially constructed and specific to our historical moment, but that moment continues to be one in which white supremacy is alive and well" (167). The methodology with which I approach this analysis of the visual politics of magazine covers is meant to keep the fact of white supremacy front and centre.

CHAPTER 4

1. For further reading on feminism and backlash, see Susan Faludi's *Backlash* (1991) and Patricia Bradley's *Mass Media and the Shaping of American Feminism, 1963–1975* (2003), which both give comprehensive accounts of the negative coverage of feminism and feminists within U.S. mass media and its effects upon the movement.

2. To be clear, drag culture is about more than simply the clothes one wears, and not all drag performances necessarily parody gender identity. I raise Butler's argument in this context to identify the centrality of the politics of fashion to feminist thought—given that *Gender Trouble* is widely considered a canonical work of feminist theory—rather than to make claims about the function of drag.

3. While containing some pertinent insights, Scott's book is, overall, quite anti-feminist and gives an overly simplistic account of what feminism "is." Her argument, for example, that "feminist criticism of images ... is full of incompetent readings masquerading as privileged insights" is an unscholarly misrepresentation, and discounting, of the rich critical traditions of feminist Cultural Studies criticism.

4. According to Linda Steiner (1996), *The New Northwest* "counted on 'intelligent' women wanting to look fashionable" and ran regular fashion columns, as well as advertising and promotion of founder and publisher Abigail Scott Duniway's millinery business (234).

5. Notwithstanding Wright Davis's disavowal of the sentimental "lady," Aronson argues that in fact many mid-nineteenth-century feminist magazines often employed a sentimental discourse in their articles on suffrage. For example, these articles frequently ended with an authorial addendum in which the author would entreat the reader directly to take some kind of action, in a way that appealed to the reader's sentiments. Early women's rights periodicals thus mobilized sentimental discourse in order to encourage reader engagement with political issues.

6. Similarly, as a specialized publication for women in the music industry, *ROCKRGRL* never published fashion pages.

7. These affective relationships between *Sassy* and *Jane* and their readers are evidenced in Jervis and Zeisler's (2006) "Pratt-fall: Ten Things to Hate about *Jane*,"

Baumgardner and Richards's (2000) *Manifesta*, and Simms's (2004) "The Secret History of *Sassy*."

8. See, for example, Mary Russo's (1989) "Female Grotesques: Carnival and Theory" and Joan Rivière's (1986) "Womanliness as Masquerade."

9. For a critical analysis of *Our Bodies, Ourselves*, see Kathy Davis's (2007/2013) "Reclaiming Women's Bodies."

10. Davis was implicated in the murder of Judge Harold Haley, through an attempted prison break by members of the Black Panthers. After eighteen months as a fugitive, she was captured, tried, and acquitted of all charges. During the period in which Davis was in hiding, she was named as one of the FBI's most wanted criminals. The "wanted" posters circulated on a mass scale and the representation of Davis on these posters has become iconic.

CHAPTER 5

1. The third-wave magazine *HUES* ceased publication in 1999, before the burgeoning of interest in craft. The magazine did not include articles on crafting and is not discussed in this chapter.

2. Classified advertisements are so named because they are typically organized by category. Classified ads are collected in one section of a periodical, as opposed to display advertising, which is generally distributed throughout the publication. Whereas display ads are usually purchased by larger businesses, classified ads allow individuals or small businesses to purchase ad space for a reasonable price. While classified ads are traditionally print-only, a hybrid form known as the "classified display advertisement" features graphics as well as print: *BUST* classifieds fall into this latter category.

3. To call knitting *new* is actually quite an old practice. In her analysis of the promotion of home craft in British women's magazines of the 1920s and 1930s, Fiona Hackney notes crafting as modern, fashionable, and new in these publications (2006, 26, 29).

4. On feminist publishing, see Murray (2004). On the growth of the feminist periodical press, see Flannery (2005). Sourcebooks on feminist periodicals include Harrison (1975) and Krichmar (1972).

5. There are also individuals and groups that engage in crafting practices that are more recognizable as traditionally "political": these include "knit in" occupations and the use of collectively made knitted, sewed, or crocheted banners in protest marches. The practice of "yarn bombing" public spaces (knitting "cozies" for lamp posts or scarves for statues, for example) works as a comment on the depersonalized and sterile environment of urban public space. Beth Pentney's (2008) analysis of feminist crafting cites the Revolutionary Knitting Circle, the Cast Off Knitting Club, and Knit4Choice as groups that have engaged in political actions concerning the G8, militarism, and abortion rights, respectively. The International Vulva Knitting Circle's invitation to knitters worldwide to create knitted representations

of their vulvas attempts to "celebrate vulva diversity" in the face of the growing trend of genital cosmetic surgery. Lisa Auerbach's open-access pattern for "Body Count Mittens" pattern invites crafters to knit the number of American soldiers killed by war into the backs of their mittens. Known as "craftivism," these political interventions are frequently feminist, genderqueer, anti-capitalist, and/or environmentalist in their orientations. In this sense, the political practices associated with traditional forms of feminist organizing find their way into, and are recast within, contemporary crafting. However, these kinds of actions also respond to the more immediate context of highly confrontational police violence that has come to mark mass protests in recent decades, with interventions that are marked by the softness of wool and the soothing clickety-clack sounds of knitting needles.

6. The idea of the feminist as bra burner stems from a theatrical protest against the 1969 Miss America pageant in which participants threw "instruments of oppression" into a "freedom trashcan" (Canning 1995, 43).

7. The chorus of "She's Crafty" is as follows: "she's crafty / she gets around / she's crafty / she's always down / she's crafty / she's got a gripe / she's crafty / and she's just my type" (Beastie Boys 1986).

8. See, for example, the craftwork of Allyson Mitchell and Allison Smith, as well as craft groups such as the Washington, D.C.–based Queer Crafting Collective and the Calgary-based Revolutionary Knitting Circle.

9. For analyses of the relationship between domesticity and postfeminism, see Genz (2009) and Hollows (2003).

CHAPTER 6

1. For more on the alternative market economies of third- and post-wave magazines, see my discussion of feminist crafting in Chapter 5.

2. Since the model's sex/gender is unknown, I will use the pronouns "they," "their," etc., to signal this gender indeterminacy. I use them/them pronouns not to reify the model's identity as genderqueer, but rather to leave open the question of gender.

3. GLBTIQ2-S = Gay, Lesbian, Bisexual, Transgendered, Intersex, Queer, and Two-Spirited.

4. I also acknowledge Cathy Cohen's (1997) important critique of the failure of queer politics to work at the intersections of race, class, and sexuality in her essay "Punks, Bulldaggers, and Welfare Queens: The Radical Potential of Queer Politics?"

5. Race is social construct with a complicated history and is thus rarely "straightforward." Skin colour is one, but not the only way that racial identity has been determined. I do not wish to imply that race is reducible to skin colour alone, here.

6. My understanding of the process of interpellation is drawn from Louis Althusser's (1971) "Ideology and Ideological State Apparatuses" and Judith Butler's critique of Althusser in *The Psychic Life of Power* (1997).

7. Adrienne Rich's (1980) now canonical "Compulsory Heterosexuality and Lesbian Existence" is perhaps the best-known feminist critique of the erasure of lesbian voices from the women's movement.

8. For an analysis of the coverage of the sex wars in *Feminist Studies*, see Basiliere (2009).

9. Although Elise Chenier (2004) persuasively argues that the lesbian sex wars receded because both the AIDS crisis and the U.S. culture wars resulted in feminists, and especially lesbian feminists, making new forms of alliance with gay men and lesbian sex radicals, I suggest that the tensions between the interrelated politics of feminism and sexuality never really disappeared, and that the 1980s sex wars continue to reverberate within twenty-first-century feminisms.

WORKS CITED

"About *Shameless*." 2014. *Shameless*. Web. 24 July. <http://shamelessmag.com/about>

"Advertise with *Bitch*—Become a Sponsor." 2015. *Bitch Media*. Web. 1 September. <http://bitchmedia.org/sponsorship>

Ahmed, Sara. 2004. *The Cultural Politics of Emotion*. New York: Routledge.

Alexander, Lili. 1996. Letter to the Editor. *HUES* (Winter): 4.

Althusser, Louis. 1971. "Ideology and Ideological State Apparatuses." *Lenin and Philosophy, and Other Essays*. Trans. Ben Brewster. London: New Left Books, 127–88.

Anderson, Benedict. 1996. *Imagined Communities: Reflections on the Origin and Spread of Nationalism*. New York: Verso.

Ang, Ien. 1985. *Watching Dallas: Soap Opera and the Melodramatic Imagination*. London: Metheun.

Ardis, Ann, and Patrick Collier. 2008. *Transatlantic Print Culture, 1880–1940: Emerging Media, Emerging Modernities*. New York: Palgrave Macmillan.

Arnsberger, Paul, Melissa Ludlum, Margaret Riley, and Mark Stanton. 2008. "A History of the Tax-Exempt Sector: An SOI Perspective." *Statistics of Income Bulletin* (Winter): 105–35. Accessed 12 September 2014. Online: <http://www.irs.gov/pub/irs-soi/tehistory.pdf>

Aronson, Amy Beth. 2002. *Taking Liberties: Early American Women's Magazines and Their Readers*. Westport, CT: Praeger Publishers.

Auerbach, Lisa Anne. (n.d.) "War Count Mittens." *Craftsanity.com*. Accessed 26 May 2008. <www.craftsanity.com/pdf/mittenpattern.pdf>

Baehr, Helen, and Ann Gray, eds. 1996. *Turning It On: A Reader in Women and Media*. New York: Edward Arnold.

Bailey, Courtney. 2003. "*Bitch*ing and Talking/Gazing Back: Feminism as Critical Reading." *Women and Language* 26 (2): 1–8.

Ballaster, Ros, Margaret Beetham, Elizabeth Frazer, and Sandra Hebron. 1991. *Women's Worlds: Ideology, Femininity, and the Woman's Magazine*. London: Macmillan.

Bannerji, Himani. 2000. *The Dark Side of the Nation: Essays on Multiculturalism, Nation, and Gender*. Toronto: Canadian Scholars' Press.

Bardot, Erika. 1997. "Wake Up and Smell the Tea Bag." She's Crafty. *BUST* 9 (Spring/Summer): 10.

Bassiliere, Jenna. 2009. "Political Is Personal: Scholarly Manifestations of the Feminist Sex Wars." *Michigan Feminist Studies* 22: 1–25.

Baumgardner, Jennifer, and Amy Richards. 2000. *Manifesta: Young Women, Feminism, and the Future*. New York: Farrar, Straus and Giroux.

Beastie Boys and Rick Rubin. 1986. "She's Crafty." *Licensed to Ill*. Columbia Records. Audiocassette.

Bell, David, and Joanne Hollows, eds. 2005. *Ordinary Lifestyles: Popular Media, Consumption and Taste*. New York: Open University Press.

Berger, Melody, ed. 2006. *We Don't Need Another Wave*. Emeryville, CA: Seal Press.

Berlant, Lauren. 1997. *The Queen of America Goes to Washington City*. Durham, NC: Duke University Press.

——. 2000. "Intimacy: A Special Issue." *Intimacy*. Chicago: University of Chicago Press. 1–8.

——. 2008. *The Female Complaint: The Unfinished Business of Sentimentality in American Culture*. Durham, NC: Duke University Press.

Berlant, Lauren, and Michael Warner. 1998. "Sex in Public." *Critical Inquiry* 24.2: 547–66.

Betterton, Rosemary, ed. 1987. *Looking On: Images of Femininity in the Visual Arts and Media*. London: Pandora Press.

"Bitch: Feminist Response to Popular Culture." 2005. *Bitch Magazine*. Home Page. 12 November. <www.bitchmagazine.com>

Bitch Magazine Records. 2003. Duke University Rare Book, Manuscript, and Special Collections Library. Sallie Bingham Center for Women's History and Culture. Box 2.

Bitch Media. 2012. "Bitch Media Sponsorship Kit." 8 May. Web. 30 June 2014.<http://bitchmagazine.org/sites/default/files/documents/bitchmedia_sponsorship_kit_060513.pdf>

Bleyer, Jennifer. 2004. "Cut-and-Paste Revolution: Notes from the Girl Zine Explosion." In Labaton and Martin 2004, 42–60.

Bold, Christine, ed. 2012. *U.S. Popular Print Culture, 1830–1918*. Oxford: Oxford University Press.

Bonacich, Edna, et al., eds. 1994. *Global Production: The Apparel Industry in the Pacific Rim*. Philadelphia: Temple University Press.

Bourdieu, Pierre. 1984. *Distinction: A Social Critique on the Judgment of Taste*. Trans. Richard Nice. New York: Routledge and Keegan Paul.

Bradley, Patricia. 2003. *Mass Media and the Shaping of American Feminism, 1963–1975*. Mississippi: University Press of Mississippi.

Bronstein, Carolyn. 2005. "Representing the Third Wave: Mainstream Print Media Framing of a New Feminist Movement." *Journalism and Mass Communication Quarterly* 82 (4): 783–803.

Brooks, Abigail. 2007. "Feminist Standpoint Epistemology: Building Knowledge and Empowerment Through Women's Lived Experience." In Hesse-Biber and Leavy 2007, 53–82.

Brown, Susan, Jeanne Perrault, JoAnnWallace, and Heather Zwicker, eds. 2011. *Not Drowning but Waving: Women, Feminism, and the Liberal Arts*. Edmonton, AB: University of Alberta Press.

Bruzzi, Stella, and Pamela Church-Gibson, eds. 2001. *Fashion Cultures: Theories, Exploration, and Analysis*. New York: Routledge.

Buhle, Mari Jo. 1983. *Women and the American Left: A Guide to Sources*. Boston: G. K. Hall and Co.

Burgin, Victor, James Donald, and Cora Kaplan, eds. 1986. *Formations of Fantasy*. New York: Methuen.

"Bust: For Women with Something to Get Off Their Chests." 2005. *BUST, Inc.* Home Page. 3 November. <www.bust.com>

"*BUST* Media Kit." Accessed 5 June 2006. <http://www.bust.com/mediakit>

Butcher, Patricia Smith. 1989. *Education for Equality: Women's Rights Periodicals and Women's Higher Education, 1849–1920*. Contributions in Women's Studies. Westport, CT: Greenwood Press.

Butler, Judith. 1993. *Bodies That Matter: On the Discursive Limits of "Sex."* New York: Routledge.

———. 1990/1999. *Gender Trouble: Feminism and the Subversion of Identity*. New York: Routledge.

———. 1997. *The Psychic Life of Power: Theories in Subjection*. Stanford, CA: Stanford University Press.

Butler, Pamela, and Jigna Desai. 2008. "Manolos, Marriage, and Mantras: Chick-Lit Criticism and Transnational Feminism." *Meridians: Feminism, Race, Transnationalism* 8 (2): 1–31.

B-Word Worldwide. *Bitch: Feminist Response to Popular Culture Records, 1996–2008*. Sallie Bingham Center for Women's History and Culture. Special Collections Library.

Canaan, Kitsey. 2003. Letter. *Bitch* 19 (Winter): 6.

Canning, Charlotte. 1995. *Feminist Theatres in the USA: Staging Women's Experience*. New York: Routledge.

Carastathis, Anna. 2013. "Identity Categories as Potential Coalitions." *Signs* 38(4): 941–65.

Carter, Julian. 2007. *The Heart of Whiteness: Normal Sexuality and Race in America, 1880–1940*. Durham, NC: Duke University Press.

Chafin, Chris. 2014. "How has *BUST* Magazine Survived?" *The Awl* (8 January). <http://www.theawl.com/2014/01/how-has-bust-magazine-survived>

Chambers, Linda B., Linda Steiner, and Carole Fleming. 2004. *Women and Journalism*. New York: Routledge.

Chapman, Mary, and Victoria Lamont. 2012. "American Suffrage Print Culture." In Bold 2012, 253–76.

Chasin, Alexandra. 2001. *Selling Out: The Gay and Lesbian Movement Goes to Market*. New York: Palgrave Macmillan.

Cheng, Lucie, and Gary Gereffi. 1994. "U.S. Retailers and Asian Garment Production." In Bonacich et al. 1994, 63–79.

Chenier, Elise. 2004. "Lesbian Sex Wars." In Summers 2004.

Church-Gibson, Pamela. 2001. "Redressing the Balance: Patriarchy, Postmodernism, and Fashion." In Bruzzi and Pamela Church-Gibson 2001.

Clark, Jessica. 2004. Letter to the Editor, *BUST* 28 (2004): 7.

"Closet Politics." 1995. *HUES*: 34.

Cohen, Cathy J. 1997. "Punks, Bulldaggers, and Welfare Queens: The Radical Potential of Queer Politics?" In Johnson and Henderson 2005, 21–51.

Cohen, Cathy J., Kathleen B. Jones, and Joan C. Tronto, eds. 1997. *Women Transforming Politics: An Alternative Reader*. New York: New York University Press.

Cohen, Nicole. 2007. Email interview. 15 January.

Cohoon, Lorinda B. 2006. *Serialized Citizenships: Periodicals, Books, and American Boys, 1840–1911*. Toronto: Scarecrow Press.

Collins, Patricia Hill. 1993. "Toward a New Vision: Race, Class, and Gender as Categories of Analysis and Connection." In Kimmel and Ferber 2014, 240–57.

———. 2000. *Black Feminist Thought: Knowledge, Consciousness, and the Politics of Empowerment*. 2nd ed. New York: Routledge.

———. 2004. "Why Black Sexual Politics?" *Black Sexual Politics: African Americans, Gender, and the New Racism*. New York: Routledge. 25–52, 311–17.

Combahee River Collective. 1980. "Combahee River Collective Statement." 7 pages. Accessed 29 September 2014. Online: <http://www.sfu.ca/iirp/documents/Combahee%201979.pdf>

Conrad, Nettie. 2001. "Third Wave Feminism: A Case Study of *BUST* Magazine." Master of Arts in Mass Communications Thesis. Northridge: California State University.

"Contents." 2008. *BUST* 51 (June/July): 3–4.

Coward, Rosalind. 1987. "Sexual Liberation and the Family." In Betterton 1987, 53–57.

Crenshaw, Kimberlé Williams. 1989. "Demarginalizing the Intersection of Race and Sex: A Black Feminist Critique of Antidiscrimination Doctrine, Feminist Theory, and Antiracist Politics." *University of Chicago Legal Forum* 140: 139–67.

———. 1995. "Mapping the Margins: Intersectionality, Identity Politics, and Violence Against Women of Colour." In Crenshaw et al. 1995, 357–83.

Crenshaw, Kimberlé, et al., eds. 1995. *Critical Race Theory: The Key Writers That Formed the Movement*. New York: New Press.

Crickett, Laura. 2003. Letter. *Bitch* 19 (Winter): 6.

Crow, Barbara, ed. 2000. *Radical Feminism: A Documentary Reader*. New York: New York University Press.

Crowley, David. 2003. *Magazine Covers*. London: Mitchell Beazley.

Curran, James, David Morley, and Valerie Walkerdine, eds. 1996. *Cultural Studies and Communication*. New York: Arnold.

Currie, Dawn. 1999. *Girl Talk: Adolescent Magazines and their Readers*. Toronto: University of Toronto Press.

Cvetkovich, Ann. 2003. *An Archive of Feelings: Trauma, Sexuality, and Lesbian Public Cultures*. Durham, NC: Duke University Press.

———. 2012. *Depression: A Public Feeling*. Durham, NC: Duke University Press.

Darms, Lisa, ed. 2013. *The Riot Grrrl Collection*. New York: Feminist Press.

Davidson, Cathy N., and Jessamyn Hatcher, eds. 2002. *No More Separate Spheres! A Next Wave American Studies Reader*. Durham, NC: Duke University Press.

Davis, Angela Y. 1994. "Afro Images: Politics, Fashion, and Nostalgia." *Critical Inquiry* 21.1 (Autumn): 37–45.

Davis, Kathy. 2007/2013. "Reclaiming Women's Bodies: Colonialist Trope or Critical Epistemology?" In McCann and Seung-kyung Kim 2013, 502–16.

Delap, Lucy, and Maria DiCenzo. 2008. "Transatlantic Print Culture: The Anglo-American Feminist Press and Emerging 'Modernities.'" In Ardis and Collier 2008, 48–65.

De Lauretis, Teresa, ed. 1989. *Feminist Studies/Critical Studies*. Bloomington: Indiana University Press.

D'Enbeau, Suzy. 2009. "Feminine and Feminist Transformation in Popular Culture: An Application of Mary Daly's Radical Philosophies to *Bust* Magazine." *Feminist Media Studies* 9 (1): 17–36.

Derrida, Jacques. 1977. "Signature, Event, Context." *Glyph* 1: 172–97.

DeSantis, Carla. 1995. "Don't Get Me Started!" Editorial. ROCKRGRL 1 (January/February): 2.

———. 1996. "Send Us Your Money!" Editorial. ROCKRGRL 10 (July/August): 3.

———. 2005. "Adieu." Editorial. ROCKRGRL 57 (Fall): 4.

DiCenzo, Maria. 2000. "Militant Distribution: *Votes for Women* and the Public Sphere." *Media History* 6 (2): 115–28.

Doan, Laura, and Jay Prosser, eds. 2002. *Palatable Poison: Critical Perspectives on* The Well of Loneliness. New York: Columbia University Press.

Duggan, Lisa, and Nan D. Hunter. 1995. *Sex Wars: Sexual Dissent and Political Culture*. New York: Routledge.

Duncombe, Stephen. 1997. *Notes from the Underground: Zines and the Politics of Alternative Culture*. Haymarket Series. New York: Verso.

Echols, Alice. 1997. "Nothing Distant about It: Women's Liberation and Sixties Radicalism." In Cohen, Jones, and Tronto 1997, 456–76.

Edut, Ophira. 1993. "The Disposable Jewish Nose." HUES 2: 3.

Edut, Ophira, and Tali Edut. n.d. "HUES Magazine." *Mediarology*. Accessed 10 November 2014. <http://www.mediarology.com/ourwork-branding-hues.html>

Edut, Tali. 1997. "HUES Magazine: The Making of a Movement." In Heywood and Drake 1997, 83–98.

Edwards, Clive. 2006. "'Home Is Where the Art Is': Women, Handicrafts and Home Improvements 1750–1900." *Journal of Design History* 19 (1): 11–21.

Eichhorn, Kate. 2013. *The Archival Turn in Feminism: Outrage in Order*. Philadelphia: Temple University Press.

Egan, Tracie. 2008. "The Struggles of *Bitch* Magazine Are Neither Surprising Nor New." *Jezebel.com: Celebrity, Sex, Fashion for Women*. 16 September. Accessed 23 July 2009. <http://jezebel.com/5050695the-struggles-of-bitch-magazine-are-neither-surprising-nor-new>

Elam, Diane, and Robyn Wiegman, eds. 1995. *Feminism beside Itself*. New York: Routledge.

Ellis, Becky. 2007. "Why Feminism Isn't for Everybody." *Briarpatch Magazine* (March): 1–4. 1 Mar. 2007 <http://briarpatchmagazine.com/news/?p=399>

Embree, Alice. "Media Images 1: Madison Avenue Brainwashing – The Facts." *Sisterhood Is Powerful: An Anthology of Writings from the Women's Liberation Movement*. Ed. Robin Morgan. New York: Random House, 1970. 175–91.

Endres, Kathleen L. 1996a. "Introduction." In Endres and Lueck 1996, vi–xxi.

——. 1996b. "No More Fun and Games." In Endres and Lueck 1996, 246–50.

——. 1996c. "Off Our Backs." In Endres and Lueck 1996, 265–73.

——. 1996d. "The Woman Citizen." In Endres and Lueck, 1996, 429–37.

——. 1996e. "The Woman's Tribune." In Endres and Lueck 1996, 478–85.

Endres, Kathleen L., and Therese L. Lueck, eds. 1996. *Women's Periodicals in the United States: Social and Political Issues*. Historical Guides to the World's Periodicals and Newspapers. Westport, CT: Greenwood Press.

Enstad, Nan. 1999. *Ladies of Labor, Girls of Adventure: Working Women, Popular Culture, and Labor Politics at the Turn of the Twentieth Century*. New York: Columbia University Press.

Faludi, Susan. 1991. *Backlash: The Undeclared War Against American Women*. New York: Crown Publishers.

Farrell, Amy Erdman. 1998. *Yours in Sisterhood: Ms. Magazine and the Promise of Popular Feminism*. Chapel Hill: University of North Carolina Press.

Faster, Twisty. 2006. "A Few Remarks on a Few Remarks." IblamethePatriarchy.com. 30 September. <http://blog.iblamethepatriarchy.com>

Ferber, Abby L., Andrea O'Reilly Herrera, and Dena R. Samuels. 2007. "The Matrix of Oppression and Privilege: Theory and Practice for the New Millennium." *American Behavioral Scientist* 51 (4): 516–31.

Ferguson, Marjorie. 1983. *Forever Feminine: Women's Magazines and the Cult of Femininity*. London: Heinemann.

Finnegan, Margaret. 1999. *Selling Suffrage: Consumer Culture and Votes for Women*. New York: Columbia University Press.

Fischer, Gayle V. 2001. *Pantaloons and Power: A Nineteenth-Century Dress Reform in the United States*. Kent, OH: Kent State University Press.

Fisher, Elizabeth. Editorial. *Aphra* 1.1 (1970): 6.

Flannery, Kathryn. 2005. *Feminist Literacies, 1968–75*. Chicago: University of Illinois Press.

Foucault, Michel. 1969. *The Archaeology of Knowledge and the Discourse on Language*. Trans. A. M. Sheridan Smith. New York: Pantheon Books.

———. 1978. *The History of Sexuality, Volume One: An Introduction*. Trans. Robert Hurley. New York: Vintage Books.

Fowles, Stacey May. 2007. "*Sassy* Fans Weigh In and Sum Up the Debate." *Shameless*. Blog post. 13 July. Web. 24 July 2014. <http://shamelessmag.com/blog/entry/sassy-fans-way-in-and-sum-up-the-jane-debate>

Franklin, Sarah, Celia Lury, and Jackie Stacey, eds. 1991. "Feminism and Cultural Studies: Pasts, Presents, Futures." *Off-Centre: Feminism and Cultural Studies*. London: HarperCollins Academic, 1–19.

Fraser, Nancy. 1997. "Rethinking the Public Sphere: A Contribution to the Critique of Actually Existing Democracy." *Justice Interruptus: Critical Reflections on the "Post-Socialist Condition."* New York: Routledge, 69–98.

Frazer, Elizabeth. 1996. "Teenage Girls Reading *Jackie*." In Baehr and Gray 1996, 130–37.

Freeman, Joreen. 2000. "The Bitch Manifesto." In Crow 2000, 226–32.

———. 2009. "Grrrl Zines in the Library." *Signs* 35(1): 52–59.

Friedan, Betty. 1963. *The Feminine Mystique*. New York: Dell.

Friedman, Susan Stanford. 1995. "Making History: Reflections on Feminism, Narrative, and Desire." In Elam and Wiegman 1995, 11–53.

Frith, Simon. 2007. *Taking Popular Music Seriously: Selected Essays*. Burlington, VT: Ashgate Publishing Company.

Frith, Simon, with Angela McRobbie. 1978/79. "Rock and Sexuality." In Simon 2007, 41–58.

Gallagher, Margaret. 2001. *Gender Setting: New Agendas for Media Monitoring and Advocacy*. New York: Palgrave.

Garrison, Ednie Kaeh. 2005. "Are We on a Wavelength Yet? On Feminist Oceanography, Radios, and Third Wave Feminism." In Reger 2005, 237–56.

Garvey, Ellen Gruber. 1996. *The Adman in the Parlor: Magazines and the Gendering of Consumer Culture, 1880s to 1910s*. New York: Oxford University Press.

Genz, Stéfanie. 2009. "'I Am Not a Housewife, but …' Postfeminism and the Revival of Domesticity." In Gillis and Hollows 2009.

Gevinson, Tavi. 2010. "Are You Tired of *Sassy* Yet? THE ANSWER IS NO." *Tavi Gevison's Blog*. Blog post. 26 April. Web. 24 July 2014. <http://www.thestylerookie.com/2010/04_01_archive.html>

Gillis, Stacey, and Joanne Hollows, eds. 2009. *Feminism, Domesticity, and Popular Culture*. New York: Routledge.

Gillis, Stacy, Gillian Howie, and Rebecca Munford, eds. 2004. *Third Wave Feminism: A Critical Exploration*. London, UK: Palgrave Macmillan.

Gilmore, Stephanie. 2005. "Bridging the Waves: Sex and Sexuality in a Second Wave Organization." In Reger 2005, 97–116.

Gilmore, Stephanie, ed. 2008. *Feminist Coalitions: Historical Perspectives on Second-Wave Feminism in the United States*. Chicago: University of Illinois Press.

Goode, Luke. 2005. *Jürgen Habermas: Democracy and the Public Sphere*. Ann Arbor, MI: Pluto Press.

Gottlieb, Agnes Hooper. 1996a. "The Revolution." In Endres and Lueck 1996, 339–45.

———. 1996b. "The Una." In Endres and Lueck 1996, 387–94.

Gough-Yates, Anna. 2003. *Understanding Women's Magazines: Publishing, Markets, and Readerships*. New York: Routledge.

Green, Barbara. 2009. "The Feminist Periodical Press: Women, Periodical Studies, and Modernity." *Literature Compass* 6 (1): 191–205.

Greider, Linda. 2001. "Not Your Grandmother's Hobby." *Washingtonian* 36 (5): 136–40. Web. 29 January 2007.

Grewal, Inderpal. 2005. *Transnational America: Feminisms, Diasporas, Neoliberalisms*. Durham, NC: Duke University Press.

Groeneveld, Elizabeth. 2011. "'Not a Postfeminism Feminist': Feminism's Third Wave." In Brown, Perrault, and Zwicker 2011, 271–84.

Habermas, Jürgen. 1962/1987. *The Structural Transformation of the Public Sphere: An Inquiry into a Category of Bourgeois Society*. Cambridge, MA: Polity Press.

Hackney, Fiona. 2006. "'Use Your Hands for Happiness': Home Craft and Make-do -and-Mend in British Women's Magazines in the 920s and 1930s." *Journal of Design History* 19 (1): 23–38.

Hale, Angela, and Jane Willis, eds. 2005. *Threads of Labour: Garment Industry Supply Chains from the Workers' Perspective*. Oxford: Blackwell Publishing.

Hall, Stuart, ed. 1997. *Representation: Cultural Representations and Signifying Practices*. London: Sage Publications.

Hall, Stuart, and Tony Jefferson, eds. 1976. *Resistance Through Rituals: Youth Subcultures in Post-War Britain*. New York: Homes and Meier Publishers.

Haraway, Donna. 1988. "Situated Knowledges: The Science Question in Feminism and the Privilege of Partial Perspective." *Feminist Studies* 14 (3): 575–99.

———. 1991. *Simians, Cyborgs, Women: The Reinvention of Nature*. New York: Routledge. 149–81.

Harris, Anita. 2003. "gURL Scenes and Grrrl Zines: The Regulation and Resistance of Girls in Late Modernity." *Feminist Review* 75: 38–56.

Harris, Sharon M., ed. 2004. *Blue Pencils and Hidden Hands: Women Editing Periodicals, 1830–1910*. Boston: Northeastern University Press.

Harrison, Cynthia Ellen. 1975. *Women's Movement Media: A Sourcebook*. New York: Bowker Company.

Hasinoff, Amy Adele. 2015. *Sexting Panic: Rethinking Criminalization, Privacy, and Consent*. Champaign: University of Illinois Press.

Hearing of the Senate Judiciary Committee on the Nomination of Clarence Thomas to the Supreme Court. 1991. 11 October. Electronic Text Center: University of Virginia

Library. Online: <http://etext.lib.virginia.edu/etcbin/toccer-new- yitna?id=Usa Thom&images=images/modeng&data=/lv6/workspace/yitna&tag=public&part=24>

Hebdige, Dick. 1979. *Subculture: The Meaning of Style*. London: Methuen.

Hemmings, Clare. 2011. *Why Stories Matter: The Political Grammar of Feminist Theory*. Durham, NC: Duke University Press.

Henkin, David M. 1988. "Introduction: Public Reading, Public Space." *City Reading: Written Words and Public Spaces in Antebellum New York*. New York: Columbia University Press, 1–26.

Henry, Astrid. 2004. *Not My Mother's Sister: Generational Conflict and Third-Wave Feminism*. Bloomington, IA: Indiana University Press.

Hernandez, Daisy, and Bushra Rehman, eds. 2002. *Colonize This! Young Women of Color on Today's Feminism*. New York: Seal Press.

Hesse-Biber, Sharlene Nagy, and Patricia Lina Leavy, eds. 2007. *Feminist Research Practice: A Primer*. Thousand Oaks, CA: Sage Publications.

Hex, Celina. 1997. "Goddess." Editorial. *BUST* 9 (Spring/Summer): 2.

Hex, Celina, and Betty Boob. 1993. Untitled. Editorial. *BUST* 1: n.p.

Hex, Celina, Betty Boob, and Laurie "Areola" Henzel. 1999. "*BUST* or Bust!" Editorial. *BUST* 12 (Spring): 4.

Hex, Celina, and Amanda Ray. 2000. "She's Crafty: Knits Are for Chicks." *BUST* 14 (Spring): 17.

Heywood, Leslie, and Jennifer Drake, eds. 1997. *Third Wave Agenda: Being Feminist, Doing Feminism*. Minneapolis: University of Minnesota Press.

Hirshman, Linda. 2006. *Get to Work: A Manifesto for Women of the World*. New York: Viking.

"History." 2015. *BitchMedia*. Web. 14 September. <https://bitchmedia.org/history-0>

"The History of Toys in Babeland." 2015. *Babeland*. Web. 1 September. <http://www .babeland.com/about/presskit/history>

Hof, Karina. 2006. "Something You Can Actually Pick Up: Scrapbooking as a Form and Forum of Cultural Citizenship." *European Journal of Cultural Studies* 9 (5): 363–84.

Holland, Samantha. 2004. *Alternative Femininities: Body, Age, and Identity*. New York: Bloomsbury.

Hollows, Joanne. *Feminism, Femininity and Popular Culture*. 2000. New York: Manchester University Press.

———. 2003. "Feeling Like a Domestic Goddess: Postfeminism and Cooking." *European Journal of Cultural Studies* 6 (2): 179–202.

hooks, bell. 1981. *Ain't I a Woman?: Black Women and Feminism*. Cambridge, MA: South End Press.

———. 1992. "Eating the Other." *Black Looks: Race and Representation*. Toronto: Between the Lines, 21–39.

———. 1994. "Theory as Liberatory Practice." *Teaching to Transgress: Education as the Practice of Freedom*. New York: Routledge, 59–75.

Humphreys, Nancy K. 1989. *American Women's Magazines: An Annotated Historical Guide*. New York: Garland Publishing.

Hutcheon, Linda. 1985. *A Theory of Parody: The Teachings of Twentieth-Century Art Forms*. New York: Methuen.

Inge, M. Thomas, and Dennis. 2002. *The Greenwood Guide to American Popular Culture*. Westport, CT: Greenwood Press.

Inness, Sherri A., 1998. *Delinquents and Debutantes: Twentieth-Century American Girls' Cultures*. New York University Press.

Jay, Karla. 2010. "Karla Jay Lavender Menace." YouTube Video, uploaded by lbranson1. March 21. Web. Accessed September 23, 2015. <https://www.youtube.com/watch?v=pKeRUG9uZIo>

Jervis, Lisa. 1996a. "Bait and Switch Sassy." Special Section: *Sassy Sucks. Bitch* 1: Web. 21 June 2014. <http://bitchmagazine.org/article/bait-and-switch-sassy>

———. 1996b. "*Sassy* Update: The New Staff of the New-and-Not-Improved *Sassy* Get Defensive in the Face of their Critics." *Bitch* 2 (1996). Web. 21 June 2014. <http://bitchmagazine.org/article/sassy-responds>

———. 1996c. "Something's Really Been Bothering Me." Editorial. *Bitch* 1 (3): 2.

———. 1996d. "This Magazine Is about Speaking Up." Editorial. *Bitch* 1 (1): 1.

———. 2000. "There Was Supposed to Be an Ad on This Page." *Bitch* 12: 91.

———. 2006. "Goodbye to Feminism's Generational Divide." In Berger 2006.

———. 2007. Email interview. 27 February.

Jervis, Lisa, and Andi Zeisler. 2000. Untitled Editorial Commentary. *Bitch* 13: 6.

———. 2001. "Gloria Steinem, Take Heart ..." Editorial. *Bitch* 14: 5.

———. 2002. "I Thought This Was a Feminist Magazine, Not a Lesbian Magazine." Editorial. *Bitch* 18 (Fall): 5.

———. 2003. "The Editors Respond." Editorial. *Bitch* 19 (Winter): 6.

———. 2006. "Pratt-Fall: Ten Things to Hate about *Jane*." In Jervis and Zeisler 2006, 285–90.

Jervis, Lisa, and Andi Zeisler, eds. 2006. *Bitchfest: Ten Years of Cultural Criticism from the Pages of* Bitch *Magazine*. New York: Farrar, Straus and Giroux.

Jesella, Kara, and Marisa Meltzer. 2007. *How* Sassy *Changed My Life: A Love Letter to the Greatest Teen Magazines of All Time*. New York: Farrar, Straus and Giroux.

Johnson, E. Patrick. 2001. "'Quare' Studies, Or (Almost) Everything I Know about Queer Studies I Learned from My Grandmother." *Text and Performance Quarterly* 21 (1): 1–25.

Johnson, Patrick, and Mae G. Henderson, eds. 2005. *Black Queer Studies: A Critical Anthology*. Durham, NC: Duke University Press.

Johnson, Sammye. 1996. "Chrysalis." In Endres and Lueck, 57–66.

Karp, Marcelle, and Debbie Stoller, eds. 1999. *The* BUST *Guide to the New Girl Order*. New York: Penguin Books.

Kate. 1998. Letter. *BUST* 11 (Summer/Fall 1998): 7.

Kearney, Mary Celeste. 1998. "Producing Girls: Rethinking the Study of Female Youth Culture." In Inness 1998, 285–310.

———. 2006. *Girls Make Media*. New York: Routledge.

Kimmel, Michael S., and Abby L. Ferber, eds. 2014. *Privilege: A Reader*. 3rd ed. Boulder, CO: Westview Press.

Kinser, Amber E. 2004. "Negotiating Spaces For/Through Third-Wave Feminism." *NWSA* Journal 16 (3) (Fall): 124–53.

Kitch, Carolyn. 2005. *Pages From the Past: History and Memory in American Magazines*. Chapel Hill, NC: University of North Carolina Press.

Klein, Melissa. 1997. "Duality and Redefinition: Young Feminism and the Alternative Music Community." In Heywood and Drake 1997, 207–25.

Klein, Naomi. 2000. *No Logo*. Toronto: Vintage Canada.

Krichmar, Albert. 1972. *The Woman's Rights Movement in the United States, 1848–1970: A Bibliography and Sourcebook*. Metuchen, NJ: Scarecrow Press.

Kuczynski, Alex. 2001. "The New Feminist Mystique; Variety of Brash Magazines Upset the Old Stereotypes." *New York Times*. 10 September. Online. <http://www.nytimes.com/2001/09/10/business/the-new-feminist-mystique-variety-of-brash-magazines-upset-the-old-stereotypes.html>.

Labaton, Vivien, and Dawn Martin, eds. 2004. *The Fire This Time: Young Activists and the New Feminism*. New York: Anchor Books.

Lafky, Sue A. "Feminist Teacher." In Endres and Lueck, 87–93.

Latham, Joyce M. 2015. "*Off / On Our Backs*: The Feminist Press in the 'Sex Wars' of the 1980s." *Protest on the Page: Essays on Print and the Culture of Dissent since 1865*. Madison: University of Wisconsin Press, 221–40.

Latham, Sean, and Robert Scholes. 2006. "The Rise of Periodical Studies." *PMLA* 121 (2): 517–31.

Laughlin, Kathleen A., Julie Gallagher, Dorothy Sue Cobble, Eileen Boris, Premilla Nadasen, Stephanie Gilmore, and Leandra Zarnow. 2010. "Is It Time to Jump Ship? Historians Rethink the Waves Metaphor." *Feminist Formations* 22 (1) (Spring): 76–135.

Lee, Carol E. 2005. "A Pastime of Grandma and the 'Golden Girls' Evolves into a Hip New Hobby." *New York Times*. 30 March. Web. Accessed 2 August 2008. <http://www.nytimes.com/2005/03/30/opinion/30wed3.html?_r=1&sq=&st=nyt&oref=slogin>

Lenn, Stefanie. 2007. Letter to the Editor. *BUST* 42 (December/January): 7.

Leonard, Marion. 1998. "Paper Planes: Travelling the New Grrrl Geographies." In Skelton and Valentine 1998, 102–119.

Leone, Viviene. 2000. "Domestics." In Crow 2000, 516–20.

Lesher, Tina. 1996. "Voice of the Women's Liberation Movement." In Endres and Lueck 1996, 413–417.

Lipsitz, George. 2006. *The Progressive Investment in Whiteness: How White People Profit from Identity Politics*. Philadelphia, PA: Temple University Press.

Lithwick, Dahlia. 2014. "'All the Issues Are Still With Us': Talking to Anita Hill, as Truthful as Ever." Slate.com. 21 March. Online: <http://www.slate.com/articles/ double_x/doublex/2014/03/talking_to_anita_hill_at_57_the_woman_who_stood_ up_to_clarence_thomas_is.html>

Logroño Guerrero, Carmela. 1995. "Red, White, and Clueless? Republican Women of Color." *HUES* 1 (5): 18–19, 56–57. Print.

Logwood, Dyann. 1995. "Ethnic Makeup: Orange No More!" *HUES* 1 (5): 9.

——. 2007. Telephone interviews. 1 and 5 October.

Logwood, Dyann, Ophira Edut, and Tali Edut. 1995. "Look How Far We've Come!" Editorial. *HUES* 1 (5): 3.

Lorde, Audre. 1984. *Sister Outsider: Essays and Speeches*. Freedom, CA: Crossing Press.

Lugones, María C., and Elizabeth V. Spelman. 1995. "Have We Got a Theory for You! Feminist Theory, Cultural Imperialism and the Demand for 'The Woman's Voice.'" In Tuana and Tong 1995, 494–507.

MacDonald, Anne. 1988. *No Idle Hands: A Social History of American Knitting*. New York: Ballantyne Books.

Mainardi, Pat. 2000. "The Politics of Housework." In Crow 2000, 525–29.

Mahmood, Saba. 2008. "Teaching and Research in Unavailable Intersections." In Scott 2008, 81–115.

Marcus, Sara. 2010. *Girls to the Front: The True Story of the Riot Grrrl Revolution*. New York: Harper Collins.

Marer, Eva. 2002. "Knitting: The New Yoga." *Health* 16 (2): 76–80.

Martindale, Kathleen. 1997. *Un/Popular Culture: Lesbian Writing after the Sex Wars*. New York: State University of New York Press.

Marzolf, Marion. 1977. *Up from the Footnote: A History of Women Journalists*. New York: Hastings House Publishers.

Matachar, Emily. 2011. "The New Domesticity: Fun, Empowering, or a Step Back for American Women?" *Washington Post*. 25 November. Online: <http://www .washingtonpost.com/opinions/the-new-domesticity-fun-empowering-or-a-step -back-for-american-women/2011/11/18/gIQAqkg1vN_story.html>

May, Vivian M. 2012. "Intersectionality." In Orr, Braithwaite, and Lichtenstein 2012, 155–72.

McBride, Andrew. 2008. "The Sex Wars." *Lesbian History*. Esther Newton et al. University of Michigan. Accessed 10 July 2009. <http://sitemaker.umich.edu/lesbian .history/the_sex_wars>

McCann, Carole R., and Seung-kyung Kim, eds. 2013. *Feminist Theory Reader: Local and Global Perspectives*. 3rd ed. New York: Routledge.

McClellan Derr, Christen. 2006. Letter to the Editor, *BUST* 37 (December/January): 8.

McCracken, Ellen. 1993. *Decoding Women's Magazines: From* Mademoiselle *to* Ms. New York: St. Martin's Press.

McGee, Heather. 2003. Letter. *Bitch* 20 (Spring): 8–9.

McGhee, Erin. 2004. "Lit Pick. *Get Crafty: Hip Home Ec*." Review. *BUST* 29 (Fall): 109.

McRobbie, Angela. 1996. "*More!*: New Sexualities in Girls' and Women's Magazines." In Curran, Morley, and Walkerdine 1996, 172–95.

——. 2009. *The Aftermath of Feminism: Gender, Culture, and Social Change*. Thousand Oaks, CA: Sage Publications.

McRobbie, Angela, and Jenny Garber. 1976. "Girls and Subcultures: An Exploration." In Hall and Jefferson 1976, 209–22.

Melville, Sally. 2001. Letter to the Editor, *BUST* 18 (Summer): 6.

Minahan, Stella, and Julie Wolfram Cox. 2007. "Stitch 'n Bitch: Cyberfeminism, a Third Place, and the New Materiality." *Journal of Material Culture* 12 (1): 5–21.

Miner, Michael. 2010. "Venus's Next Wave." *Chicago Reader*. 25 March. Web. 26 July 2014. <http://www.chicagoreader.com/chicago/venus-magazine-amy-schroeder-sarah-beardsley/Content?oid=1570058&showFullText=true>

Minkler, Meredith, Lawrence Wallack, and Patricia Madden. 1987. "Alcohol and Cigarette Advertising in *Ms.* Magazine." *Journal of Public Health Policy* 8 (2) (Summer): 164–79. Web. 7 July 2014. <http://www.jstor.org/stable/3342199>

Mitchell, A. Claudia, and Jacqueline Reid-Walsh, eds. 2008. *Girl Culture: An Encyclopedia, Volume 2*. Westport, CT: Greenwood Press.

Mohanty, Chandra. 2003. *Feminism Without Borders: Decolonizing Theory, Practicing Solidarity*. Durham, NC: Duke University Press.

Monem, Nadine Käthe. 2007. *Riot Grrrl: Revolution Girl Style Now!* London: Black Dog Publishing.

Moraga, Cherríe. 1981. "Preface." In Moraga and Anzaldúa 1981, xiii–xx.

Moraga, Cherríe, and Gloria Anzaldúa, eds. 1981. *This Bridge Called My Back: Writings by Radical Women of Colour*. Watertown, MA: Persphone Press.

Morton, Donald, ed. 1996. *The Material Queer: A LesBiGay Cultural Studies Reader*. Boulder, CO: Westview Press.

Mott, Frank Luther. 1970. *A History of American Magazines, Volume II: 1850–1865*. 1936. 4th ed. Cambridge, MA: Harvard University Press.

Munford, Rebecca. 2004. "'Wake Up and Smell the Lipgloss': Gender, Generation and the (A)politics of Girl Power." In Gillis, Howie, and Munford 2004, 142–54.

Muñoz, José Esteban. 1999. *Disidentifications: Queers of Color and the Performance of Politics*. University of Minnesota Press.

Murphy, Caryn. 2008. "Sassy." In Mitchell and Reid-Walsh 2008, 516–18.

Murray, Simone. 2004. *Mixed Media: Feminist Presses and Publishing Politics*. London: Pluto Press.

Nakamura, Lisa. 2015. "The Digital Afterlife of *This Bridge Called My Back*: Woman of Color Theory and Activism on Social Media." PACTLAB, University of Victoria. 4 March. Web. <http://pactac.net/2015/03/the-digital-afterlife-of-this-bridge-woman-of-color-theory-and-activism-on-social-media/>

Nash, Jennifer C. 2008. "Re-Thinking Intersectionality." *Feminist Review* 89 (June): 1–15.

Nelson, Cary, and Larry Grossberg, eds. 1988. *Marxism and the Interpretation of Culture*. Urbana: University of Illinois Press.

Nguyen, Mimi, ed. 1997. *Evolution of a Race Riot* 1. Web. 24 July 2014. <http://issuu
.com/poczineproject/docs/evolution-of-a-race-riot-issue-1>

———. 2012. "Riot Grrrl, Race, and Revival." *Women & Performance: A Journal of
Feminist Theory* 22 (2–3): 173–96.

Ohmann, Richard. 1996. *Selling Culture: Magazines, Markets, and Class at the Turn of
the Century*. New York: Verso.

Orr, Catherine, Ann Braithwaite, and Diane Lichtenstein, eds. 2012. *Rethinking
Women's and Gender Studies*. New York: Routledge.

"Our History." 2014. *Bitchmedia*. Web. 25 July. <http://bitchmagazine.org/history>

"Our Outfits, Ourselves." 2006. *BUST* (August/September): 55–63.

"Out-of-Barbie Experience." 1993. *HUES*: 14–15.

Parker, Richard Guy, and Peter Aggleton, eds. 1999. *Culture, Society, and Sexuality: A
Reader*. London: UCL Press.

Pearce, Lynne. 1997. *Feminism and the Politics of Reading*. New York: St. Martin's Press.

Pentney, Beth Ann. 2008. "Feminism, Activism, and Knitting: Are the Fibre Arts a
Viable Mode for Feminist Political Action?" *thirdspace* 8 (1) (Summer). Online.
<http://www.thirdspace.ca/journal/article/viewArticle/pentney/210>

People of Color Zine Project. 2014. Mission Statement. Web. 24 July. <http://poczine
project.tumblr.com>

Phelan, Peggy. 1993. *Unmarked: The Politics of Performance*. New York: Routledge.

Phizacklea, Annie. 1990. *Unpacking the Fashion Industry: Gender, Racism, and Class in
Production*. New York: Routledge.

Pie Chart. 2001. *Bitch* 13: 7.

Piepmeier, Alison. 2009. *Girl Zines: Making Media, Doing Feminism*. New York
University Press.

Puar, Jasbir. 2002. "A Transnational Feminist Critique of Queer Tourism." Oxford:
Antipode. Web.

———. 2007. *Terrorist Assemblages: Homonationalism in Queer Times*. Durham, NC:
Duke University Press.

Radicalesbians. 1971. "The Woman-Identified-Woman." In Crow 2000, 233–37.

Radway, Janice. 1984. *Reading the Romance*. Chapel Hill, NC: University of North
Carolina Press.

———. 2001. "Girls, Zines, and the Miscellaneous Production of Subjectivity in an Age of
Unceasing Circulation." *Speaker Series* 18. Online: <http://www.infoamerica.org/
documentos_pdf/radway01.pdf>

Railla, Jean. 1999. "Cheap Thrills." She's Crafty. *BUST* 12 (Spring): 22.

Razack, Sherene H. 1998. *Looking White People in the Eye: Gender, Race, and Culture in
Courtrooms and Classrooms*. Toronto: University of Toronto Press.

Razack, Sherene, Malinda Smith, and Sunera Thobani, eds. 2010. *States of Race:
Critical Race Feminism for the 21st Century*. Toronto, ON: Between the Lines Press.

Redstockings Manifesto. 1969. In Crow 2000, 223–25.

Reger, Jo, ed. 2005. *Different Wavelengths: Studies of the Contemporary Women's Movement*. New York: Routledge.

Rentschler, Carrie A., and Samantha C. Thrift. 2015. "Doing Feminism in the Network: Networked Laughter and the 'Binders Full of Women' Meme." *Feminist Theory*.

"Revolution, Girl Style." 2014. *Newsweek* (orginally published 22 November 1992; published online 13 March 2010). Web. 24 July. <http://www.newsweek.com/ revolution-girl-style-196998>

Rich, Adrienne. 1980. "Compulsory Heterosexuality and Lesbian Existence." *Journal of Women's History* 15 (3): 11–48.

Riviere, Joan. 1929. "Womanliness as Masquerade." In Burgin, Donald, and Kaplan 1986, 35–44.

Rockwell, Paige. 2006. "Feminists Just Want to Have Fun." *Salon.com*. 16 October. <http://www.salon.com/mwt/broadsheet/2006/09/29/fun/index.html>

Rodier, Katharine. 2004. "Lucy Stone and *The Woman's Journal*." In Harris 2004, 99–120.

Romero, Lora. 1997. *Home Fronts: Domesticity and Its Critics in the Antebellum United States*. Durham, NC: Duke University Press.

Roth, Benita. 2003. *Separate Roads to Feminism: Black, Chicana, and White Feminist Movements in America's Second Wave*. Cambridge, MA: Cambridge University Press.

Rubin, Gayle. 1984. "Thinking Sex: Notes for a Radical Theory of the Politics of Sexuality." In Parker and Aggleton 1999, 143–78.

Rundle, Lisa B. 2005. "Subversive Stitchery." *Herizons* 18 (4) (Spring): 31.

Russo, Ann, and Cheris Kramarae. 1991. *The Radical Women's Press of the 1850s*. New York: Routledge, Chapman, and Hall.

Russo, Mary. 1989. "Female Grotesques: Carnival and Theory." In De Lauretis 1989, 213–29.

Sampath, Sheila. 2016. Email message to author. 18 February.

Savage, Candice. 1998. *Beauty Queens: A Playful History*. Vancouver: Greystone Books.

"Save Bitch." 2008. *BitchMedia*. 14 September. <http://www.youtube.com/watch?v= WpteWcREVVA>

Scelfo, Julie. 2004. "Rock-and-Roll Knitters: They May Have Blue Hair, but They're No Grannies." *Newsweek* (24 January): 54.

Schafer, Debbie. 2003. Letter. *Bitch* 19 (Winter): 6.

Schilt, Kristen. 2003. "'I'll Resist with Every Inch and Every Breath': Girls and Zine Making as a Form of Resistance." *Youth & Society* 35 (1) (September): 71–97.

Schmidt, Dorothy. 2002. "Magazines." In Inge and Hall 2002, 989–1017.

Schroeder, Amy. 2001. "Magik on Venus: An Interview with Amy Schroeder." Interview with M. Handren. *Grrrl Zine Network*. Web. 22 June 2014. <http://www.grrrlzines .net/interviews/Venus.htm>

——. 2006. Email interview. 21 November.

Scott, Anne Crittenden. 1972. "The Value of Housework: For Love or Money?" *Ms.* 1 (1) (July): 56–59.

Scott, Joan Wallach, ed. 2008. *Women's Studies on the Edge*. Durham, NC: Duke University Press.

Scott, Linda M. 2006. *Fresh Lipstick: Redressing Fashion and Feminism*. New York: Palgrave Macmillan.

Shameless. 2014. "Ad Kit 2014." Web. 30 June. <http://shamelessmag.com/files/AdKit_2014.pdf>

Sharrock, Justine. 2003. "The Revolution Will Not Be Sanitized." *Bitch* 19 (Winter): 60–63, 93–94.

Siegal, Erin. 2003. Letter. *Bitch* 19 (Winter): 6.

Simms, Molly. 2004. "The Secret History of *Sassy*." *BUST* (Fall): 69–73.

Sinor, Jennifer. 2003. "Another Form of Crying: Girl Zines as Life Writing." *Prose Studies: History, Theory, Criticism* 26 (1–2): 240–64.

Skelton, Tracey, and Gill Valentine, eds. *Cool Places: Geographies of Youth Culture*. New York: Routledge.

Smith, Barry Wise. 1996. "The Lily." Endres and Lueck 1996, 174–86.

Smith, Cherry. 1996. "What Is This Thing Called Queer?" In Morton 1996, 277–85.

Smith, Malinda. 2010. "Gender, Whiteness, and 'Other Others' in the Academy." In Razack, Smith, and Thobani 2010, 37–58.

Smith, Malinda, and Fatima Jaffer. 2012. *Beyond the Queer Alphabet: Conversations on Gender, Sexuality, and Intersectionality*. Teaching Equity Matters E-Book Series. 28–31.

Snyder, R. Claire. 2008. "What Is Third-Wave Feminism? A New Directions Essay." *Signs* 34 (1) (Autumn): 175–96.

Solanas, Valerie. 1967/1971. *SCUM Manifesto*. London: Olympia Press.

Somerson, Wendy. 2007. "Knot in Our Name: Activism beyond the Knitting Circle." *Bitch* 34 (Winter): 36–41.

Spencer, David R. 1996. "The Woman's Journal." In Endres and Lueck 1996, 468–78.

Spivak, Gayatri Chakravorty. 1988. "Can the Subaltern Speak?" In Nelson and Grossberg 1988, 271–313.

Spivey, Marilyn. 2004. Letter. *Bitch* 20 (Spring): 89.

Springer, Kimberly. "Third Wave Black Feminism?" *Signs* 27 (4) (2002): 1059–98. Print.

Staggenborg, Suzanne, and Verta Taylor. 2005. "Whatever Happened to the Women's Movement?" *Mobilization: An International Journal* 10 (1): 37–52.

Steiner, Linda. 1996. "The New Northwest." In Endres and Lueck 1996, 232–37.

Stockburger, Ingrid Z. 2011. "Making Zines, Making Selves: Identity Construction in DIY Autobiography." Dissertation. Washington, DC: Georgetown University.

Stoller, Debbie. 2002. "Fightin' Words." *BUST* (Spring): 4.

———. 2003. *Stitch 'n Bitch: The Knitter's Handbook*. New York: Workman Press.

———. 2005. "The Shiz-Knit: Join the Knitting Revolution." *BUST* (Spring): 15.

———. 2006. "The Devil Wears Nada." Editorial. *BUST* (August/September): 6.

———. 2009. "Future Shock." Editorial. *BUST* (January/February): 6.

Stone, Lucy. 2004. "'Our Office': *The Woman's Journal*, 15 January 1870." In Harris 2004, 121–22.

Summers, Claude J., ed. 2004. *GLBTQ: An Encyclopedia of Gay, Lesbian, Bisexual, Transgender, and Queer Culture*. Chicago, IL: glbtq, inc. Online. Accessed 10 July 2009. <www.glbtq.com/social-sciences/lesbian_sex_wars.html>

Tartakovsky, Flora. 2000. "That Clicking Sound: Grandma's Favorite Hobby Hooks a New Generation of Young, Urban Go-Getters." *Time*. 31 January. Accessed 2 August 2008. <http:www.time.com/time/magazine/article/0,9171,995957-1,00 .html>

"The 3rd Wave: Feminism for the New Millennium." 2006. <http://www.3rdwwwave .com> 16 September.

Thom, Mary. 1997. *Inside* Ms.*: Twenty Five Years of the Magazine and the Women's Movement*. New York: Henry Holt and Company.

Tiffany, Laura. 2009. "Crafting: A Silver Lining in a Tough Economy." *Entrepreneur*. 9 March. Accessed 5 July 2009. <http://www.entrepreneur.com/startingabusiness/ businessideas/article200450.html>

Tobias, Vicki. 2005. "Blog This! An Introduction to Blogs, Blogging, and the Feminist Blogosphere." *Feminist Collections: A Quarterly of Women's Studies Resources* 26 (2–3): 11–17.

Todd, Mark, and Esther Pearl Watson. 2006. *Watcha Mean, What's a Zine?* Boston, MA: Graphia.

Tolman, Deborah. 2002. *Dilemmas of Desire: Teenage Girls Talk about Sexuality*. Harvard University Press.

Toys in Babeland. 2002a. "Make a Splash." *Bitch: Feminist Response to Popular Culture* 17 (Summer).

——. 2002b. "Pet Your Bunny." *Bitch: Feminist Response to Popular Culture* 18 (Fall).

——. 2003. "I Started My Own Sexual Revolution." *Bitch: Feminist Response to Popular Culture* 21 (Summer).

Tuana, Nancy, and Rosemarie Tong. 1995. *Feminist and Philosophy: Essential Readings in Theory, Reinterpretation, and Application*. Boulder, CO: Westview Press.

Up from Under. 1970. 1.1 (May/June): 1–2.

van Zoonen, Liesbet. 1994. *Feminist Media Studies*. London: Sage.

Valverde, Mariana. 1985. *Sex, Power and Pleasure*. Toronto: Women's Press, 75–108, 209–10.

"Venus: Advertising Information." 2007. *Venuszine.com*. 18 March. <http://www .venuszine.com/advertise>

VenusZine.com, Press Kit, Accessed June 19, 2011. <http://venuszine.com/advertise>

"Violence: Our Stories." *HUES* 1.5 (Spring and Summer 1995): 23–27.

Waickman, Elizabeth. 2008. "Knitting Hobby Attracting More Men and Younger Devotees." *Point Park News Service* (September 24). <http://pointparknewsservice .com/?p=247>

Walker, Alice. 1984. *In Search of Our Mother's Gardens: Womanist Prose*. San Diego: Harcourt Brace Jovanovich Publishers.

Walker, Nancy A. 1998. *Women's Magazines, 1940–1960: Gender Roles in the Popular Press*. The Bedford Series in History and Culture. Boston, MA: Bedford/St. Martin's.

———. 2000. *Shaping Our Mothers' World: American Women's Magazines*. Jackson: University Press of Mississippi, 2000.

Walker, Rebecca. 1992. "Becoming Third Wave." *Ms*. 2 (4) (January/February): 39–41.

Warner, Michael. 2002. *Publics and Counterpublics*. New York: Zone Books.

Warrior, Betsy. 2000. "Housework: Slavery or Labour of Love." In Crow 2000, 530–34.

Waters, Melanie. 2004. "Sexing It Up? Women, Pornography, and Third-Wave Feminism." In Gillis, Howie, and Munford 2004, 250–65.

Werker, Kim. 2007. *Crochet Me: Designs to Fuel the Crochet Revolution*. Interweave Books.

Willdorf, Nina. 2001. "*BUST* Goes Bust." *The Phoenix.com*. 15–22 November. Accessed 25 April 2007. <http://72.166.46.24//boston/news_features/this_just_in/ docu ments/02006468.htm>

Wilson, Elizabeth. 1985. *Adorned in Dreams: Fashion and Modernity*. London: Virago.

Winning, Joanne. 2002. "Writing by the Light of *The Well*: Radclyffe Hall and the Lesbian Modernists." In Doan and Prosser 2002, 372–93.

Winship, Janice. 1980. *Inside Women's Magazines*. London: Pandora.

———. 1987. "'A Girl Needs to Get Street-Wise': Magazines for the 1980s." In Betterton 1987, 127–42.

Wise, Anna. 2006. Letter to the Editor. *BUST* 36 (December/January): 8.

Worick, Jennifer. 2007. "From Rags to Riches." *BUST* 47 (October/November): 25.

Zeisler, Andi. 2007. Email interview. 20 November.

———. 2008. *Feminism and Pop Culture*. Berkeley: Seal Press.

Zeisler, Andi, and Rachel Fudge. 2006. "Editor's Letter." *Bitch* (Summer): 5.

Zeisler, Andi, Lisa Jervis, and Rita Hao. 1999. "10 Things to Hate about *Jane*: New Rag From Former *Sassy* Editor Raised Our Hopes and Then Dashed Them on the Jagged Rocks of the Newsstand." *Bitch* 9. Web. 21 June 2014. <http://bitchmagazine.org/ article/ten-things-hate-about-jane>

Zobl, Elke. 2009. "Cultural Production, Transnational Networking, and Critical Reflection in Feminist Zines." *Signs* 35 (1): 1–12.

Zuckerman, Mary Ellen. 1998. *A History of Popular Women's Magazines in the United States, 1792–1995*. Westport, CT: Greenwood Press.

INDEX

Abzug, Bella, 93, 95, 108, 109. *See also* "Fashionable Feminists"

advertisements: and archiving, 73; classifieds, 61, 120, 173n2; number and percentage, 171n8; revenue from, 63, 64, 84. *See also* vibrator advertisements

advertisers: alternative market cultures and, 141–42; appealing to, 52, 53, 61, 65; and complimentary copy, 63; and economic downturn, 40; lack of, 18; and niche marketing, 84–89; readers become commodities for, 64; rejection by, 84; and *Sassy* boycott, 25–26; and style of publication, 60; and subscription lists, 63; and systemic racism 18; and target demographics, 59, 60; troubles appealing to, 61

advertising, 43–44, 47, 84; and ad location, 143; and ad rejection, 61, 141; and alternative market cultures, 141–48; and amount, 60, 105, 107; and reader backlash, 62; growth of DIY, 120; history in feminist periodicals, 62–65; photo cropping in, 147; politics of, 58–65; revenue from, 9, 52, 55, 58, 59, 60, 63, 64, 84, 90, 102, 141; sexualized imagery in, 147; success with, 59–61. *See also* niche marketing; Pet Your Bunny; selling out

advertising policies, 61, 64, 65, 139, 149, 157. *See also Bitch*

ageism, 127

agency, 9, 10, 111; in *BUST*, 115; and sexuality, 150

alternative market culture, 135, 141–48

alternative market economies, 135, 142

Anthony, Susan B., 51, 64, 125

anti-capitalism, 134, 173n5

archives and archiving: *Bitch* archives, 23, 28, 83, 152, 165; and feminist materials, 7, 13–17, 72–74; inclusion and exclusion in, 14, 72, 73; and race, 73; and third-wave feminism, 72–74; unofficial, 13

archives of feelings, 5–7

Babeland. *See* Toys in Babeland

backlash: and advertising, 62; and feminism, 12, 19, 94–95, 114, 172n1; lifestyle feminism as, 114–15

Bailey, Courtney, 15

Barnard Conference on Women and Sexuality (1982), 157–58

Barnard Zine Library, 13, 72

Berlant, Lauren, 4, 80, 129, 141, 142, 144, 154, 155

Big Mama Rag, 54, 55

Birkenstock feminism, 94, 95

BOOKS IN THE FILM+MEDIA STUDIES SERIES
PUBLISHED BY WILFRID LAURIER UNIVERSITY PRESS

Image and Identity: Reflections on Canadian Film Culture / R. Bruce Elder / 1989; Paper edition 2012 / xviii + 484 pp. / ISBN 978-1-55458-469-7

Image and Territory: Essays on Atom Egoyan / Monique Tschofen and Jennifer Burwell, editors / 2006 / viii + 418 pp / photos / ISBN 978-0-88920-487-4

The Young, the Restless, and the Dead: Interviews with Canadian Filmmakers / George Melnyk, editor / 2008 / xiv + 134 pp. / photos / ISBN 978-1-55458-036-1

Programming Reality: Perspectives on English-Canadian Television / Zoë Druick and Aspa Kotsopoulos, editors / 2008 / x + 344 pp. / photos / ISBN 978-1-55458-010-1

Harmony and Dissent: Film and Avant-garde Art Movements in the Early Twentieth Century / R. Bruce Elder / 2008 / xxxiv + 482 pp. / ISBN 978-1-55458-028-6

He Was Some Kind of a Man: Masculinities in the B Western / Roderick McGillis / 2009 / xii + 210 pp. / photos / ISBN 978-1-55458-059-0

The Radio Eye: Cinema in the North Atlantic, 1958–1988 / Jerry White / 2009 / xvi + 284 pp. / photos / ISBN 978-1-55458-178-8

The Gendered Screen: Canadian Women Filmmakers / Brenda Austin-Smith and George Melnyk, editors / 2010 / x + 272 pp. / ISBN 978-1-55458-179-5

Feeling Canadian: Nationalism, Affect, and Television / Marusya Bociurkiw / 2011 / viii + 184 pp. / ISBN 978-1-55458-268-6

Beyond Bylines: Media Workers and Women's Rights in Canada / Barbara M. Freeman / 2011 / xii + 328 pp. / photos / ISBN 978-1-55458-269-3

Canadian Television: Text and Context / Marian Bredin, Scott Henderson, and Sarah A. Matheson, editors / 2011 / xvi + 238 pp. / ISBN 978-1-55458-361-4

Cinema and Social Change in Germany and Austria / Gabriele Mueller and James M. Skidmore, editors / 2012 / x + 304 pp. / photos / ISBN 978-1-55458-225-9

DADA, Surrealism, and the Cinematic Effect / Bruce Elder / 2013 / viii + 766 pp. / ISBN 978-1-55458-625-7

Two Bicycles: The Work of Jean-Luc Godard and Anne-Marie Miéville / Jerry White / 2013 / x + 204 pp. / ISBN 978-1-55458-935-7

The Legacies of Jean-Luc Godard / Douglas Morrey, Christina Stojanova, and Nicole Côté, editors / 2014 / photos / ISBN 978-1-55458-920-3

Detecting Canada: Essays on Canadian Crime Fiction, Film, and Television / Jeannette Sloniowski and Marilyn Rose, editors / 2014 / xxiv + 318 pp. / ISBN 978-1-55458-926-5

Reverse Shots: Indigenous Film and Media in an International Context / Wendy Gay Pearson and Susan Knabe, editors / 2014 / ISBN 978-1-55458-335-5

Making Feminist Media: Third-Wave Magazines on the Cusp of the Digital Age / Elizabeth Groeneveld / 2016 / ISBN 978-1-77112-120-0